Praise for
Fearless

"As a rule, we don't endorse books or movies or anything regarding the command where I work—and Adam Brown worked—but as the author writes in *Fearless*, you have to know the rules so you know when to bend or break them. This is one of those times. Read this book. Period. It succeeds where all the others have failed."

—ANONYMOUS, SEAL Team SIX operator

"Adam Brown's zest for life led him down a few dark alleys and more than one dead end. Kindhearted and wild, Adam led a life that lacked direction. God, a woman, and the U.S. Navy gave it to him. *Fearless* is a love story...several love stories: a man for his woman, a warrior for his team, parents for kids, and soldiers for their country. There is no greater love than that a man lay down his life for his friends. Be warned—reading *Fearless* will change the way you see the world."

—STU WEBER, veteran Green Beret, pastor, and author of *Tender Warrior*

"When people know they are going to die, often their one regret is that they didn't say 'I love you' enough. Adam Brown never had to worry. His life was about love: love of God, family, friends, country, his fellow SEALs, and the Afghan children who worshiped him. In *Fearless*, Eric Blehm does a marvelous and moving job uncovering the man—the men—beneath the SEAL mythology of elite, rock-hard warriors renowned for their courage and skill. The SEALs in *Fearless* hug their children, seek comfort from their wives, wear Batman briefs, answer to names like Big Bird and Fozzy, mourn lost buddies, and risk their lives to rescue civilians from the field of fire. This is a stirring, revelatory, heartbreaking story."

—JAMES CAMPBELL, author of *The Final Frontiersman*
and *The Ghost Mountain Boys*

"*Fearless* is a vivid account of one man's journey from all-American boy to all-American hero. Blehm's writing takes you beyond the battlefield and right to the heart of the personal battles, sacrifices, and triumphs of one of America's elite warriors. Anyone looking for an inspiring story of inner strength and courage will be richly rewarded by this book."

—ERIC GREITENS, former Navy SEAL and *New York Times*
best-selling author of *The Heart and the Fist*

"This is not another SEAL book about ego; this is a powerful book about perseverance that will absolutely inspire everybody. Adam was a warrior in the truest sense—courageous, compassionate, intrepid, and humble. And his dedication to God, country, family, and the Brotherhood was genuine and exceptional. This book will motivate you to challenge yourself to be…fearless."

—SEAL teammate of Adam Brown, BUD/S Class 226

"*Fearless* stands unique among works of modern combat literature through author Eric Blehm's masterful weaving of a fallen Navy SEAL's professional war-fighting life with his complex personal victories and travails. Rich in detail and captivating in its honesty, you won't put *Fearless* down once you read the first page. Read it and prepare to learn a whole new world of life as a Navy SEAL."

—ED DARACK, author of *Victory Point: Operations Red
Wings and Whalers—The Marine Corps' Battle for
Freedom in Afghanistan*

"*Fearless* is a *timely* book for Americans transfixed by our military elite and the fight against terrorism. Author Eric Blehm provides an intimate look at the stamina, toughness, and mindset of Adam Brown, who, against all odds, became a Navy SEAL. *Fearless* is also a *timeless* book about the human condition. This true story is an emotional roller coaster about betrayal and love, despair and faith, tragedy and triumph, life and death, the grace of God. This story will bring tears to your eyes, and yet your spirit will soar. *Fearless* is destined to be a classic—a story about hope, now and forever."

—LARRY BECK, PHD, professor, San Diego State University, and author of *Moving Beyond Treeline*

"A rare look into the highly secretive and incredibly demanding world of special operators, *Fearless* profoundly captures the heart and mind of an elite warrior who bravely overcame obstacle after obstacle—then paid the ultimate price for the freedoms we all enjoy in America and the rest of the free world."

—W. E. B. GRIFFIN AND WILLIAM E. BUTTERWORTH IV, best-selling authors of Men at War, Presidential Agent, and other *Wall Street Journal* and *New York Times* best-selling series

"Eric Blehm's *Fearless* is an unforgettable tale of bravery, loss, redemption, joy, sorrow, serenity, and integrity. As topical as today's headlines, *Fearless* at its heart deals with eternal verities that are timeless in their importance and significance."

—JIM O'NEILL, author of *Laus Deo,* BUD/S 62, UDT-21, SEAL Team TWO

FEARLESS

ALSO BY ERIC BLEHM

The Last Season

The Only Thing Worth Dying For: How
Eleven Green Berets Fought for a New Afghanistan

Molly the Owl

FEARLESS

The Undaunted Courage and Ultimate Sacrifice
of Navy SEAL Team SIX Operator Adam Brown

ERIC BLEHM

New York Times Best-Selling Author of *The Only Thing Worth Dying For*

WATERBROOK
PRESS

FEARLESS

All Scripture quotations, unless otherwise indicated, are taken from the New King James Version®. Copyright © 1982 by Thomas Nelson Inc. Used by permission. All rights reserved. Scripture quotations marked (NIV) are taken from the Holy Bible, New International Version®, NIV®. Copyright © 1973, 1978, 1984 by Biblica Inc.™ Used by permission of Zondervan. All rights reserved worldwide. www.zondervan.com.

Some dates, locations, times, distances, and names (including those of some civilians) have been changed; faces in photographs obscured; and military tactics, techniques, and procedures altered in order to maintain operational security for the safety of the U.S. Navy SEALs and those who work alongside them.

Trade Paperback ISBN 978-0-307-73070-1
Hardcover ISBN 978-0-307-73069-5
eBook ISBN 978-0-307-73071-8

Copyright © 2012 by Eric Blehm

Cover design by Kristopher K. Orr; cover image of Navy SEAL Trident by Corbis

Published in the United States by WaterBrook, an imprint of the Crown Publishing Group, a division of Penguin Random House LLC, New York.

WATERBROOK® and its deer colophon are registered trademarks of Penguin Random House LLC.

The Library of Congress has catalogued the hardcover edition as follows:

Library of Congress Cataloging-in-Publication Data
Blehm, Eric.
    Fearless : the undaunted courage and ultimate sacrifice of Navy SEAL Team Six operator Adam Brown / Eric Blehm. — 1st ed.
        pages cm
      ISBN 978-0-307-73069-5 — ISBN 978-0-307-73071-8 (electronic)
  1. Brown, Adam, 1974–2010. 2. Bin Laden, Osama, 1957–2011 — Assassination. 3. United States. Navy. SEALs — Biography. 4. United States. Navy — Commando troops — Biography. I. Title.
    VG87.B58 2012
    359.9/84092 B
                           2012006655

Printed in the United States of America

30 29 28 27

SPECIAL SALES
Most WaterBrook books are available at special quantity discounts when purchased in bulk by corporations, organizations, and special-interest groups. Custom imprinting or excerpting can also be done to fit special needs. For information, please e-mail specialmarketscms@penguin randomhouse.com or call 1-800-603-7051.

*This book is dedicated to the fallen
American heroes killed in action
on August 6, 2011,
in Wardak Province, Afghanistan.*

CONTENTS

Author's Note xiii

Prologue 1

1 Foundations 4

2 Something Special 13

3 The Wolf Pack 26

4 Slipping 36

5 The Dark Time 47

6 In God's Hands 59

7 Kelley 77

8 Rising Up 99

9 Pays to Be a Winner 112

10 A SEAL Is Born 123

11 The Calling 139

12 War 156

13 Something Important 176

14 Green Team 193

15 Top Secret 211

16 Heart of a Warrior 236

17 Objective Lake James 254

18 I Got It! 272

19 Unconquerable Soul 287

Epilogue 306

Afterword 319

Acknowledgments 323

In Memoriam 325

Adam's Legacy: Reader Comments on the
    Hardcover Edition of *Fearless* 329

AUTHOR'S NOTE

Adam Brown's civilian and military life has been recounted to me by his family, friends, and teammates—all eyewitnesses to each event portrayed in this book, including what Adam told them directly about his history and spiritual testimony. I also used official documents, statements, military records and reports, criminal records, family archives, letters, e-mails, and journal and diary entries. Some dates, locations, times, distances, and names (including those of some civilians) have been changed; faces in photographs obscured; and military tactics, techniques, and procedures altered in order to maintain operational security for the safety of the U.S. Navy SEALs and those who work alongside them.

All information about the Naval Special Warfare Development Group, the SEALs, and individuals (including the use of real names) has already been published widely by the media and is deemed common knowledge. Nearly a dozen active-duty SEAL operators—including those in leadership roles—have unofficially, but no less meticulously, reviewed this manuscript for factuality and to point out any issues that might endanger lives in future operations. I have removed or rewritten sections to their approval, and in the few cases of discrepancy among the operators, I went with the majority. Any vagueness in the manuscript is intentional, to protect these men and their allies.

All quotes, slang, inner thoughts, dialogue, and descriptions have been conveyed to me by those intimately involved in the story to the best of their ability and individual memories. Nothing has been contrived, dramatized, or fabricated.

What you are about to read is the account of an American hero who bravely gave permission in his final written requests to share his journey, from small-town America to the gutter to jail to Jesus to war to the top tier of the U.S. military: SEAL Team SIX.

Prologue

FROM MAY THROUGH JULY 2011, when it seemed that every journalist on the planet was scrambling to get an inside angle on the Osama bin Laden kill mission in Pakistan, I was making my way around the United States interviewing over a dozen U.S. Navy SEALs. Although most were from the Naval Special Warfare Development Group or, as the Obama administration announced to the world, SEAL Team SIX—the team that had taken out bin Laden—I was meeting with them for a different reason altogether.

I traveled from California to Pennsylvania to Alaska to Virginia to Arkansas, interviewing each of the SEALs for several hours. Although the mission of a lifetime that some had taken part in only days before was still on their minds, we weren't there to focus on bin Laden. They'd met with me, an outsider to their ranks, for something equally important and deeply personal to them: the family of one of their fallen SEAL brothers—Chief Special Warfare Operator Adam Brown—wanted his story told.

And if the world was to learn about Adam Brown, the SEALs wanted it done right. As one of the men, Thomas Ratzlaff, humbly said to me while we stood in the rain watching the muddy currents of the Copper River flow through the Alaskan wilderness, "Adam is the one SEAL from our command whose story absolutely deserves a book."

"When I first heard about Adam's past," Matt Mason said, looking out over the stormy Atlantic Ocean, "I didn't believe it. It was hard for me to wrap my mind around what he overcame, and how Kelley stood by his side."

"You need to tell the whole story," John Faas admonished me as we ate at a favorite restaurant of Adam's near the Virginia Beach boardwalk. "There are enough books that show how tough SEAL training is, there's enough Tom Clancy fiction. What there isn't enough of is the humanity. When you start digging, you are going to find a whole lot of humanity in Adam Brown."

Slapping his hand against the desk in a small hotel room, Kevin Houston said, "You need to promise me: don't start this story at BUD/S— that is so cliché. You *have* to go to Hot Springs and tell those stories."

"Has anybody told you about his last mission?" Chris Campbell asked as he prepped his gear for a week of training in Alaska. "The whole purpose of that op was to protect our brothers, these conventional Army guys who were just getting pounded by this thug, that was the mission. But then within that, you've got what we do individually for our troop, and that's protect each other. That's what Adam was doing."

In back-to-back interviews, Brian Bill, "Big Bird" to Adam's children, explained how Adam made him want to be a better person and was the model of the father he himself hoped to be one day, while Heath Robinson said Adam was both fearless and compassionate on operations. Adam was the first to volunteer to go through that "black hole," a breached doorway into an enemy building; the first to help carry an Afghan's load; and the first to sit down and try to calm women and children after a raid.

For days I heard similar accounts from Adam's family, friends, and teammates—all of whom had one goal: to honor him by ensuring that his legend among the SEALs lived on.

Since many of the SEALs from Adam's squadron were about to embark on yet another rotation into Afghanistan, they wanted to speak with me sooner rather than later. As warriors, they were firmly grounded in the reality of their job.

"We're about to deploy," one of Adam's closest SEAL buddies said as we began our interview in June. "You never know what might happen—I could get killed on my next mission. I want to do Adam right, so let's get it done."

"Where would you like to start?" I asked him.

"Let's begin with March 17," he said. "Let's get that out of the way first."

Foundations

WHEN ADAM BROWN WOKE UP on March 17, 2010, he didn't know he would die that night in the Hindu Kush mountains of Afghanistan—but he was ready.

Seven thousand miles away, in a suburb of Virginia Beach, his ten-year-old son, Nathan, was worried about him. From the moment he'd opened his eyes that morning, he felt something bad was going to happen to his daddy, but he kept it to himself, rolled out of bed, and got ready for school. It was Saint Patrick's Day, and he made sure to wear something green so he wouldn't get pinched.

On a previous deployment, Adam had written in his journal to both Nathan and Savannah, Nathan's seven-year-old sister, a letter they weren't meant to see unless the worst happened:

> I'm not afraid of anything that might happen to me on this Earth because I know no matter what, nothing can take my spirit from me.... How much it pains me...to think about not watching my boy excel in life, or giving my little baby girl away in marriage.... Buddy, I'll be there, you'll feel me there when you steal your first base, smash someone on the football field, make all A's. I'll be

there for all of your achievements. But much more, Buddy, I'll be there for every failure. Remember, I know tears, I know pain and disappointment, and I will be there for you with every drop. You cannot disappoint me. I understand!

Adam Brown did understand what it meant to disappoint, to feel the shame he'd experienced on a hot, humid August afternoon years earlier when his parents had him arrested. "It's time for you to face what you've done," his father had told him in 1996, just before Adam was handcuffed and escorted to the backseat of the Garland County sheriff's cruiser. When the deputy slammed the car door shut, Adam watched his mother's legs buckle, and as she collapsed, his dad caught her and held her tightly against him. She began to cry, and Adam knew he had broken her heart.

That vision—of his mother sobbing into his father's chest—would haunt him for the rest of his life, but it also sparked the journey that defined who he would become.

Officially known as a Chief Special Warfare Operator (SEAL), Adam Brown was one of the most respected Special Operations warriors in the U.S. Navy. He worked for the Naval Special Warfare Development Group (NSWDG), a.k.a. DEVGRU. Before May 2011, details about Adam's unit—popularly called SEAL Team SIX—were neither confirmed nor commented on by the Pentagon and the White House. One night changed everything; the wave of publicity following Osama bin Laden's death thrust the little-known unit into the spotlight.

When Adam's team deployed to Operation Enduring Freedom in March 2010, the SEALs were spread across Afghanistan to cover a range of responsibilities dictated to them by the generals and admirals in charge of strategic operations. Adam and part of his team were stationed at an assaulters' base in a remote corner of northern Afghanistan. This region along the Pakistan border was still, after nearly eight and a half years of the War on Terror, a safe haven for Afghan insurgents, foreign jihadists, and terrorist cells—often working in concert. It was a land of high-value targets: raids in the region almost always resulted in fruitful intelligence, which led to further dismantling of the insurgency against the Afghan government and yielded more pieces to the puzzle that eventually revealed the whereabouts of bin Laden.

Since late 2009, intelligence networks had been tracking a Kunar Province Taliban leader—code-named Objective Lake James—who had already taken credit for numerous deaths among coalition forces. The most recent intelligence confirmed that "James" planned to attack a U.S. Army battalion preparing to relocate from its current position adjacent to the Pech River Valley. The valley was a deadly piece of real estate where insurgents could strike coalition forces and then retreat into their mountain strongholds—villages and valleys whose inhabitants, in many cases, had never seen an American. There were lines on the map beyond which the insurgents knew they would not be pursued.

That was about to change. Intelligence pinpointed James's current location, a compound in a secluded village in the mountainous Chapa Dara district of Kunar Province. Even though this particular hamlet was a *way*-over-the-line safe haven for insurgents, Adam and his teammates began planning to either capture or kill James.

First they viewed images of the compound. Confirming details of the landscape and structures was always difficult until the SEALs were on the ground, but the target residence didn't appear any more problematic than the hundreds of other compounds they'd raided during multiple deployments. Further surveillance of the valley revealed men armed with rifles, mostly AK-47s, as well as light machine guns and rocket-propelled grenades. The men in the photographs were of fighting age, which in the past had meant men with beards. Lately, however, the insurgents and jihadists had begun shaving to appear younger and were even donning burkas to disguise themselves as women, to better their chances of escape. So it was difficult to accurately determine overall enemy numbers.

In the target compound, roughly five males, six females, and six children were present at various times of day. James and his men were expected to fight rather than be captured, so the civilians complicated the raid. History had shown that this enemy used both women and children freely as human shields, but the SEALs were trained to handle these scenarios.

What made Objective Lake James one of the three most difficult (described by Command as "audacious") missions in the war up to then were two facts. Located in a narrow valley deep within wooded mountains, the objective was surrounded by enemy who had chiseled their homes into formidable, often terraced slopes and rocky cliff faces. This meant the SEALs could not fly in, land or fast rope near the target, perform their mission, and fly out—their usual modus operandi. They would have to infiltrate by foot a great distance over extremely difficult enemy-occupied terrain, hit their target, and hike out to the helicopter landing zone (HLZ).

Adam and his team were prepared to do whatever it took not to alert the village or the rest of the valley's residents. That meant staying as quiet as possible and using suppressed weapons or knives to kill or capture the targeted individual. Once they had completed their task, they would search the premises for intelligence and detain the civilians. If doors did need to be blown open or the enemy fought back, the entire valley would hear and come out with weapons blazing, and it would be a battle all the way to the HLZ—a thirty- to sixty-minute hike. The SEALs knew that length of time under fire would feel like an eternity.

An easier way to take out James and his men would have been to drop a bomb, but that was not an option because of the women and children in the compound and the families in adjacent homes. This had to be a surgical strike, aimed at one insurgent and his cell of fighters who, if not eliminated by Adam's team, would continue to attack American or coalition forces.

That much was certain.

While prepping his equipment for the mission, Adam folded the Arkansas flag his brother, Shawn, had given him. He always carried it into battle, tucking it proudly between his body armor and his uniform.

Every SEAL who encountered Adam Brown knew in short order where he was from. He loved his home state right down to the dirt. "It is the one state in our country that can sustain itself," he'd tell you while explaining his Arkansas Bubble Theory. "Y'all could put a bubble over it, cut us off from importing anything from the rest of the world, and we would not only survive, we would eat well and prosper."

The one thing Arkansas doesn't have is an ocean, and when Adam entered the U.S. Navy's grueling twenty-seven-week Basic Underwater Demolition/SEAL (BUD/S) training course in 1999, he'd swum in the sea only a handful of times. At the beginning of BUD/S, an instructor had told his class, "The reputation you forge here will follow you to the teams. Your reputation here will define you."

Adam's reputation certainly did define him, but the stories that made him a legend began long before BUD/S in the southern proving grounds of Hot Springs, Arkansas. That was where he earned the nickname Psycho for taking on the biggest players on his peewee football team, where he boldly faced a loaded shotgun, where he jumped from a moving vehicle off an interstate bridge into a lake, where he saved a life, eluded capture, and performed his first nighttime raids. Says Adam's high school football coach, Steve Anderson, "He did things a Navy SEAL would do long before he was a SEAL."

His reputation continued among his SEAL buddies in DEVGRU.

"He didn't have a 'fear bone' in his body," says Kevin Houston. "Tough as nails" is the way Brian Bill describes Adam. Heath Robinson likens him to a bored-out engine without a regulator: "He was a machine, wide open in everything he did—full throttle." With that mindset came injuries, but according to Dave Cain, a SEAL who was there when Adam's fingers were severed in Afghanistan, "He could endure pain better than anybody I've ever known...if he felt it at all."

In truth, Adam did feel pain—lots of it. He was just incredibly determined and resilient, a toughness that began at birth. "He came out injured," says his mother, Janice. According to his father, Larry, Adam was ready to be born three minutes after his twin sister, Manda, when "the doctor discovered he was breech. So they had to dislocate his shoulder in order to get him out."

"He barely cried," says Janice. "The doctor put his shoulder back in place, and while Manda was still crying after coming into this cold and bright new world, little Adam was quiet, sort of curious, looking around, like he was saying, 'Okay, what *else* you got for me?'"

Adam Lee Brown was born on February 5, 1974, in Hot Springs, Arkansas. His father, Larry, had grown up there, the second of six children in a blue-collar Baptist family that went to church on Wednesday night and twice on Sunday. Larry's father, Elmer, was a World War II veteran who drove a truck for an oil company, a business he ran for months when the owner was out with a serious illness. Larry told his father that he should insist on a raise, but Elmer replied that it would be taking advantage of an unfortunate situation.

"It wouldn't be right," Elmer said when his family gathered around the dinner table one night, "and you do what's right, no matter what." Then he reminded them, "God is watching us, all the time."

Once dinner wrapped up each weeknight, Larry's mother, Rosa, would rush off to the night shift at a nearby shoe factory, coming home in time to make breakfast and send Elmer off to work. Larry began contributing to the family coin jar in elementary school with a paper route, and later, as a teen, he baled hay in the summer and worked in chicken houses year-round. He attended Hot Springs High School—in the same class as future Arkansas governor and U.S. president Bill Clinton, though they didn't know each other. During his campaigns, when Clinton talked about the character-building life of hard-working Arkansans, Larry knew firsthand what that meant. His junior and senior years in high school, he washed logging trucks on the weekends and the other five days worked three to eight in the morning at a doughnut shop, finishing the shift with just enough time to run to school.

It was a hard life, but the siblings were tight, the parents loving, and as a family, they were content—never wanting for anything, even though they didn't have much to speak of. "You gotta do what you gotta do," Elmer would tell Larry, "and when you're done, you'll be stronger for it."

After high school Larry became an electrician's apprentice, and a year later he began dating Janice Smith, a high school senior who had grown up only a few blocks away but with a very different family situation. She never knew her father and was raised mostly by her maternal grandparents instead of her mother, who had to work two jobs in order to support her three children. The situation didn't really bother Janice, though. She loved her grandparents dearly and respected their values, one of which was "Always do the right thing."

As she grew older, Janice realized that her mother's priorities centered around money. Even though it was out of necessity, it still "didn't feel right." Following her heart did, and she eloped with Larry Brown her senior year.

Their relationship was all about fun and young love, but Janice knew she wanted a family someday. Larry was already working hard to be a provider, making money as an electrician and attending night school in Little Rock to earn his license so he could join the union.

His maturity did little to endear him to Janice's mother or grandparents, however, who didn't like the idea of Janice being married while still in high school and persuaded her to have the marriage annulled. They broke up, and within a week a heartbroken Larry was notified that he was a potential draftee for Vietnam. He didn't wait to be drafted, so he went to the recruiting office in downtown Hot Springs and chose the Navy, whose signals intelligence and radio operator schools seemed most in line with his work as an electrician. Also, everybody he knew, including his father, an infantryman who helped hold the line at Bastogne in World War II, advised him to stay off the ground.

He and Janice wrote back and forth while he was in boot camp, and when she closed a letter with "Love ya," he proposed again. This time they were married in the backyard garden of her grandparents' home. He was twenty; she was nineteen. After the wedding they drove to Florida and moved into a trailer near Naval Air Station Jacksonville, where Larry was based.

He was ordered to war as a radioman on a P3 bomber that patrolled the coastal waters of Vietnam, eavesdropping on and hunting Chinese submarines and other enemy watercraft. Returning home from his tour in time for the arrival of their first child, Larry Shawn Brown, on December 13, 1968, he deployed again less than a year later. He didn't see much action, but he did see the shell shocked, the wounded, and the body bags as they passed through his air base en route to hospitals or home. He also watched small teams depart for secret missions—elite volunteers from the Army Special Forces, Air Force Commandos, and Navy SEALs, all operating in the dark and dangerous jungle and its waterways.

When Larry flew his missions, he imagined what the men "submerged" in the jungle below were facing. He held them in the highest regard, and he thought of them every night when he ate a warm meal and crawled into a dry bed.

Once Larry completed his four years of service, he put the war behind him and moved with Janice from Florida back to Hot Springs, finished his electrician's apprenticeship, and began working for a local contractor. Determined to provide for his family without Janice having to work, Larry earned enough so they could save a little money each month. After three years of frugal living, they had scraped together the down payment on a thirty-thousand-dollar starter house in a subdivision two hundred yards from Lake Hamilton. It wasn't large, maybe fifteen hundred square feet, but following nearly a decade of tiny apartments and trailers, it felt like a mansion—the perfect home in which to expand their family.

A month before the due date of their second child, the doctor gave Janice some startling news.

"Mrs. Brown," he said with a smile, "there's a little something extra I failed to notice before."

"Extra? Like what?" Janice asked.

"Extra, like an extra baby. You're having twins, ma'am."

2

Something Special

WHEN ADAM'S TWIN SISTER, MANDA, was born three minutes ahead of him on February 5, 1974, it was the last time she beat him at anything. Adam was the first to scoot, first to crawl, first to walk, and first to climb out of the crib...and plummet to the floor.

The first time Adam smacked his head as he escaped the confines of his crib was at nine months. While goose eggs and bruises bred caution in Manda, they didn't faze Adam. He'd cry a bit, then be off exploring. After three such escapes, Larry cut a foot off the legs of the crib to shorten Adam's fall.

That was one of many safety precautions Janice and Larry implemented to prevent Adam from injuring himself. Janice would often recruit Shawn, older by five years, as a second set of eyes while she rushed to prepare dinner. "Keep an eye on Manda," she'd tell him, "but watch Adam like a hawk."

Adam didn't come with brakes. He loved to climb, be it stairs, fences, or a ladder in the garage. If Adam was missing, the first place his parents would look was up. Soon after his second birthday, Janice glanced out the living room window and saw that Adam had pushed a chair across the back porch and was using it to climb up on the railing—twelve feet above the ground. Before she could react, he stood up tall and jumped out of

Brown family archives

Janice and Larry didn't know Adam had launched himself
off the roof of the family car until the roll of film, photographed
by seven-year-old Shawn, was developed weeks later.

sight. Horrified, Janice charged outside and down the steps, to find Adam rolling on the ground and laughing. The spanking she gave him was so hard it left a handprint on his bottom. "Never, *ever* do that again!" she yelled.

A few days later, he did it again.

At age three, Adam climbed onto the kitchen counter and dug into an open can of peaches, slicing his hand on the sharp edge. He stayed calm during the car ride to the emergency room, as they waited to see the doctor, through the exam—all the way until he was about to get stitches and the nurse insisted on strapping him into a papoose-like straitjacket. Crying and screaming, he struggled like a wild animal until he was soaked with sweat and panting. "Help me, Mommy. Help me," he pleaded with Janice, his lower lip quivering.

"That was Adam's soft side," Janice says with tears nearly thirty-five years later. "It was also when we knew this was a kid that could not be held down."

In spite of his strong-willed, unstoppable nature, Adam was a sweet child. As a toddler, he would sit patiently while "Meme"—his name for Manda—wiped his face after meals, then give her a big hug. Well into elementary school, he would climb into his mother's lap and cuddle. From the moment he learned to talk, he was full of praise for others, complimenting Manda's crayon coloring, telling Janice how good dinner was, always using "please" and "thank you," and exhibiting impeccable manners in holding doors open for others and saying "sir" and "ma'am."

Janice and Larry modeled good behavior for their children. If they were out shopping and a woman dropped her coin purse, Janice would pick it up and hand it back. In case her kids missed the point, she would say to them, "If someone drops something, you help them pick it up." Other golden words of wisdom were taught at opportune moments: "If somebody falls over, you offer them your hand." "Would you like it if somebody called you that?" Upon noticing a kid being bullied on the playground, Larry would say, "If you don't help, you're no better than the bully."

"From those little lessons we tried to pound into them," says Janice, "some of them stuck."

Through hard work and a tight budget, Larry was able to support his family so Janice could be the full-time, dependable, engaged mother she'd never had. But in the late seventies a bad economy took a toll on construction in Arkansas, the main source of income for Larry, and the family's savings dwindled. On November 4, 1979, just after the evening news announced that five hundred militants had seized the U.S. Embassy in Tehran, Iran, Janice and Larry sat down at their dinner table to discuss their own crisis: Larry's work as an electrician had dried up—he'd collected his final paycheck—and their savings would last little more than a month. Christmas was on the horizon, and with a mortgage *and* a family to feed, Larry had no choice but to follow others in his Arkansas union and find work out of state. He soon left for a four-month contract at a powerhouse in Craig, Colorado.

The kids really missed their daddy, and while the circumstance was completely different from that of Janice's childhood, the situation of a missing parent was still sadly reminiscent of work taking precedence over family. But she put on her game face and cheerfully reminded the twins, who were four, that it was temporary, while Shawn, who was nine, learned the family mantra: "You gotta do what you gotta do, and when you're done, you'll be stronger."

When the contract ended in Colorado, the closest job to home Larry qualified for was a six-month position in Missoula, Montana. Even on a shoestring budget they could barely pay their bills, so Larry began to entertain the idea of selling or renting out their house in Hot Springs and taking the family on the road. He leased a small house in Missoula, left his Bronco in its driveway, and on April Fools' Day—fifteen years to the day after his first date with Janice—flew back to Hot Springs to drive his family to Montana.

Be strong, Janice thought, fighting tears as their house—with a For Sale or Rent sign in the front yard—shrank behind them in the rearview mirror. *We're together. That's what's important.*

Crammed into the front seat of a U-Haul truck, the Browns traveled light: a stack of mattresses, a wooden porch glider, their television set, and a few boxes of kitchen items, toys, and clothes. They rolled into Missoula the day before Easter, taking less than an hour to unload their belongings. Setting up their bedrooms, which meant plopping mattresses on the floor, could have been a depressing start to their new life, but Janice and Larry were determined to make it business as usual. The next day three delighted kids woke up to find a dusting of snow outside and a trail of candy and Easter baskets hidden throughout the house.

By the following week, Shawn, Manda, and Adam were back in school and playing sports, Larry was in his new job putting in as much overtime as he could, and Janice was holding them all to a schedule.

Larry's contract ended, and the Browns stuck around Missoula long enough for Shawn to finish his baseball season. Then they hitched a horse trailer—loaded with their meager belongings—to the Bronco and headed for Lake Charles, Louisiana. When Larry called his mother, Rosa, to tell her luck was with them and he'd gotten a job at a powerhouse there, she replied that it wasn't by luck but rather "by God's grace." Though Rosa didn't often thump the Bible at her son, she was quietly concerned for him, his young family, and the road they were on. He hadn't read the Bible since he'd returned from Vietnam, and her grandchildren had rarely, if ever, seen the inside of a church. As such, finding a church was not an issue for the Browns, whose priorities upon arriving in Lake Charles were renting a cheap house and enrolling the kids in school.

By now it was football season, and Adam was old enough for the youngest division. Manda signed up for the pep squad, and Shawn joined Pop Warner. Whenever Shawn came home from practice, Adam would ambush him in the living room, trying to tackle his older brother, who at eleven was twice the size of the six-year-old. No matter how many times Shawn pushed him away, Adam would come right back at him. Eventually, Shawn would sit on him to get him to stop.

Adam's relentlessness crossed over onto the football field, where he was the star tackler and earned the defensive player of the year award before the Browns moved again, this time to Indian Springs, Nevada.

Another job, another school, another sport, and in another blink of an eye, Nevada was a memory, and it was on to Loveland, Colorado. The twins continued to decorate the blank walls of their new rooms with prized art projects from various schools—the backs of which were marked with names, dates, and locations—and Janice and Larry marveled at how well their children had taken to life on the road. Their imaginations blossomed, transforming blank corners in rooms into castles, a tree stump into the plank of a pirate ship, or a scraggly backyard into the perfectly manicured football field of their dreams, with an end zone that begged for game-winning catches.

One snowy Sunday morning in December, the Browns trudged out into the woods and cut down a small evergreen for their living room. They spent the day making ornaments and strings of popcorn, then decorated its boughs to the smell of hot cider with cinnamon sticks simmering on the stove.

"We had pretty much nothing but homemade gifts that year," says Janice, "but it was so, so much fun. We loved that little tree, and how we dolled it all up with paper ornaments, a tinfoil star, and whatever the kids wanted to hang on it.

"It was lovely. It was…Christmas."

After two years of bouncing from state to state, Janice and Larry bought a used thirty-five-foot trailer to live in. From campgrounds to trailer parks—and sometimes Grandma Smith's driveway in Hot Springs—the family continued a nomadic existence, following work around the country and never maintaining an address for more than six months, sometimes as little as two. Larry built bunk beds for Shawn and Adam in a tiny room at the trailer's rear, while Manda had a cubbyhole within the cabinetry the size of her little mattress, and a curtain for a door. Their parents slept on the foldout couch in the ten-by-ten space that also served as the living/dining/do-everything room.

Another two years had passed when Shawn got into a fight at school in Tucson, Arizona. Now fourteen, he had been a trouper through all the moves, but Janice and Larry knew it was time to settle down. It was easier for Adam and Manda, being younger, to make new friends, while Shawn was the quiet kid who was the add-on at the end of every teacher's roll call and every coach's roster. As a solid catcher and power hitter in baseball, and a talent in almost any position on the football field, he eventually made friends and a name for himself, but then the family would move and he'd have to start again. His eighth-grade year alone, he went to six different schools—fifteen schools in all over the years.

"Shawn is miserable," Janice told Larry. "He won't complain, but he's miserable."

Shawn wasn't the only one worn out by life on the road and the constant struggle to make ends meet. "Well," said Larry, "if we're going to starve, let's do it at home. Let's go home to Hot Springs."

Six-year-old Adam insisted on wearing his "Arkansas" T-shirt on picture day.

Brown family archives

—

The Browns moved back to their house in Arkansas in time for Shawn to enter the ninth grade and Manda and Adam to begin fifth. Janice and Larry started a new business out of the garage—All Service Electric—with any and all jobs welcomed. Janice answered the phone and kept the books: in those nascent months, literally *a* book. Slowly, as they pinned their business cards on bulletin boards, tucked them under windshield wipers, and handed them out at the local grocery store, the book filled with work orders, each one a celebration.

And for every month spent at the same address, the family sank its roots deeper into the Arkansas soil, which was particularly rich in Hot Springs, a small city of some thirty-five thousand located in the scenic Ouachita Mountains and known for the natural thermal waters that flow from forty-seven springs on Hot Springs Mountain.

The kids reentered the local school system, where Adam's protective nature began to shine. Each weekday, the twins were dropped off with Shawn and had to make their way past the middle school handball courts in order to get to the elementary school. Any smaller kids within range would be bombarded with tennis balls hucked—and hucked hard—by older kids playing wall ball. "Adam would spread his arms out and side shuffle, guarding me, keeping me in close to him, so the balls couldn't hit me," says Manda. "He'd get hit a lot, but he wouldn't flinch till he got me to safety."

That first fall back home, Adam joined the YMCA's peewee tackle football program—assigned to the fifth-and-sixth-grade team, the Lake Hamilton Wolf Pack. Toward the end of their first practice with pads and helmets, Coach Mike Glisson, known as Coach Nitro, gathered the team, marked off a thirty-by-ten-yard lane, and asked for volunteers for a blocking-tackling drill called Blood Alley. The first kid to raise his hand was Adam Brown, whom Coach Nitro describes as being "not much bigger than a number two pencil." Deeming Adam either suicidal or "too big for his britches," he chose a more size-equitable boy, and when practice ended, Adam still hadn't gotten a turn.

At home Adam said to his mom, "That coach won't even let me play; he thinks I'm too little."

"Well, Adam, you know how to make somebody notice you," Janice replied. "You go back in there and keep trying. They'll let you play."

From then on, Adam made it his mission to take on the biggest players of the team every chance he got. "He just wouldn't quit," Glisson says.

Coach Nitro wasn't the only one to notice Adam's guts and reckless abandon on the field.

"Guess what my teammates called me today," Adam told his parents proudly one evening after practice. "Psycho!"

In sixth grade Adam was playing touch football on the school playground and, because Adam Brown didn't do anything half speed, the casual game became rough touch, and then *really* rough touch. Adam dived for a pass that "Superman himself couldn't have caught," says his friend Ryan Whited, and hit the ground chin first.

He got up and ran over to Ryan, mumbling something incoherently, blood dripping from the corners of his mouth. When he opened it and the blood poured out, Ryan could see that Adam had bitten most of his tongue off—all the way through, except for a little flesh on one side. "I'm going to the nurse" was what he was trying to say.

"Anybody else would have been on the ground wailing," says Ryan, "but Adam didn't even cry. He just walked to the nurse, went home, and got it sewn back on."

Every day after school, Manda and Adam would walk from their middle school over to the high school and watch Shawn at football practice.

At Lake Hamilton High School, with around seven hundred students in grades ten through twelve, "Big Bad Shawn Brown" was a star athlete whose ability to crush adversaries both on and off the field was legendary. Shawn played defensive lineman for the Lake Hamilton Wolves—the nose guard—and Adam would say, in his best Mr. T. impersonation, "I pity the fool who tries to run up the middle against my brother."

Adam was such a die-hard fan of his brother and his brother's team that the coaches made him the ball boy and gave him a team jersey. "You couldn't have slapped the smile off his face," says Shawn. "As far as Adam was concerned, he was hanging out with the NFL."

One afternoon Adam showed up to help with practice, eyes red from crying. "What happened?" Shawn asked. Adam explained how a junior varsity player had cornered him in the locker room and given him a swirly—shoved his head into a toilet bowl and flushed. "It was disrespectful," Adam said, staring at the ground.

Lifting Adam's chin up with his hand, Shawn said, "We'll see what we can do about that later."

After practice, Shawn was driving them home when he noticed the JV player's car parked outside the Busy B's Café. He pulled over and, with Adam in tow, walked up to the booth where the kid was eating a burger with a buddy. Glancing up, the kid saw Adam and Shawn, and like a deer in the headlights, he froze. Shawn leaned in and stared him in the eye.

"If you *ever* touch my little brother again," said Shawn, loud enough

Adam and Manda, age three, with their big brother, Shawn, age seven.

for every patron in the restaurant to hear, "I will break both of your legs."
He stepped away and said again, "Both of them."

The café was silent. Avoiding Shawn's ferocious gaze, the JV player
nodded his head. Outside in the parking lot, Shawn put his arm around
his little brother, who was still grinning. If Adam had looked up to Shawn
before, from that day forward he was a giant.

During the summer of 1987 a new kid showed up in Hot Springs. His
name was Jeff Buschmann, and he was a football player and a Navy brat
who'd been born in Italy, lived at Guantánamo Bay, Cuba, and bounced
around the United States from San Diego and Washington on the West
Coast to Florida and Maine on the East. He'd attended six schools, the last
in South Carolina, before his father—Commander Roger Buschmann—
took command of the Navy recruiting district based in Little Rock.

Janice had met Jeff's mother after a football practice and suggested to Adam that he do something with the new kid to make him feel welcome in Hot Springs. But instead of Adam showing Jeff around, Jeff took Adam to the monster of a rope swing he'd discovered by the pylons of the I-70 West bridge over Lake Hamilton. The rope was long, frayed, knotted, and affixed somehow to the underside of the bridge some forty feet above them. Even the intrepid Adam Brown eyed the thing and muttered "I don't know…" while Jeff dove into the warm water, grabbed the string trailing from the rope, and swam with it to the nearest pylon. "It looks like quite a ride," he said to Adam as he climbed to the starting point atop the fifteen-foot pylon. "I'll go first."

This giant pendulum took its rider full speed toward the water before arcing into the air over the lake. "At the apex you were a good twenty feet up," says Jeff. "That's when you let go if you really wanted some air time, or you could just hang on and ride it out. You couldn't slam into a tree or anything." According to Jeff, "It was completely safe," something he told Adam several times, egging him on as he took turn after turn himself.

For whatever reason, Adam didn't trust the rope, but Jeff had seen Adam on the football field and knew he had the courage. Finally, Adam relented. Climbing to the top of the pylon, he grabbed the rope high at a knot, pulled on it a few times, jumped into the air, and held on for dear life. Down he swooped, and at the lowest point, when the speed was greatest and the rope stretched the tightest, it snapped and Adam hit the calm surface of Lake Hamilton in a watery explosion of arms, legs, and gurgled curses.

"Oh shit!" Jeff said, diving off the pylon and swimming to the water's edge. "I am so sorry!" he told Adam, who was visibly shaken by the incident but tried to brush it off by saying, "It's all right; at least now I know what an enema feels like."

"I don't get it! How could I do it all those times, and then it snaps right when you try?" Jeff said.

Adam just shrugged.

It's the only time Jeff would remember Adam backing down from anything or anyone.

Once school started in the fall, Adam introduced Jeff to everyone as his new friend. He told them about "Busch" taking on the 70 West bridge rope swing, something that, Adam admitted, "scared me half to death." Such praise, coming from Adam Brown, gave the new kid instant street credibility and forged a lifelong friendship.

"At thirteen, when most kids are heartless and downright mean, Adam knew what it meant to be nice," says Jeff. "He would go out of his way to make you feel good about yourself." And Adam was friends with everybody. "He transcended cliques. I never heard him say anything mean about anybody, but he always stood up for people."

During that eighth-grade year, Adam was hanging out with friends in front of the school one morning when a school bus pulled up and students poured out. Most of the kids headed to the front doors, but three boys stopped Richie Holden, who had Down syndrome, and taunted him by calling him names. Smaller than any of the bullies, Adam nevertheless marched over and stood in front of Richie. "If you want to pick on someone," he said, "you can pick on me—if you think you're big enough."

"The three backed off," Richie's father, Dick Holden, says, recounting the story as told to him by Richie and his older sister, Rachel. "Adam put his arm around Richie and walked with him through the door, then all the way to his class. Richie never forgot that, and I remember thinking, *That Brown boy—he's something special.*"

3

The Wolf Pack

EVER SINCE ADAM HAD WATCHED SHAWN play varsity football in Lake Hamilton High School's Wolf Stadium under the Friday night lights, it had been his "field of dreams."

Walking the sidelines as an eleven-year-old ball boy, Adam had fantasized about the day he would suit up, clash against their rivals, and earn his own "stick marks"—multicolored paint streaks on his maroon helmet from colliding with the helmets of opposing schools' teams. To paint over them was sacrilege.

In the summer of 1989, Adam finally stepped onto the grass at Wolf Stadium as a player. It was eight o'clock in the morning and already ninety degrees, with T-shirt-soaking humidity, when assistant coach Steve Anderson surveyed the talent that had shown up for practice. Coach Anderson, the offensive line coach at Lake Hamilton, had his eyes peeled for players like Shawn Brown, who was now playing college ball on a partial scholarship at Henderson State University in nearby Arkadelphia. He'd seen the name *Adam Brown* on the junior varsity roster and wondered if their enthusiastic ball boy from two years before had finally put some meat on his bones.

Adam's beaming smile was unmistakable. So was his size; Coach Anderson doubted he'd grown at all since eighth grade. Even with pads on, Adam looked like "an itty bitty kid," says Coach Anderson. "All helmet."

Toward the end of their first practice, the coaches laid two blocking dummies side by side on the grass, creating a lane or "alley," and both junior varsity and varsity gathered around to cheer on their buddies during "Alley Drill." First a coach called out two equal-size players, who faced each other in three-point stances. The whistle blew and they sprang forward, collided, and tried to either bowl each other over or muscle each other out of the alley. "It's a very physical drill," says Coach Anderson, "a gut check. Football's a testosterone sport, and the guys are up there to prove their manhood and who can beat who."

Historically, the big guys—linemen, linebackers, running backs— gravitated toward this drill while the less aggressive and less meaty types prayed they wouldn't get called out. The junior varsity guys hung back as far as they could, quiet with the crickets.

Except Adam. Just as in his peewee football days with Coach Nitro's "Blood Alley," he was up front day after day, begging the coaches to put him in against the bigger varsity players. "C'mon, c'mon, let me take this one. I got It," he'd yell. The coaches, whose job included not letting the kids hurt themselves, never called on Adam and he'd ultimately stomp off angry.

"Every day he'd give it a shot," says Coach Anderson, "until finally, toward the end of summer, he wore us down."

The usually boisterous team lining the alley was almost silent as Adam faced off against one of the bigger varsity linemen. "On the whistle, they crashed into each other," says Coach Anderson. "Adam did fire out, but this guy hit him hard, drove him back harder, and rolled him up."

Fully expecting Adam to limp to the back of the line, Coach Anderson blew the whistle. Instead, Adam jumped up, slapped the side of his helmet, and said, "Let's go again! You want some more of me?"

The coaches looked at each other, and the team responded with a cry of "Let him go!"

Again Adam was pummeled, and again "he popped back up and jumped into his three-point stance, like he wasn't going to take no for an answer," says Coach Anderson.

"Let's go again—I'm gonna whip you this time," Adam grunted through his mouthpiece.

After the third time, the coaches called the drill, surprised that Adam wasn't beat up enough to stop on his own. Before heading off the field, Adam ran over to the offensive lineman he'd been pitted against and thanked him for not going easy on him.

The four coaches present that day knew they'd witnessed something remarkable. Says Coach Anderson, "That one little sophomore taught our whole team more about character in a few minutes than any of us coaches could have in an entire season. He wasn't going to be the big star lineman that his brother was, but what impressed me was this kid was not scared. He was determined that he was not going to let his size keep him from doing whatever he wanted to do."

Adam's tough, daring reputation was rivaled only by his propensity for kindness. He went out of his way to give Richie Holden, the boy with Down syndrome, a high-five whenever he saw him. At school functions he'd ask the wallflowers to dance, and there wasn't a woman in Hot Springs who opened a door for herself if Adam was in the vicinity. And he always stood up for the underdog—never realizing that because of his size he was one himself.

Just before tenth grade started, Adam was invited to a boat party at the Buschmanns' lake house. Despite the fact Jeff had become one of Adam's closest friends, Janice was having reservations about allowing her fifteen-year-old son to attend. To say Janice neither trusted Adam's swimming ability nor liked the idea of a bunch of teenagers in boats out on the lake was an understatement, but he begged until she agreed he could go—as long as he wore a life jacket. He promised he would.

A couple dozen guys and girls partied in the warm summer waters Lake Hamilton style, on a flotilla of pontoon boats and speed boats, various inflatables or skis in tow. With ice chests overflowing with cold drinks and music blaring, the girls sunbathed and the guys showed off with back-flips. And in the middle of it all was Adam, life jacket fastened securely. His buddies taunted him, "Dude, Adam, your mom's not here!" To which Adam replied, "Naw. It's no big deal, I promised."

"Adam was like no other kid I ever met," says Roger Buschmann, who was privy to Adam's resolve that day. He was even more impressed a few months later when Adam was one of five buddies invited to the Buschmann home for a sleepover. "At two in the morning I heard a knock

Jeff Buschmann and Adam after running a logging road in the Ouachita woods. Jeff recalls that the stick had something to do with fending off rattlesnakes.

on our bedroom door," he says. "It was Adam, holding a phone. Ends up the boys had snuck out to crash a girls' slumber party but got caught by the mother, who was not pleased when she called me to come get them."

As Roger Buschmann was leaving the house, he asked Adam why he hadn't gone with his buddies.

"My parents told me not to leave the house without permission, sir."

They might be able to out-party Adam, but none of his buddies could beat his crazy stunts. While they'd all jump from the 70 West bridge forty feet into the lake, Adam would add flips and gainers, a forward dive with a reverse rotation. At football camp he was the undisputed belly-flop king, doing five in a row—off the high board.

Then there was his penchant for jumping into (not out of) trees. On his first attempt off a twenty-five-foot-tall bridge into a thirty-foot elm, he missed entirely the branch he was aiming for. The one he did hit snapped, along with others that slowed his fall to the base of the tree, where he landed feet first, a shower of leaves fluttering down around him.

Figuring he'd chosen the wrong genus of tree, Adam tried leaping into a large evergreen off the second-floor deck of a friend's house a few weeks later. The branch bowed under his weight, then broke. Jeff Buschmann, on hand to witness the carnage, heard a succession of grunts as Adam hit branch after branch on his way down.

"Please don't do that again," he told Adam, who walked away bruised but not broken. "You're going to hurt yourself."

Adam considered his friends—including Jeff, Heath Vance, and Richard Williams—an extension of his family, and they bonded like brothers in what all of them felt was an idyllic country-boy upbringing. Playing football, swimming and boating in the lake, hiking in the woods, making out with girls, drinking beer, having bonfires, backyard basketball games, house parties, and fistfights—usually with each other—and pulling pranks.

One night when they were sixteen, Jeff, Richard, and Adam rolled a house in an entire case of toilet paper, then tore through the woods to get back to the car they'd left discreetly parked on a different street. Their escape was almost complete when a dark figure materialized by the car, waiting patiently.

Moments later, they were in the backseat of a police cruiser, Jeff and Richard squeezed in on either side of Adam, who kept saying, "My momma and daddy are going to be so disappointed."

"He started crying like a baby," says Richard, "and Buschmann looks over at him and says, 'Adam! Stop your crying! Don't you have any more respect for your father than that?'"

He cried most of the way to the station, and when Larry showed up, he started again. Early the following morning Larry drove him over to the house to help clean up the mess with the other culprits. No other discipline was necessary, because "the ride in the police car did the trick," says Janice. "He apologized for weeks."

At the beginning of the summer before their senior year, Adam sat down with Jeff, Heath, Richard, and a few of the other varsity football players. In one year Adam had shot up to almost six feet out of the six foot two he'd eventually reach. He was lean and lanky and, on the field, anything but graceful. "He was proof that you didn't have to be the biggest or the fastest to be a leader," says Richard. "It was his heart—his spirit—that drew people to him."

Indeed, Adam was passionate about his final year as a Wolf. In his junior year, they'd made it to the state semifinals, which wasn't bad, but Adam was emphatic: if they really wanted to put Lake Hamilton High on the map, they needed to make the finals. The only way to accomplish that would be to work out, eat right, not drink a drop of beer, and hold conditioning practices on their own before the start of the football season. A pact was made, and to the beat of songs like "Kickstart My Heart" by Mötley Crüe and "Eye of the Tiger" by Survivor, the teammates pumped iron in the weight room, ran the bleachers and did wind sprints, and cranked out push-ups, sit-ups, and leg lifts.

When the official two-a-day practices began in late August, "We were stunned by the team's level of fitness," says Coach Anderson.

"We would have been mediocre that season if we hadn't rallied the way we did," says Richard. "It took leaders like Adam to inspire so many guys to get out there and sweat their summer away for a long shot."

The Lake Hamilton Wolves won their first game. Then their second, and third—and they kept winning, all but one game, landing them in the state finals and inspiring Adam to shave his jersey number, 24, into the cropped sides of his mullet.

Although the team ultimately lost the state championship, as Arkansas State runner-up champions, it surpassed everyone's expectations and earned bragging rights throughout Garland County. The 1991 Wolves would forever be remembered as the players who put Lake Hamilton on the high school football map in Arkansas.

Over the Christmas holiday break, Richard and Adam were watching a video at the Williamses' house when they saw an action-packed preview for the movie *Navy SEALs,* which began with Lieutenant Dale Hawkins (played by Charlie Sheen) jumping from the back of a speeding Jeep off a

In 1991, the Lake Hamilton Wolves seniors led the team in a historic season to become runner-up Arkansas State champions; #24 Adam, #20 Heath Vance, #19 Jeff Buschmann, and #16 Richard Williams.

highway bridge into water at least fifty feet below. This spectacular stunt was followed by gunfire, explosions, and a deep, melodramatic voiceover and monologue: "When danger is its own reward, there are men who will go anywhere, dare anything. They're Navy SEALs, a unique fighting force who doesn't know how to lose.... Navy SEALs get paid to take risks; they're paid to die if necessary.... Together they are America's designated hitters against terrorism. Born to risk, trained to win... Navy SEALs..."

Danger is its own reward? Go anywhere, dare anything? *Hell,* Richard thought immediately, *they aren't talking about the Navy SEALs— they're talking about Adam.*

Adam, on the other hand, was most inspired by the stunt. "I'm gonna do that," he said to Richard. "I'm going to jump out of a car when we're crossing the 70 West bridge."

"You're crazy," said Richard.

As senior year progressed, every time Adam drove across the bridge, he brought the topic up to whichever buddies he was with.

"We all jumped off that bridge," Jeff says, "but to do it from a speeding vehicle…let me tell you, it's scary enough standing still and doing it."

"I don't want any part of it," Jeff informed Adam. "And you are not using my Jeep."

As Adam and his friends walked out to the school parking lot following the end-of-year athletic banquet, Adam announced he was ready for the bridge. Jeff remained steadfast in his refusal to allow Adam to jump from his car, and Richard, who was driving a Pontiac Grand Am, didn't have the right type of vehicle. Another friend volunteered his Suzuki Samurai, and they headed out into the night, a convoy of a half-dozen vehicles with Adam riding in the back of the open-topped Samurai.

Richard drove directly behind the Samurai, nervous but also confident that nothing would happen to Adam. "He'd bend, he'd get hurt," says Richard, "but he never broke. He never didn't get up."

The convoy slowed to about thirty miles per hour halfway across the bridge. The water below was dark, making it impossible to spot any boats or floating debris—not that Adam cared. Richard watched the Samurai edge closer and thought, *Maybe this isn't such a good idea.* The Samurai was now in the bike lane, just a foot or so away from the waist-high concrete wall. Then the silhouette of Adam rose up in the back, held on to the roll bar for a second, and dived into the abyss.

Richard threw on his hazard lights and screeched to a halt as Jeff sped past to get to the other side, where Adam would exit the water. The other cars pulled over as well, and Adam's buddies scrambled out and leaned against the bridge wall, scanning below. There was just enough ambient light for Richard to see Adam swimming to shore.

"You all right, Adam?" he shouted.

"Yeah!" Adam yelled up.

Sprinting down the trail, Jeff reached the water's edge the same time Adam did. "Damn, Adam," he said, offering a hand. "How was it?"

Adam explained that when he'd dived out of the Samurai, he had hoped to straighten out and land feet first. Instead, he'd hit the water sideways, which from that height and with the forward momentum was more than he'd bargained for.

"I don't think I'll do that again," was his response. "Slapped the water pretty hard, but I'm glad I did it—it would have eaten at me forever."

4

Slipping

DECKED OUT IN WOLF COLORS, MAROON AND GOLD, the Hot Springs Convention Center was the only building in town that could hold the crowd for Lake Hamilton High School's 1992 graduation ceremony. Along with the rest of the school board, Larry Brown was seated on stage, taking turns presenting diplomas as principal Curtis Williams called out the graduates' names. In the audience Janice nudged Shawn when Larry stood up and approached the podium. Adam's and Manda's names were coming up; they were both graduating with honors.

"Adam Leroy Brown," Principal Williams spoke into the microphone. The nearly three hundred graduates erupted in laughter.

"I didn't know Adam's middle name was Leroy," Shawn said to his mother.

"It's not," replied Janice, shaking her head and a little perturbed as she watched Adam strut up to his dad to receive his diploma.

"He grinned real big when he shook my hand," says Larry, "because he had just put one over on the principal by telling him his middle name was Leroy, not Lee."

Once the laughter subsided and people stopped shouting "Leroy Brown!" Manda's name was called, and when she shook her father's hand, she smiled and rolled her eyes.

At the end of the ceremony, the grads threw their caps in the air. Adam ended his high school career with a bang, literally, as he walked out the door, but once Manda and he had posed for photos and said their good-byes to friends, Adam became melancholy. Always sentimental, he made sure to tell Jeff, Richard, and Heath, "No matter where we are, no matter what we're doing, we'll always be there for each other."

Right before heading off to college, Richard drove Adam home through the winding roads of Hot Springs. It was dusk, the windows were rolled down, the warm summer wind was on their faces, the familiar woods of their youth blurred by, and they hung on to every chord of Hank Williams Jr.'s guitar as they sang along to "Country Boy Can Survive."

Soon after, the country boys from Lake Hamilton scattered in pursuit of their educations. Jeff went to the University of Arkansas in Fayetteville with plans to attend Officer Candidate School and become a Navy pilot. Heath headed to the University of Central Arkansas in Conway, where he had mapped out an education in sports medicine in order to stay involved with football. Having earned a full-ride football scholarship to Ouachita Baptist University, Richard was living the dream—as well as studying accounting.

While Adam had dreamed of playing college football for the University of Arkansas Razorbacks, a scholarship wasn't in the cards for him. "Adam was like Rudy wanting to play for the Fighting Irish," says Richard, referring to the true story of Daniel "Rudy" Ruettiger, a steel mill worker's son who had all the heart but not the size, financial means, or grades to attend, much less play for, Notre Dame. "That movie [Rudy] came out around that time, and when I saw it, all I could think about was Adam. His desire far outreached his size and skills, just like Rudy."

Still, Adam was pleased to attend Arkansas Tech University, a smaller college two hours from home, where he was confident he would be a star on the football team. He "walked on" for the Wonder Boys, and his toughness earned him a spot on defense, but he barely touched the field the entire season, playing just a few downs in three of the games.

"It was the first time Adam realized he wasn't everything he thought he was on the football field," says Larry, who with Janice attended all his home games and some of the away ones. "He wasn't fast enough or big enough to compete at the college level."

In high school Adam was a popular standout who had thrived on his crazy, unstoppable reputation. But at Arkansas Tech he was just another student, another face, and another forgettable jersey on game day. His grades were mediocre: biology, C; chemistry, D; college algebra, C; sociology, B. In a family where Cs were unacceptable, Adam was slipping.

He vowed to his parents that he would do better second semester, but his grades were the same for the follow-on courses in biology, chemistry, and algebra: C, D, and C. His one A was in bowling. He worked at a retail store as a clerk to help offset the expenses paid by his parents, and in his free time he would go to parties and hang out at the bars and clubs around campus with friends he'd made in class or on the team. But for the first time in his life, he seemed out of sync.

"Adam went through his awkward stage later than most," remembers Manda. "We'd talk on the phone, and you could tell he was unhappy, didn't really fit in with any one group, and that's what I mean by 'awkward.' Adam had always been friends with everybody, and in college that changed. Lots of acquaintances but no real friends."

The summer after his freshman year, Adam returned home to work for his father. Being in Hot Springs recharged his batteries for the fall of 1993, when he transferred to Henderson State University in Arkadelphia—the same college where Shawn had been on a football scholarship until he'd blown out his knee.

Although Adam had never quit anything in his life, he read the writing on the wall. He could not stand being sidelined and made the hard decision to put football behind him. His new sport was drinking, and his new "party friends" had a hard time matching Adam's abilities with a beer funnel.

Over Christmas break their sophomore year, Adam, Jeff, Heath, and Richard slid into the bench seat of Adam's black Ford F-150 pickup to head to a party across town. Within moments of their reunion—the first time they'd all been together since the previous summer—Adam elbowed Jeff in the ribs and said, "It's like a day hasn't passed, and here we are together again."

Around midnight they were returning home on Central Avenue when a truck sped up to their tail, swerved back and forth, then nearly ran them off the road as it passed.

"They can't do that in our town!" Jeff said angrily.

"Hell no!" said Adam. "Let's slow these guys down." Stepping on the accelerator, he pulled alongside the truck and shouted, "Slow down!"

Four guys in their early twenties looked over. "Yeah?" the driver yelled back. "Pull over!"

Both vehicles pulled off the road near McClard's Bar-B-Q, then, as though straight out of a scene in a movie, the two groups of four got out and moved slowly toward each other from the black night into the dim white glow of a nearby streetlight. The driver was the biggest, and like the others, he had both hands balled up in tight fists and came in swinging. "We're from Little Rock!" he yelled. "You don't want to f— with us!"

A solid right jab from Adam hit the guy square in the mouth, and a full-on brawl erupted between the two groups. Jeff took a hard punch to his ribs. Shoving back, he saw a stiletto blade in the shaking hand of the guy who had hit him, and felt warmth moving down his side. When he tore open his flannel shirt to look, the white undershirt was turning dark red and blood was pooling at his beltline. Anger surged to rage, and Jeff grabbed the guy by the hair, yanked him to the ground, and began pounding his face with the other fist.

"What the hell are you doing?" Adam yelled, pulling Jeff away. "You're going to break his skull open!"

"He f—ing bladed me, man!" said Jeff, holding his shirt open and beginning to stumble.

Just as the guys from Little Rock jumped back in their truck and slammed the door, Adam let out what Jeff describes as a "primal roar," charged straight at the front of the vehicle, and launched himself into the air. Clearing the hood, he rammed his head like a torpedo into the windshield, which caved in with a sickening thud—a spiderweb of cracks extending from the hole. After rolling off the side of the hood, Adam stood up.

The truck door swung open and there was a loud, ominous *chu-chunk*. One of the guys had chambered a round in a shotgun and leveled it at Heath, who raced for cover behind Adam's truck.

Boom! Boom! the shotgun went off, and Richard scrambled under Adam's truck. When he stood up on the other side, he saw Jeff stumbling toward him, noticed the blood, and assumed he'd been shot. "Richard!" yelled Jeff. "Help me."

Half carrying, half dragging a nearly unconscious Jeff to a retaining wall beside the truck, the friends ducked down as two more shotgun rounds blasted off. Blood had now soaked the front of both of Jeff's shirts.

"If we don't do something, Busch is going to die," Richard said. Adam immediately jumped over the wall and ripped off his shirt. Shaking his fists in the air, he walked toward the guy with the gun, yelling, "If you're going to shoot me, f—ing shoot me!" Visibly shaking, the guy didn't say anything but also didn't put down the gun, so Adam kept walking until the barrel was only a couple of feet away and pointed straight at his chest. "Then I'm going to take my friend to the hospital."

The guy lowered the gun.

By the time they'd rushed Jeff to the emergency room at St. Joseph's Hospital, he was having trouble breathing and almost passed out while the doctor probed the wound. The knife had entered between his ribs—inches from his heart—and into his left lung, which was filling with blood and required immediate surgery.

As Jeff lay on a gurney in the pre-op room, a surgical nurse read his chart. "You're a lucky young man," she told him.

"Yeah," he said weakly. "My friend saved my life."

Details of the incident made the local paper the following day. Minutes after Adam and his friends had sped to the hospital, the police showed up at the scene. "They found a massive pool of blood, some brass knuckles, and a library book that had been checked out by guess who," says Richard. "Adam Brown. It must've fallen out when he'd opened the door to his truck."

Adam, Jeff, Richard, and Heath were questioned by deputies at the hospital and counseled to leave the speeding tickets to them and not pull over reckless drivers looking for a fight. Adam, in particular, was told that in the future he should "run from a loaded gun."

That spring, Adam transferred to the University of Central Arkansas in Conway and changed his major from engineering to business administration. His heart wasn't in either discipline. "He was pretty lost, no direction," says Heath, who was continuing his degree in sports medicine at the same college. "The one thing he said he didn't want to do was end up working for his dad the rest of his life. He said he wanted to do something big, something important; he just couldn't figure out what that was."

In the summer of 1994, Janice and Larry announced to their kids that they were renting a big beach house in the resort town of Destin, Florida, an opportunity for the entire family to have its first five-star trip together. Not long before they left, however, Adam told his parents he should stay home and get ready for school instead.

Though sad that her son would be missing this special vacation, Janice was proud of Adam's maturity. "We're going to go and have fun," she told him, handing him two hundred dollars when she hugged him good-bye. "Your dad and I want you to have some fun too. Go out to dinner, see some movies—you enjoy it."

While the rest of the Browns enjoyed the beach in Destin, Adam planned a huge party at their house.

The two hundred dollars covered the kegs.

Word of the August 4 party spread widely, even to neighboring counties. By nightfall the house and backyard were a sea of people. Soon the roof was doubling as a high dive for the shallow pool, with Adam cheerfully leading the charge with a front flip to laid-out belly flop.

The crowd continued to swell, pushing the fence over to make more room in the side yard. Drunken youths were in the street when police arrived to send most of the partygoers on their way. "That party," says Heath Vance, "was a raging success, but it was also a disaster." Aside from the destruction to the Browns' home—a toilet ripped from the floor, a window shattered, the fence trampled—Adam reconnected with a young woman he'd known in high school named Cindy Gravis.

At age twenty, Adam had drunk his share of beer and was no stranger to southern whiskey, but he could count on the fingers of one hand how many times he'd smoked marijuana, which he'd told his buddies always made him feel like a loser. After a night of "getting friendly" with Cindy, however, when she pressed up against Adam and suggestively said, "You wanna get high?" his response was, "Well, yeah. Absolutely."

The following morning when Adam's uncle Charlie drove to work at All Service Electric, which was still based in the Browns' garage, people were sprawled on the front yard, sleeping it off among the shrubs. Inside, Charlie found Adam with a trash bag, picking up cups and beer cans.

"Please don't tell my mom and dad," said Adam, his eyes wide at his uncle's arrival.

"You get this all cleaned up—and fix that toilet," Charlie said, surveying the damage. "But if they ask me, I'm going to have to tell them. I'm not going to lie."

When Adam went to Wal-Mart to pick up the supplies he would need, Grandma Brown was working at the front door as a greeter, a job she'd had for years. Feeling guilty, Adam fessed up, telling his grandmother that he was trying to clean up the aftermath of a party that had gotten out of hand.

"Just how bad is it, Adam?" she asked as he exited the store with a cartful of cleaning supplies, a Wal-Mart employee following him with the new toilet on a dolly.

Not wanting to spoil the Browns' vacation, Grandma Brown waited until their last day in Florida to break the news: "Adam had a big party while you were away. I thought you should be aware."

All the way home, Manda steadfastly defended Adam to their parents, maintaining that it was no big deal if Adam had some friends over for a little party—till she found that her closet had been rifled and some clothes were missing, her jewelry box had been pillaged, and her bed had been more than just slept in. Adam suffered his sister's angry glare and the disappointed looks from Janice and Larry, especially once Janice discovered that more than fifty items had been stolen or broken, including a family heirloom quilt so stained that a partygoer had tossed it in the trash.

That Adam felt terrible was obvious. He told his family he'd make it right, and Janice replied that some of this could never be made right. He was going to have to earn their trust again.

For the rest of the month, Adam hung out with his new girlfriend, Cindy, and her friends after work and on weekends. "They were a different group than Adam knew in high school," says Larry. "They'd never stick around for long; they'd come by the house, grab Adam, and off they'd go."

Then Adam informed his parents that he'd decided to take a break from school to figure out what he wanted to do with his life. The truth was he didn't want to leave Cindy. He began to party away his paychecks from All Service Electric and was soon learning the ropes of the drug world in and around Hot Springs with Cindy as his partner and guide. On weekends, after work, or in the middle of the night, they'd go for a drive that always ended at a drug house, hanging out for hours on dirty couches around coffee tables cluttered with beer cans, ashtrays, and drug paraphernalia.

At first Adam stuck to marijuana and alcohol, but then Cindy introduced him to crystal meth, followed by her drug of choice, crack cocaine. She told Adam that he could never fully understand her unless he did the drug too.

"The first time I did it," Adam explained to a friend, "I knew I had sold my soul." For a few minutes he experienced what he described as "euphoria," and from that moment forward he smoked crack almost every day. Each time he came down off the high, the only thing he could think about was when he could do it again.

Too enamored of the drug to fear it, Adam believed he would simply quit when he wanted to. He viewed this world of drugs as something he was just passing through. It didn't bother him that the two thousand dollars he'd earned working for his parents was gone less than two weeks after his first taste of crack, money that was spent supplying himself, Cindy, and many of the addicts he met—buying single hits for them the way one buys a round at a bar.

Adam continued to live at home and work for All Service Electric until the end of 1994, when Janice and Larry moved to a nearby farm with a big barn for the offices and workshop of their business, which had continued in its success. Still hiding his addiction from his parents and closest friends, Adam couldn't ignore it himself. At work, he couldn't concentrate and felt a quiver in his muscles, a yearning that, try as he might, he could not ignore. As soon as the day ended, he would temper the shakiness with alcohol until he could smoke some crack, and once again life was beautiful.

The Brown family had no idea what was going on under their noses: outwardly, Adam was the same old Adam, though perhaps a bit distracted and a little paler than normal. Aside from work, his parents didn't see much of him, and Manda and Shawn were off living their own lives, Manda attending college and Shawn employed as a pharmacist in Little Rock.

Likewise, close buddies Jeff, Heath, and Richard saw Adam only occasionally. They knew Cindy was a bad influence and that he spent a lot of time getting high with her and had even tried cocaine, but their concern was limited because on the phone he sounded the same as always.

Adam would get over it soon enough, they figured, with no clue as to the full extent of his addiction. And get over *her*. After all, he'd always done the right thing.

"He'll be all right," Jeff told Heath during a discussion about Adam. "He'll figure it out."

5

The Dark Time

JANICE AND LARRY HAD ALWAYS HAPPILY employed Adam, not only because he was their son, but also because he'd been a dedicated worker for as long as they could remember. Once, when Adam was four, Larry had to string wire under a house. It was a tight squeeze—two feet tops—beneath the foundation and the flooring, and when he peered across the darkness through the hole he'd cut into the house's siding, he saw it was too far for a wire pusher to reach.

"You want to do it?" he asked Adam, half joking. "You're not scared of spiders, right?"

Adam lit up. "Yeah! Do I get to use your big flashlight?"

With Larry's flashlight grasped in one hand and the end of the wire in the other, Adam pushed through the cutout and started crawling. Halfway in, some thirty feet or so, he called back, "Dad, there's something dead here in front of me."

"What is it?"

"Either a giant rat or a possum."

"Well," said Larry, "he won't hurt you then. Just go around him."

Once Adam was nearly across, Larry darted to the other side of the house. He grabbed the wire that Adam threaded through a marble-size hole.

"Now what?" Adam called through the hole.

"Turn around and go back."

"Past the possum?" said Adam.

"Unless you can squeeze through this hole."

"And that was Adam's debut performance as my helper," says Larry. "He was our tunnel rat."

In high school Adam did just about everything for the company, from manual labor to delicate wiring learned from Larry. He was both punctual and a model employee.

"But then he started slipping," says Janice. "That year he stopped going to college after the big party. That was what tipped us off something was wrong. First it was his work ethic, then it was his attitude."

It started with Adam's being late by a few minutes, then an hour, but he'd always apologize and have an excuse: he'd run out of gas or forgot his watch. When he began disappearing for an entire day or two, he no longer bothered apologizing or offering an explanation. He'd just show up and go to work "like he was entitled to come and go as he pleased," says Larry. While Larry did tell Adam this was unacceptable and disruptive behavior, he didn't tell his son that he was also embarrassed. His boy should have been the hardest worker in the family business.

On a day Adam hadn't appeared for work again, Larry walked into the house and asked Janice if she'd seen him.

"He's soaking in the hot tub," she said.

Uncertain if he was more mad or disappointed, Larry shook his head and stepped out on the back deck, where Adam was lying in the tub looking up at the night sky. "Adam...," he began.

"I don't want to hear it!" Adam shouted.

"Don't you raise your voice to me," Larry yelled back, his frustration getting the better of him.

"Look who's calling the kettle black," Adam said with a scoff.

Inside the house Janice could hear the heated conversation—and was pretty sure half of Hot Springs could too. "I am sick and tired of your attitude!" shouted Larry. "You're unreliable. You've got no motivation. You don't finish anything you start!"

Adam yelled back, "A lot of kids take some time off from school. Why can't I just have some fun? I think you've devoted your life to make sure I don't have any fun!"

Momentarily stunned, Larry hesitated. Adam grinned and submerged his head in the hot water, and Larry didn't wait for him to surface. He walked inside and saw Janice standing motionless by the window, too sad for tears.

"What has happened to Adam?" she said quietly. "That little boy I love is gone."

Later that night Janice told Larry, "Remember earlier this year when we were talking about how lucky we were getting all our kids through without any drug problems? I think we spoke too soon."

"I'm thinking the same thing," said Larry. "He's got to be on drugs. That's just not Adam."

They agreed not to confront Adam but instead wait until the next time he disappeared, which ended up being the following week. When he returned to work several days later, Janice marched up to him and said, "I want you to come with me down to the medical center."

"Why, Mama?" Adam said sweetly.

"I want you to take a drug test. You're an employee here—you need to take one just like the rest of the fellas."

"I am not on drugs, Mom!"

"Well," said Janice, "then let's get this done."

The following day, after Janice and Larry found out that their son had tested positive for cocaine, marijuana, and amphetamines, Adam was already gone again.

He showed up at Heath's apartment in Conway and stayed for two days, during which time he told Heath how hard he and Cindy had been partying and that his parents had sent him for a drug test. Heath was shocked—and relieved that Janice and Larry knew what was going on.

For his part Jeff had been concerned that Adam seemed content to stick around Hot Springs crashing high school parties. His concern turned into disbelief when Adam told him during a phone call soon after that he'd begun to shoot up meth and crack because injecting them made the high last longer.

"Cindy showed me how to do it," Adam said. "We do it for each other. I shoot her up, and she shoots me up." It had "bonded" them, Adam explained.

When Jeff shared this new development with Heath, Heath decided that Cindy Gravis was not just a loser but "pure evil" as well.

Two weeks after the drug test, Adam returned to the farmhouse. He was repentant and wanted to come home. "It will never happen again, Mama," he said to Janice. He promised he'd stopped the drugs—he knew they'd been a mistake. That meant something to his parents, because as far as they knew, Adam had never broken a promise. They forgave him, but continued to keep a wary eye out for signs of drug usage.

Unbeknownst to Janice and Larry, Adam proceeded to break his promise. He supported his addiction by cleverly stealing from his family, using the All Service Electric account at local supply shops and hardware stores to buy tools and other items he then sold for cash. Soon he was taking credit card checks from Janice's purse or Larry's desk, making them out to himself and forging his parents' signatures for cash or goods that he could sell. Over a month passed before they figured out what he was doing. When they confronted him, he disappeared.

He suddenly reappeared, then disappeared, reappeared, again and again, always weaseling his way back into Janice and Larry's home and hearts. They allowed it because they were relieved he was alive and because they remembered the pure, sweet boy they'd raised to always do the right thing. They believed that the Adam they knew would eventually decide to kick his addiction in the butt.

This cycle continued well into 1995.

During one of his disappearances, Janice and Larry recruited Shawn and Manda, and together they combed the streets of Hot Springs until they found him—and Cindy—strung out in a "borrowed" All Service Electric truck parked beside a convenience store. Noticing his family, Adam and Cindy got out and walked over.

"Adam, you need to come home," Janice pleaded through her open window. "You two don't need to be together. You're not ever going to get well this way."

Adam looked at Cindy, put his arm around her, looked at his folks, and said, "Nope." Staring at the Browns, Janice in particular, Cindy snickered.

"Adam," Janice said, "you are going nowhere good with her. You come home. Now!"

Cindy pulled away from Adam and leaned in the window. "You don't hear so well, do you? He said no. He's staying with me!"

Janice was furious. Never had she spit in someone's face, but—shaking with anger over what this drug addict had done to her baby—that's exactly what she did. Jerking away, Cindy wiped at her face and cursed while Adam glared at his mom, a look she hadn't thought he was even capable of.

Angry and disheartened, the Browns drove off, leaving Shawn to bring the truck home. "Look at what you're doing to Mom and Dad," he told Adam quietly as he got behind the wheel. "They don't deserve this. You disgust me."

Shawn was done; he wanted nothing more to do with his brother. He would have "beat the tar" out of Adam right then and there, but he knew that would only add to his parents' pain, so instead he drove away, leaving Adam standing in the parking lot with Cindy.

Around this time Shawn quit his job as a pharmacist in Little Rock, went to work for his father, and bought a home with his wife, Tina, near Hot Springs. Adam was no longer employed at All Service Electric, and Shawn made it clear that he didn't want anyone telling Adam where he lived. "We don't want him coming around," he said. "I don't trust him."

Manda, who was still working on her bachelor's degree, just wanted her twin brother back. It felt as if a part of her was dying. One day when she was home during spring break, Adam came by to pick up some clothes and she tried to talk sense into him about Cindy and his lifestyle. They argued heatedly, and finally he threw up his arms and said, "I'm done. I'm out of here." He headed for the door and Manda begged him, "Please, Adam, please don't go!" Never before had Adam failed to try to make her feel better, to hug her when she was hurting or sad. This time he left without looking back.

Later that day she found a card tucked under the windshield wiper of her car. On the back Adam had written, "Meme, you know I love you."

She tucked the note into her wallet and treasured it for years. The small piece of paper reminded her that the Adam she knew and loved was still in there somewhere.

—

For most of the first half of 1995 Adam lived and slept wherever he could flop himself down: the airport terminal, a crack addict's trailer in the woods, or the house of a friend he hadn't yet stolen from.

At a loss as to how to help him, Adam's friends did what they could, taking him in, getting him odd jobs that lasted only until the schedule and responsibility overwhelmed him. The longest stint was working the pit at Stubby's BBQ, a job that high school buddy Chris Dunkel procured for him at his family's restaurant in hopes that good southern food would encourage Adam to eat more. Adam moved in with Chris, who tried to keep him on a healthy schedule, but once more, he disappeared.

In May 1995 Adam showed up at Jeff's apartment in Fayetteville, where he was attending the University of Arkansas. Cindy had recently broken up with Adam because he couldn't give her what she needed, according to Adam. Jeff interpreted this to mean that Adam couldn't give her enough drugs or drug money.

"Hearing they were apart," says Jeff, "was the best news I'd had all year."

But Adam continued his hard-core drug usage, splitting his time either being depressed or trying to forget how depressed he was by shooting himself up with speedballs—a mixture of cocaine and an opiate, usually heroin. He confided in a friend that at times he'd wake up from a drug-induced stupor and have to ask another addict where he was.

Only Adam's family and closest friends knew the full extent of his problem. Janice and Larry didn't talk about it openly, instead shouldering most of the stress themselves—all the anxiety, sleeplessness, and obsessive worry.

If a fatal car accident was reported on the radio, Janice immediately thought of Adam. If a body was found floating in a lake, she'd half expect a sheriff to pull up and break the news. When she heard crime reports, she thought of Adam. With any news related to illegal drugs, her mind shifted to Adam.

Most of all, she wondered.

She wondered if she and Larry were doing everything they could for their baby, the precious little boy they'd brought into this world almost twenty-two years earlier. They had talked extensively about intervention, but most of what they'd read said that Adam had to be ready, that the only person who could help Adam was Adam himself. He was an adult; they could not commit him to a lockdown treatment program unless he was a danger to himself or others.

And the knowledge that he was using a dangerous drug—crack cocaine, Adam's best friends confided to the Browns—only added to her stress. Crack is nasty stuff, as Janice discovered in her research. A user can become addicted after just one try, it alters the brain's chemistry, and it renders the user powerless against an intense need for more. The side effects, both short term and long term, are horrifying: increased blood pressure and heart rate, anxiety and paranoia, insomnia, severe depression, delirium, psychosis, auditory and tactile hallucinations, respiratory failure, brain seizures, heart attack, stroke, and sudden death. One of the most unnerving effects Janice read about was "coke bugs," a tactile hallucination in which users sense, and sometimes see, bugs moving about beneath their skin and will do anything to get rid of them: scratch, cut, poke, stab, even kill themselves in the process.

When Janice went to bed on New Year's Eve 1995, the last thing she wondered before drifting off was where her wayward son would sleep that night, or if he would sleep at all.

—

That night Adam was at a friend's house on Morphew Road, not far from his mom and dad's. He had become so addicted that he couldn't go half a day without experiencing withdrawal symptoms. Several hits of crack were stashed in his pocket to ring in the New Year, and he began smoking them at midnight.

Around two o'clock in the morning, Adam went into the bathroom with a knife. Sometime later, his friend checked on him, and when Adam didn't answer, he kicked in the door and found Adam crouched on the floor covered in blood, continually stabbing at his neck with the knife.

Instinctively, the friend balled up his fist and punched Adam squarely in the face, disarmed him, and yelled down the hall, "Call an ambulance!"

The first police officer to respond found Adam bleeding profusely from his neck and arm. "Applied direct pressure to wounds until Life-mobile Personnel arrived," he wrote in his report. "Ran subject for wants/warrants. Subject had an active felony warrant for his arrest and was placed in custody after his wounds were taken care of by St. Joseph's ER staff."

Upon receiving the call that their son was in the hospital with self-inflicted stab wounds, as well as wanted by the law for forging checks and

Adam being "processed" at the Garland County jail during his dark time.

stealing property, Janice and Larry paid the ten thousand dollars in bail and restitution and requested that an officer drive Adam from the Garland County jail to a lockdown drug treatment center. Months before, they had looked into the center but could not persuade Adam to check himself in—and there wasn't evidence that he should be committed against his will. Now that he was clearly a danger to himself and bound for jail if his parents hadn't paid the restitution, he had no choice.

When the drugs left his system and the fog cleared, Adam found himself in a hospital with a staff whose recovery strategy included the twelve-step program of Alcoholics Anonymous. Adam began his first step toward sobriety by admitting he was powerless over the drug and that his life had become unmanageable.

"He couldn't argue that one," says Larry, who along with Janice kept their visits to a minimum, stopping in only a handful of times.

Adam began by answering questions in a mini-autobiography highlighting the significant events in his life. "This tends to put your life in perspective," stated the instructions.

Sitting at the small desk in his room, Adam started with his childhood and preteen years. He noted that he had "always wanted to impress everyone and be the very best. Enjoyed showing off to my parents and brother in sports and cared for my sister very much." He recounted his earliest attitude about alcoholism or chemical dependency by stating, "Only losers let it happen to them."

While Adam was working through these questions, Manda visited him. "He was so sad," she says, "and just lost." She put her arms around her brother and hugged him. He started to cry. She hugged him harder when he told her that he hated himself. "Adam, you can get through this," she said, offering him the same advice their mom had once given her, the shy and quiet sister in Adam's shadow who wondered if people liked her or if she even liked herself. "First of all, you need to get over this," she said, repeating Janice's words. "You are a likable person, and you need to like yourself. Remember who you are."

For months Manda had been praying for Adam. However, she never told him she had been praying for him, because she knew it would have had little or no impact, but "it was what got me through and gave me hope," she says. "I prayed for my mom and dad too, because they were carrying such a weight on their shoulders with Adam. It was eating them up inside."

When her parents would tell her "Only Adam can help Adam," she inwardly believed that what Adam was up against was too big for even him. Leaving the hospital that day, she thanked the Lord for getting Adam off the street and prayed that he would continue to watch over her brother.

Grandma Brown and Larry's sister, Becky, had begun taking Adam and Manda to church on Sundays when they'd moved back to Hot Springs after those years living on the road, and as young teenagers both of them had accepted Jesus Christ as their Savior and been baptized. Manda had stayed on the path, but somewhere Adam had veered off.

The questions in the autobiography forced Adam to examine each stage of his life. Regarding his relationship with his parents and siblings before his drug addiction, he answered "good" every time. Asked what major values his parents had passed on to him, he wrote, "Be the best you can be. You can be anything you want to be. Hard work will overcome anything."

He perceived himself to be "very shy" with girls, but felt he had had lots of close guy and girl friends in high school. He felt he was a "good person" during the high school phase of his life, which was when he began to experiment with alcohol, "so I could feel at ease with myself," he wrote. On the subject of his current life, he wrote that for the first time ever, he had let his parents down and taken advantage of them. As for Shawn, "I lost my relationship with my brother."

"I can't be depended on anymore," he continued. "I was once a crazy, unique, hard-working person, but now I'm a miserable drug addict that hurts other people. I feel very alone, but I have many, many people that really care about me."

Most of the twenty-two-year-old's answers were a barrage of self-deprecation without an ounce of hope. Only the very last line in the workbook allowed a sliver of light to penetrate the dark storm of self-hatred: "But I will climb out of this hole and be somebody."

Fighting shivers, sweats, and the severe shaking of physical drug withdrawal, Adam worked his way through the First Step of Alcoholics Anonymous. He sat in group sessions, met daily with a counselor, and made it his goal to return to college. Fourteen days later, Janice and Larry paid the six-thousand-dollar bill and were told by doctors that Adam was ready to go as long as he continued the twelve-step program.

"Really?" said Janice incredulously. "You think he's okay to go out into the world this soon? Can he go back to college?"

"We've provided him with the tools," said one of the program's counselors, and Adam agreed, saying, "I'm ready to get back on track."

Skepticism overshadowed Janice and Larry's hope: expensive as the hospital had been, two weeks didn't seem long enough.

6

In God's Hands

ON THE FIRST DAY OF MARCH 1996, Janice and Larry returned home from searching for Adam after hearing from the University of Central Arkansas that he had not attended classes for weeks.

Nobody they knew had seen or heard from Adam. Larry was distraught and Janice was at her wit's end. She kept telling herself that she'd felt this way before, that even though she would worry herself sick Adam was dead somewhere in a ditch, he always showed up. But they couldn't—and Adam couldn't—keep going on like this, so Janice and Larry sat down at their kitchen table to figure out a course of action.

As Janice brainstormed aloud how they would save their son, Larry had an epiphany. Reaching across the table, he took his wife's hand. "We've tried everything we can do," he said. "We can't fix Adam. God is going to have to fix Adam. We've got to go to church."

Janice hadn't been raised to know God. She didn't even *think* about God. With Larry's words, however, a light bulb switched on. "You're right," she replied.

Larry slapped both his knees and said, "We'll go this weekend."

The next Sunday morning Larry found the Bible his mother had given them as a wedding gift, wiped some thirty years' worth of dust off the spine, and brought it with them to Second Baptist Church in Hot

Springs—the church Manda attended when she was home from college.

A woman about Janice's age greeted the Browns by the front door. "Good morning! Welcome," she said. "My name is Helen Webb. Come on in and let me show you around."

Larry, who hadn't gone to church since Vietnam, was a bit rusty on his knowledge of Scripture, and Janice had never read the Bible, but after that first sermon, both of them felt lifted up. The peace Larry experienced returned him to occasional times in his youth when he had leaned on God.

They went home with an invitation to come back soon.

The associate pastor, Mike Smith, knocked on the Browns' front door three days later to thank them for being guests of the church. Over a cup of coffee, Janice and Larry shared Adam's story. "We are failing our baby," Janice said as she shook her head and wiped at tears.

For more than an hour, Pastor Smith listened while they explained their family past and their spiritual past. As a child Larry had gone to church three times a week but stopped once he entered the military. Janice had attended church only for weddings, funerals, and a Christmas Mass or two and said she knew nothing about religion. "I don't know how to pray," she said, "so I've just been talking to God nonstop in my head since church on Sunday, asking him to look after Adam."

"You're doing fine," said Pastor Smith. "Just open up your heart to Jesus. He knows exactly what you're up against; your struggles are not uncommon. And he has a plan."

Pastor Smith understood intimately what Adam was up against with addiction and cocaine, but he left the Browns' home without sharing his personal history. Back at the church he called Helen Webb, who was in charge of the prayer chain. "Helen, we need to pray for a couple," he told

her. "Their son was arrested, he's battling drugs, and they desperately
need our prayers."

The following Sunday Janice and Larry attended separate Bible studies
before the worship service. In the women's class, "most of them were
mature Christians," says Janice, "and they started talking about 'I read
this scripture, and it revealed to me that I need to do this today.' It was
totally foreign to me, but what I saw was that they were living their lives
through the Bible and laughing and having fun—and I didn't think
Christians *could* have fun."

She became intrigued with the Bible, who Jesus was, and why all these
people were so enamored of him. When she shared a little about Adam,
one of the women told her to "give some of that weight you're carrying to
Jesus. You can't do it all by yourself. Just like your son can't do it all by
himself."

So she did. Right then and there, Janice prayed silently, and she
could not deny the peace she felt. Larry experienced the same liberating
freedom from his own debilitating guilt and failure as a father. "God is in
charge," Larry said to Janice afterward. "That's what going to church reminded me of today."

Although Janice had gone for one reason only, to help Adam, "it
ended up helping me," she says. "Once I realized I needed Jesus, it wasn't
for Adam; it was for me."

Scripture by scripture Janice devoured her new Bible, until one
morning, as she stood in her kitchen, she asked Jesus into her heart. She
shared the news with Larry, who said he had recommitted himself to
God and reconfirmed that Jesus Christ was his Lord and Savior. Together
they prayed, asking Jesus to save Adam.

Only then were they able to stop chasing him. "We quit," says Janice.

"We were like, 'Lord, you're in charge, and we're going to back away and let you be in charge.'"

For the first time in her life, Janice understood what it meant to have "blind faith."

Two weeks later Adam's boyhood friend Ryan Whited was driving south on Highway 7 in Hot Springs when he heard a horn honking from behind. The driver in the blue Toyota truck tailing him waved him over.

Ryan pulled off to the side of the road and the Toyota rolled up alongside. "Adam Brown!" Ryan said through the open window. "What's been going on?"

In high school, though not a football player, Ryan had been rowdy right along with Adam. He had mellowed some as a senior and become more active in his church, and in fact had invited Adam along a few times. When Adam had been working on his workbook in drug rehab three months earlier, he had answered the question "Name the spiritual mentors in your life" with three names: Grandma Brown, Aunt Becky, and Ryan Whited.

But it had been years since Adam had seen Ryan, who had attended the local community college after graduation, then traveled around the world, living in a commune in Switzerland before returning to Hot Springs.

"Sorry for pulling you over like that," Adam said, "but I saw you driving and I kind of need to talk to you." He hopped into Ryan's car and proceeded to unload what had been going on in his life, that he'd stolen from virtually everyone he knew in order to support his drug habit. When Adam confessed he'd stolen from his parents, he started crying. "I'm really addicted to crack," he told Ryan. "I can't stop doing it. I need your help."

Adam asked if he could move in with Ryan and his brother, David. "I know y'all will be a good influence, and I'll get myself well," he said. "I won't be a problem."

Yes, Ryan said immediately, then he called David, who was four years older and a youth pastor at a local church, to confirm. David had known Adam as a kid and agreed to let him stay, with some basic ground rules: no drugs or drug friends allowed in the house.

Adam, not trusting himself, asked if Ryan could drive with him to where he'd been staying to pick up his belongings. Along the way he pointed out five crackhouses. "If I disappear," Adam said, "can you come get me out of there?"

In a wooded area outside town, they turned down a narrow road of broken blacktop that led to a trash-strewn clearing. "This is it," said Adam, pointing to the centerpiece of the dump—a dilapidated trailer.

The inside looked as bad as the outside and smelled even worse. Dirty dishes covered with rotting food were piled in the sink. There was a crib in the living room. The floor was littered with garbage. Adam waded through the tiny rooms, grabbing clothes and stuffing them into a black Hefty bag.

"It was in a state that animals shouldn't be living in," says Ryan. "It was just nasty. The clothes that we gathered were on the floor. It wasn't like we got out specific things from the closet that had been put away. It was a disaster. I was just sitting there in this place thinking, *What in the world is going on in Adam's life that he could live here?*"

Over the following four months, Ryan went out and found Adam a half-dozen times and took him back in. Adam continually suffered severe mood swings ranging from excitement about living and what he would do after conquering drugs to depression and a "Why bother?" attitude.

Ryan talked with him for hours, sometimes through the night, and a recurring topic was the philosophical "problem of evil."

"Adam had a hard time wrapping his head and heart around it," says Ryan. "How could a fair, just, and loving God allow so much evil and suffering in the world?" This was a question Ryan had also struggled with, eventually arriving at the conclusion that there could be both evil and a loving God. While some use the existence of evil to discount the existence of God, he believed the opposite—that evil was an unfortunate but necessary element in God's world.

"That's where faith comes into play," Adam said to him, "and I'm having a hard time with that." They would go in circles, with Ryan contending that you can have strong faith and still have questions.

On August 12, 1996, Ryan called Janice and Larry after spending three days searching for Adam around Hot Springs. This time Adam had disappeared with David's car and thousands of dollars' worth of camping gear, stereo equipment, CDs, two checkbooks, and a Smith & Wesson .38 Special handgun that had belonged to the Whiteds' grandfather. Janice and Larry agreed that Ryan and David should call the police. When they resisted, Janice told them that Adam needed to hit rock bottom. "That is the only way he's going to come back up," she said. "It's either that, or he's going to end up dead or somebody's going to get hurt or killed."

Praying that they were doing the right thing, Ryan and David filed a formal complaint against Adam. One discussion Ryan had had with Adam brought him a measure of peace with the decision: they had talked about "how beautiful grace is and how God's grace can redeem so much darkness and what was so ugly can be made beautiful," says Ryan.

Two days later, Janice and Larry received a phone call from a friend who had spotted Adam in David's car at the same house on Morphew Road where Adam had been on New Year's Eve. Immediately, Janice called the Garland County Sheriff's Department and advised a deputy of the active warrant for Adam's arrest, refusing to hang up until the officer agreed to send a car to his current location.

"We'll meet you there," she told him. "We're leaving right now."

The Browns parked down the street from the two-story house shortly after noon. Following the plan they'd formulated on the way over, Janice walked around the house to cover the back door while Larry knocked on the front door. A few seconds later the back door swung open and Adam nearly ran into Janice. "Don't run, Adam," she said, reaching for his wrist.

When Larry came hustling around the side of the house, Janice was holding Adam's hand. "I got him," she said as Larry put his hand on Adam's shoulder. The two of them flanked their son as they walked to the front of the house and stood facing the street.

"Adam," said Larry, "there's a warrant for your arrest. We've called the sheriff. It's time for you to face what you've done."

Sadness washed over Adam's face, and he squirmed some when a sheriff's car pulled up and a deputy approached them, but his parents held him tight.

"Adam Brown?" the deputy asked.

"Yes sir," was Adam's subdued response.

"Put your shirt on, son."

Adam pulled the sweaty, dirty shirt over his slouched shoulders. After being placed under arrest and handcuffed, he was led to the cruiser.

When the deputy slammed the car door, Adam watched Janice's legs buckle and Larry catch her and hold her tight. She buried her head in his chest and sobbed.

Knowing he had broken his mother's heart, Adam slumped in the backseat, trying to hide his face from the world. But when they passed through the heavy gates of the Garland County jail, he couldn't run anymore. The one person he had to face now was himself.

Pastor Smith was sitting in his office at Second Baptist Church when Larry knocked on the door.

"I've done the hardest thing in my life today," Larry told him. "I've had my son arrested."

"That's the toughest kind of love you could have given Adam," said Pastor Smith, "but let me tell you something—I did the same thing with my daughter just a year ago." His daughter's cocaine addiction had led to stealing, forging checks, and, ultimately, arrest. "We could have paid her bail, but we left her in there. It broke my heart, but I knew it was the best place for her."

They talked and prayed together at length, then Larry hugged his pastor, thanked him for confiding, and asked him what had happened with his daughter.

"She served most of her sentence," he said. "She was released through the prosecuting attorney, charges dropped with an agreement to go to Teen Challenge, a Christian drug treatment program. She's our daughter again now. She's much better."

"Mike," said Larry, "when you have the opportunity, would you go by and visit Adam?"

"Of course," said Pastor Smith. "I'll get over there as soon as I can."

The first night Adam was in jail was the best night of sleep Janice and Larry could remember. "We knew where he was," says Janice. "We knew he was safe."

Adam didn't sleep a wink. That day reality sank in as he'd had his mug shot taken and his body fully searched, taken a supervised shower, and dressed in an orange jumpsuit with PRISONER stenciled on it. After staring at a tray of food during dinner and being pegged by the other inmates as the new "cracker head," he was led to his cell.

When the steel-barred door slammed shut, he sat alone on a thin mattress, his back against a cool concrete wall, facing eleven felony counts. In the morning, feeling the quiver of withdrawal, he called home.

"Okay, Mom," he said. "I messed up. When are you getting me out?"

"We're not," said Janice.

"What do you mean, you're not? You can *bail* me out."

"Nope." Janice stood firm despite Adam's angry voice. "You can stay in there till you see the judge."

Later that day Adam had a visitor. He didn't recognize the name Mike Smith or the face of the man sitting on the other side of the glass partition. Elbows on the concrete counter, Pastor Smith leaned in and said through a phone, "Hello, Adam. Your parents asked me to pay you a visit."

Adam was initially standoffish. "Yes sir," he said. "Are you a lawyer?"

"No, I'm an associate pastor at your parents' church. Your dad shared confidentially with me what's happened, and I want you to know having you arrested was the hardest thing they have ever done. Adam, they didn't want to do this and it was out of tough love, pure love, that you are here. Whatever pain you are feeling, I can guarantee they are feeling it double."

Jaw clenched as he fought back tears, Adam shook his head.

"I know the hurt they're feeling, Adam," Pastor Smith continued, "because that's exactly what I did to my own daughter. She was right here at the Garland County Detention Center, just like you, for the same reasons."

His interest piqued by the similarity of their stories, Adam asked how the pastor's daughter had gotten out of jail and where she was currently.

"Even though she was brought up in a Christian home, she strayed. There was something missing in her life, big time, and that was the Lord Jesus Christ."

Adam nodded.

"Jesus was missing in your parents' life too," Pastor Smith said, "and I believe, Adam, that as horrible as these last years have been for them, you helped lead them to God. Your father has recommitted his life to Jesus, and your mother has been saved. They reached out, and I feel certain that he gave them the strength to have you arrested. God is at work here, just as he was for my daughter. He miraculously provided a way for her to get out of jail and into a Christian drug treatment program that worked."

Respectful and receptive through the rest of their meeting, Adam asked Pastor Smith as he was leaving to deliver a message to Janice and Larry. "Tell them I'm sorry," he said. "And that I love them."

Arrested on a Wednesday, Adam simmered in the jail cell through the weekend. During this time Janice and Larry received just one call from him.

"I want you to know," he told them, "I got beat up yesterday."

"Well, I'm sorry to hear that," Janice responded, trying hard to sound nonchalant.

The Browns consulted an attorney and spoke with the Whiteds, arriving at a plea to present to the judge: they agreed to drop the charges if restitution was paid and if Adam would consent to one year in Teen Challenge instead of the year in prison he was facing.

Five days in jail seemed to have humbled Adam, thought Pastor Smith on his second visit, when Adam immediately began sharing his spiritual history. Though Adam's attendance at church was sporadic throughout his childhood, at age fourteen he had invited the Lord into his heart and been baptized at Center Fork Missionary Baptist Church, where he was taught that God forgave his sins and offered him eternal salvation. At the time, Adam's Sunday school teacher had been Wanda Holden, mother of Richie, the boy with Down syndrome he had stood up for. "Almost every day at the end of Bible study," says Wanda, "Adam requested we say a prayer for his parents—that they be drawn to the Lord and be saved."

Now Adam said he was ready to recommit his life to Jesus and asked the pastor if he could help.

"I've been here before with other people in jail," Pastor Smith said. "They've prayed like we're about to, but Adam, I want you to know that God can and really does want to change your life. But it begins with an honest and open desire from you to say, 'God, no more is it about me; it's about you.' Are you ready for that commitment?"

"I am," said Adam, and on the other side of the glass partition he got off the chair, knelt down, bowed his head, and repeated after the pastor,

God, for the first time in my life, I trust you. And God, I thank you that I'm here in jail. God, whatever you've got planned for my life, I trust you. God, I'm sorry for my sins. And today, the best way I know how, I ask you to come into my life. Come into my heart and save me. I want to begin a brand-new life. Amen.

Pastor Smith visited Adam again after several days. "Adam had questions," he says. "Lots of questions, but the biggest one was, 'After all I've done, how do I begin to live this Christian life? How do I turn my life around?'"

"Well, the bad news is you can't," Pastor Smith said to Adam. "But the good news is Christ *can* turn it around for you, and he'll give you the strength and power to do it."

"How?" Adam asked.

"Let me just show you a verse in the Bible. 'I can do all things through Christ who strengthens me.' That's Philippians 4:13. If we try to do it within our own power, Adam, we're going to fail."

One week later Adam faced the judge, who sentenced him to a total of forty-five days in the Garland County Detention Center, after which he would attend the Teen Challenge drug treatment program at an out-of-state location. Teen Challenge—a faith-based nationwide residential program that treats all ages, despite the name—was not a lockdown program, the judge explained. Adam could leave anytime he wanted, but if he did, he would be back in jail for an additional year. As for the restitution, it was more than ten thousand dollars, which Janice and Larry paid once again.

After Adam served the entire forty-five-day sentence, Larry picked his son up from jail. Adam was stoic as they hugged, then walked to the car, but once they began to drive, he broke down and cried. Larry told him they weren't going home but instead heading to a father-son weekend retreat run by Second Baptist Church. Knowing that Adam, too, had recommitted his life to Jesus, Larry believed the retreat would be a safe environment for reconciliation before Adam left on Monday for Teen Challenge.

They arrived at a local lake in time for the hamburger cookout and found forty ten- and eleven-year-old boys eating at picnic tables with their thirtysomething fathers. "We at the right place, Dad?" Adam asked, and the two began to laugh, the first time in a couple of years. They laughed again when the boys expressed their delight at having Adam on their team for the fathers-versus-sons soccer game.

The night was spent in a group Bible study, roasting marshmallows around a fire pit, and sharing a cabin dormitory. Early the next morning, with cups of coffee in hand, Adam and Larry walked to the edge of the lake and had a heart-to-heart. Adam apologized for the pain he'd put his parents through in the past two years, and Larry apologized for the harsh words he'd spoken to Adam. What haunted Larry most was when he'd called Adam "simpleminded" and "lazy" during one heated argument.

Adam told him he probably deserved it at the time, but Larry was firm that it had been hurtful, and he'd meant it to be hurtful, and that was wrong.

They agreed to leave the past behind them and prayed together. "That's done, Lord," Larry said. "We're going forward from here, and we are putting all of our trust in you."

On Sunday Adam reconnected with his mother, receiving too many hugs to count. Manda, who had graduated from college and was working as an x-ray technician at a local hospital, did the same when she joined them at church. Though happy about Adam's sentencing to rehab, Shawn still had his reservations about his brother and chose not to see him. "I was behind him," he explains. "I just wasn't ready to face him."

The following day, as Janice and Larry saw Adam off at the airport, she told her son she was proud of him. "For what, Mom?" Adam said. "I just got out of jail."

"Because I know what you're fighting is real hard," she said. "You keep fighting."

Larry sent his son off with Proverbs 3:5–6: "Trust in the LORD with all your heart, and lean not on your own understanding; in all your ways acknowledge Him, and He shall direct your paths."

At the Sanford, Florida, Teen Challenge, Adam was one of a hundred mostly young men receiving treatment for "life-controlling" behaviors and addictions. There were no fences around the suburban neighborhood property that looked like a small school with a central basketball court. The doors were not locked in the dormitory-style housing, which consisted of bunk beds, lockers, and a communal bathroom. "When we first got there, it felt like Bible boot camp," says Kenny Marsten, a recovering crack addict who roomed with Adam in 1996. "But it was a safe haven, and we needed that."

This safe haven at first isolated Adam from any outside pressures. Phone calls were prohibited the initial month, while letter writing was encouraged. No visitors were allowed in the first four months, then family visits were permitted on prearranged weekends for a few hours, and then, with good behavior, eight-hour passes for day excursions were issued. Otherwise, Adam was ensconced in the program.

What little free time there was consisted of half-hour to one-hour blocks that could be used for exercise, working out in the weight room, or playing a pickup game on the basketball court—where Adam usually gravitated. Five days a week, Adam rose at 5:00 a.m., ate breakfast, and was driven to the program's auto-detailing shop at the Manheim Auto Auction in Sanford, where he waxed and buffed cars with a heavy commercial buff pad from 7:00 a.m. to 3:00 p.m. On the ride back to the center, he would get in a quick nap before attending Bible-related classes with titles such as "Attitudes," "Overcoming Temptation," "Growing Through Failure," "How to Study the Bible," and "Loving and Accepting Myself"—followed by one-on-one counseling and chapel. After that it was a cafeteria-style dinner, quiet time for personal devotions, and lights out at 10:00 p.m.

That first week at Teen Challenge, Adam heard the parable of the prodigal son. This story from the book of Luke would become his favorite, one he returned to repeatedly for inspiration while attending the rehab program.

In the parable, Jesus told how a man's son brazenly asked for his inheritance while his father was still alive, a rebellious and selfish thing to do. The father complied, and the young man left home and squandered all his money in "wild living." A severe famine came, and the young man, now broke, ended up feeding pigs in order to support himself. He'd hit rock bottom.

Destitute and starving, the young man finally decided to return home, hoping for forgiveness from his father but expecting anger. To his surprise, his father welcomed him home with open arms, saying that his son had been "dead and is alive again; he was lost and is found" (see Luke 15:11–32, NIV).

In an early phone call to check on Adam's progress, Janice and Larry spoke with the program's director and Adam's counselor, Wayne Gray, who said that "Adam is really embracing a relationship with Jesus Christ. Because of that, I believe Adam will find true meaning and purpose. He's learning that God loves him and God will guide him through this dark time."

Adam began to earn a reputation among the staff and his peers for his enthusiasm, empathy, and—while he could be lighthearted and goofy— competitive nature and drive, which really shone on the basketball court. Most Sundays, when Adam traveled with Teen Challenge's small choir, singing at churches across central and northern Florida, he would volunteer to give his personal testimony, "how his drug addiction had impacted his family," says Gray. "He cried every time he told of driving away in the backseat of a police car while he watched his mother crying so hard that his father had to hold her up.

"He always volunteered for our community/street outreaches. We owned a fifty-by-eighty-foot tent and would put it up in housing projects and parks to witness, do kids' programs, and serve meals. In short order Adam was in charge of the tent crew. I'd watch him bark orders to make sure things were done safe, and then he'd play with the inner-city kids for hours."

Says Kenny, "During outreach, Adam really connected with the kids, and he'd use that to impart some wisdom: 'Stay on the basketball court—stay off the drugs,' that kind of thing."

Two weeks into Teen Challenge, Adam sent his parents a letter, which they put on their refrigerator door to read and reread in the months that followed.

Dear Mom and Dad,

We're having quiet time at 9:30 p.m. I don't think we have to go to work tomorrow. Everyone is going on pass or something. I think every third Saturday in a month we're up for an eight-hour pass.

A man graduated tonight. It was a wonderful thing. He spoke for a while then his mom got up and asked to say something. She said, "I am so proud of you." I got chills that ran all through my body and a tear fell down my cheek. I wiped it away and realized the day that happens to me will absolutely be the greatest day I have ever had. I know it is sad that graduating from

a drug rehab is your greatest goal, but it is more than that. It is the
first day I will be able to look at you with no shame. It is a new
chance at life. It is a new beginning for all my family and friends.
It is a day I will be totally living for Christ and not ashamed and
thankful. I don't want to hear you say one time you are proud
of me until that day because that day I will be able to respect it.
Praise God. Dad, you remember how you always just wanted me
to finish one thing I started? Well here it is, not because I can do
it, but because God is going to do it for me, for you dad, you
mom and for everyone that ever believed in me. Read Luke 15:11
(parable of the lost son). That is how I will come to you and I
know that is how y'all will rejoice.

Only 352 days to go.

Lights out and God Bless you. I'm doing fine.

Love, Adam

In August 1997, after nearly eleven months in the program, Adam was
granted a special leave—a two-day visit home to attend Manda's wedding
to Jeremy Atkinson, whom she had begun dating in college.

At the ceremony Adam and Shawn escorted Janice into the church
and seated her, then together they lit the candles. At the reception Janice
was impressed by Adam's poise when he graciously deflected any focus
that came his way from relatives and friends aware of his recovery and
sobriety. "Thank you, but this is Manda's time," Adam would say. "We'll
talk about it later." All had been forgiven in the Brown family. "The past
is the past," Larry had told both Shawn and Manda. Shawn agreed but
was still wary and cordial at best when he was one on one with his brother.

On the last Saturday in September, Adam celebrated a year of sobriety by returning to Hot Springs for good. The next morning, he stood

before his parents and the congregation at Second Baptist Church. Although he had been sharing his testimony publicly for months back in Florida, he was especially nervous to thank the people who had been praying for him since his parents began attending the church.

"I don't think I've ever had such beads of sweat rolling off me before I tell this story to people I know have loved me and prayed for me and been such a determining factor in changing my life," he began. Adam then told how he got off track in life and ultimately became an addict. "You never know what hopelessness means until you get there, and I got there," he said through tears.

He talked about how he ended up stealing from his parents, others in his family, and friends so he could buy drugs. Finally, he reached rock bottom with his arrest for eleven felonies.

"I got on my knees in jail, and I accepted Jesus Christ back into my heart, and God has changed my life. It was a little over a year ago that I accepted the Lord back into my life. I went to a program called Teen Challenge, a safe haven away from the world where you can learn the Word of God, and how much God loves you, and how God will never leave you or forsake you. I have true confidence now, not in me, but in the One who lives in me."

"Amen," the congregation said.

"My paths are straight now in Jesus Christ. I just praise God and thank you all so much for your prayer. There is a purpose for it all, and I just try and encourage you to remember this, and all of you who prayed for me. What you have done for me was not idle. It changed my life."

7

Kelley

WHILE ADAM SPIRALED TOWARD DRUG ADDICTION in Hot Springs, a young woman a year and a half younger named Kelley Tippy was living a life somewhat paralleling his, though not as dark or wild.

Born in Georgia and raised in Little Rock, Kelley was an A and B student through high school, a cheerleader who was active in her church, barely drank, and never smoked. She attended the University of Central Arkansas in Conway but dropped out after one semester because she "lacked direction," she says. She moved to an apartment back in Little Rock, where her life revolved around work and partying, which continued heavily when she and some girlfriends road tripped to Panama City Beach, Florida, for spring break. "You know what?" one of her friends said after a week. "Wouldn't it be great to move here for the summer—really have some fun?"

That's just what Kelley did right after school let out, renting an apartment, finding a waitressing job, and diving into a carefree lifestyle that almost always called for a miniskirt or a bikini. She would wait tables in the evening, dance and party the rest of the night away, sleep until afternoon if she slept at all, hang out at the beach, and repeat the process seven days a week. It was so much fun she didn't want the summer to end. Occasionally she felt a twinge of guilt for not returning to

Kelley Tippy in Little Rock shortly
after returning from Florida.

college, but for the most part she was content in the now, with nothing on the horizon but good times.

The thought of home was particularly dreary. Though Kelley's childhood had been wonderful, everything had changed at age thirteen when her parents began fighting. Kelley's mother would leave for days and even weeks at a time, and her father would shoulder the responsi-bility of raising Kelley and her younger brother. Arguments were nearly constant whenever Kelley's mother returned, and Kelley was no longer relaxed in her own home. Family had become a source of anxiety, not comfort.

One Sunday well into September, Kelley woke up in the middle of the day, looked around the dirty apartment her father was helping her rent in Panama City Beach—piles of laundry on the floor and party fliers taped to a fridge holding more alcohol than food—and thought, *This isn't normal. This isn't right. I'm going nowhere.* "I felt pathetic," she says.

The next week she was out with friends when a fight broke out and a male friend was badly beaten. That jolted her. *I don't hang around people like this,* she thought. *Where am I? What am I doing here?* Only days later another friend, a "very GQ, Mr. Muscle, flashy, super cocky" type, was shot during a drug deal gone bad. Kelley visited him in the hospital, and he was "so scared and humbled," she says. "I could almost see the innocent boy he used to be before he got all wrapped up in this seedy world."

Late for work, Kelley hurried home to her apartment to change. As she fumbled through her closet for a pair of matching shoes amidst the disarray, she happened upon her Bible—the one book she'd brought with her from home. She picked it up, brushed off the sand and dust, sat on the bed with it on her lap, and said out loud, "Lord, it's time for me to get out of here, isn't it?"

Hurricane Opal slammed into the Florida coast on October 4, 1995, with hundred-mile-an-hour wind gusts and a massive storm surge. That morning Kelley packed up her belongings and joined the evacuating throngs heading west through torrential rain and howling wind on gridlocked highways. She didn't stop driving until she'd reached Little Rock fifteen hours later.

After moving back in with her father, Kelley mended her relationship with her mother over long talks and reconnected with her spirituality. She began attending Otter Creek Assembly of God. She read her Bible. She searched for direction. "God," she prayed, "what is my path?"

Kelley took a job as a travel agent in early 1996 and enrolled in college courses at the University of Arkansas at Little Rock, but she didn't finish her classes. Her heart just wasn't in it. Occasionally, she'd go out clubbing with friends but drank little, always volunteered to be the designated driver, and never again watched the sun come up after partying all night.

On October 17, 1997, two years after Kelley returned home, she and her friend Stephanie headed to the hippest nightspot in Little Rock to meet up with Heath Vance, whom Stephanie had gone to college with. Inside the smoky building, where an act reminiscent of *The Rocky Horror Picture Show* was being performed on the stage, Kelley and Stephanie located Heath Vance standing with several buddies.

Kelley was instantly enamored with one of Heath's friends, a young man he introduced as Adam. Leaning toward Kelley, Stephanie quietly said, "You can have any of them you want, but stay away from that one. He's *crazy*. Stay away from him."

"Ooh," said Kelley, "but he's the one I like."

"Don't say I didn't warn you," Stephanie said. "He's trouble."

Adam chose that moment to take his shirt off and begin whirling it over his head, hooting at the transvestite act onstage. *Who is this guy?* wondered Kelley. *He's hilarious.* She kept staring at his crooked smile and deep blue eyes, smitten. What she didn't know was that Adam had been home from Teen Challenge for only three weeks. He had been clean and sober for just over a year. "I still question the wisdom," says Heath. "What in the world compelled me to bring Adam to a bar in Little Rock a couple of weeks out of drug rehab?"

Likewise, Adam couldn't take his eyes off Kelley, a tall brunette with a girl-next-door face. Eventually, he walked over and stood near her. "Y'all havin' a good time?" she asked him.

"Sure am," said Adam. "I don't get out much."

Kelley laughed. *Yeah, right*, she thought.

They talked for a while, then out of the blue Adam said, "You smell so good, Kelley. What kind of perfume are you wearing?"

Overhearing the question, Stephanie rolled her eyes at what sounded like an obvious pickup line, but Kelley replied, "That's funny. I have on three types of perfume tonight."

"Yeah? What are they?"

"Heaven, Pleasures, and Forever."

Without missing a beat Adam said, "Hmm. That *is* funny. That's exactly how I picture us: heaven, pleasures, and forever."

Adam went home that night with Kelley's number.

The phone rang the following afternoon at Kelley's home.

"Hello," said Adam. "May I speak with Kelley, please?"

"This is Kelley."

"I thought so! Hey, this is Adam. Adam Brown—we met last night? What are ya doin'?"

"Oh, I just got home."

"Ah. Where you been?"

Kelley wanted to be honest and say that she'd just returned from teaching Sunday school, but she was nervous. She'd met this guy at a place that was, well, not where you'd expect a God-fearing Southern Baptist Sunday school teacher to be hanging out—and giving out her phone number, no less.

"Well, Adam, I just got home from church."

There was quiet, then a gigantic sigh of relief. "I am *so* glad to hear you say that," Adam said. "I'm a Christian and I go to church too. And that's super important to my life. Figured I'd get that out in the open right off the bat."

———

Kelley had been on a handful of dates with Adam and never experienced an awkward moment of silence or boredom. He was quirky, funny, and silly, but at the same time a perfect gentleman who saw to her every need—from opening the car door to making sure her popcorn had enough salt at the movies. She went to church with him too, and met Janice and Larry.

Then one night they were to meet for dinner at the Waffle House in Benton and Adam didn't appear. He finally showed up forty minutes late, apologized as he grabbed a menu, and wouldn't meet her eye. It took Kelley only a minute to clue in.

"Are you on something?" she asked.

"Funny story about that," he said, looking up at her with disappointed eyes. "I actually am."

While Kelley made him eat waffles and drink coffee, Adam explained how he had finished a drug treatment program only two months earlier. "This is the first time I've done it in over a year. I drove through this part of town on the way here, and I parked in front of this house I used to go to. I got tempted and couldn't fight it. I went in, smoked some, and now I feel horrible. It will not happen again."

He was talking so fast and so oddly that Kelley became worried—not for her safety but for his. He was acting "weird, crazy weird," she remembers. Just what Stephanie had warned her about. When his behavior hadn't changed after two hours, she made a decision.

"You aren't going home like this," she said, then drove them to a nearby hotel.

"I'm so sorry," he said at least a dozen times. In the room he wrote a check to cover its cost but she wouldn't accept it, so he shoved it in her purse.

Kelley kept Adam talking into early morning, telling him about her parents' fighting and their recent divorce, and Panama City Beach and how she'd come home and made amends with her mother and thanked her dad for being there for her. Adam choked up when he told her about his own mother and father, how much they loved each other and everything they had done for him, how awesome his older brother was, and what a great friend and supporter his twin sister had always been. He broke down and cried as he admitted he'd already let his family down and now he was doing it again.

"This isn't you," Kelley said. "It's the drug. You have so much more to offer than this, Adam Brown. You know what? I'm going to pray for you."

"That sounds like I won't be seeing you again," he said.

After hugging him for a long time, she wiped his tears and said, "You just have to fight this."

At four in the morning, she drove them back to the Waffle House,

Brown family archives

From the start, Adam was smitten and comfortably goofy with Kelley.

fed Adam breakfast, and dropped him off at home. As she backed out of the driveway, he ran up beside the car and she rolled down the window. "I love you," he said.

"You know, it's funny, but I love you too," she said, all the while thinking, *What in the world are you doing, Kelley Tippy?*

She prayed for guidance as well as for Adam, but she knew her heart belonged to him and nothing told her to run from the situation. The moment she'd laid eyes on him, she had fallen in love. It simply didn't matter that he came with baggage. Major baggage.

When Kelley got home, she retrieved Adam's check from her purse and laughed because it was made out in pencil. Then she sighed heavily as she read the memo line where Adam had written, "I'm very sorry I disappointed you."

For the next few weeks, Adam was on time for every date, which included taking Kelley's dog, a chocolate Lab named Sidney, to swim at the lake, attending church, and holding hands on long walks. Says Kelley, "He'd just do sweet little things," like adjusting her car's air vents so the heat would blow on her when it was cold. "But the sweetest was how he'd make me feel important. He'd stare at me and I'd catch him, and he'd smile and tell me I was beautiful. He'd tell me over and over again how lucky he was."

One day she arrived at work to find a rose on her desk, with a note: *I love you—and am always thanking God for placing an angel in my heart. Adam.* On another day a gigantic box of a dozen Jungle Roses arrived, overnighted from the Amazon. When Kelley chastised Adam for spending that kind of money, he told her, "You deserve the best."

Then, in early December, Adam stood Kelley up. "It was the second time he'd relapsed," she says. "And I was thinking, *But wait! You're so sweet and perfect! Why? It's like two personalities.*"

Adam resurfaced two days later, as remorseful and apologetic as before: "a moment of weakness," he explained. Like he'd done with Ryan Whited nearly two years earlier, he drove Kelley by the crackhouses where she could look for him if he disappeared again.

"But it's not going to happen again," she said to him. A statement, not a question.

He nodded, his head hung low.

It did happen again, the week before Christmas, and Kelley found him in one of the drug houses. He was "dirty, disheveled, and gross," she says. "He smelled, and I told him, 'You have so much more to offer than this, and you know it. You are so much better than this.'"

The third time it happened, "it was as if he was cheating on me," she explains. "It almost felt like a girl."

"I'm getting jealous over this drug because it's taking my place," she told him.

"I'm sorry!" Adam pleaded with her. "I don't want to do it, I really don't. It calls my name. I just start driving, and then I'm there—and it's too late."

The fourth time, Kelley was beside herself. "How can I do this?" she cried to Adam. "How can I stay with you?"

"Please don't," he said. "Really. I'm only going to bring you down."

At the beginning of 1998, Kelley informed Janice and Larry of the relapses and they told her to break up with Adam. "He's lost, and you don't need that in your life. We're going to keep praying for a miracle, but we just don't know what's going to happen with Adam. We don't want him to drag you down with him."

"But I love him," Kelley said.

The three of them put their heads together and decided to encourage

Adam to return to Teen Challenge for the six-month voluntary cap to the yearlong program, a segment that helps individuals assimilate back into society. They had an intervention dinner with Adam, and he agreed he needed the help. "I don't want to lose you," he told Kelley while he packed. He left for Teen Challenge that week.

"I will be here waiting for you when you're done," Kelley assured him. "Six months is nothing."

Adam stayed in Florida less than a month.

"I've done my stint," he said to Kelley when they reunited. "I know what I'm doing is wrong. Teen Challenge is a very secure place; it's a safe haven. You work, there's structure, you learn the Bible, you have no freedom. It's a safe environment, and then you get thrown back into reality. Okay, I've been guarded and protected and all this, and now I'm just back where I started. Even though I have all this knowledge and this wisdom I've gained from God and from my experience there, those demons are still calling my name. It takes over. So how do I live here, in the real world?"

"'Trust in the LORD with all your heart, and lean not on your own understanding,'" Kelley replied, quoting Proverbs 3:5–6. "'In all your ways acknowledge Him, and He shall direct your paths.' You just have to trust in God and don't give in," she said.

For six months, Kelley spent the better part of her days either baby-sitting Adam or searching for him during his relapses, which occurred every week or two. Since being in Hot Springs seemed a big part of the problem, Adam moved fifty miles east to Little Rock, got his own apartment not far from Kelley and her father, enrolled in classes at the University of Arkansas at Little Rock, and found work as a waiter at the Steak and Ale. Kelley handled his money, requiring receipts for every dime he spent—

but it was easy for Adam to squirrel away tips for the next time he heard the drug call his name.

On July 11, 1998, Kelley and Adam attended Richard Williams's wedding in Arkadelphia, an hour south of Hot Springs. Adam was a groomsman, along with Jeff Buschmann, Heath Vance, and other friends from high school, so the reception resembled a Lake Hamilton High class reunion. Richard had earned a bachelor's degree and an MBA; Jeff had gotten his bachelor's, had graduated from the Navy Officer Candidate School, and was currently attending Navy Flight School in Texas. There were more stories of college degrees and good jobs.

"Everybody had moved on to the next level," says Jeff, "but Adam was at the same place he was when he graduated high school, and I could tell it bothered him. People who didn't know asked him what he'd been up to, and he'd say, 'Still working with my dad, off and on.'"

Throughout the festivities Kelley stayed by Adam's side, making sure he didn't drink anything besides the champagne toast; they both knew what that would lead to. While Adam seemed saddened by the reminiscing, Kelley loved hearing about his crazy stunts—the belly flops, the bridge jump—but she was deeply touched by the story of his refusing to take the life jacket off at the lake because his mother had told him not to. *He was so honest and so pure,* Kelley thought.

At one point during the night Richard took Kelley aside. "I'm sure you're hearing all these crazy stories about Adam," he said. "But let me tell you, the one thing you're probably not hearing is how he would jump in front of a truck for any one of us. He's got a heart of gold."

With so many others advising Kelley to run from Adam, it was nice to hear something positive. "Thank you, Richard," she said. "I can't tell you how much that means to me."

Two days after the wedding, Adam disappeared. The day after that, Larry called Kelley because one of his work trucks and a bunch of tools were missing. "It's Adam," she said before he could finish. "I'll go find him."

"No, Kelley," Larry said. "You've done this how many times? I don't want you to go off and get yourself killed on account of Adam. I think the only thing that's going to stop him is prison."

"I'm sorry, Mr. Brown," she said firmly, "but Adam's not going to get off that easy."

Nine months of patience, encouragement, and empathy had finally left Kelley feeling "crazy angry." She hung up the phone before Larry could say another word. As she hurriedly got ready, she rehearsed aloud what she was going to tell her boyfriend when she tracked him down: "I am sick and tired of this, Adam Brown! You are not going to do this to me! You are not going to do this to your family! I don't care if you're in trouble with some dealer, I don't care what your problem is, you are *not* going to go hock all your dad's stuff. It's not fair!"

Finished with her planned tirade, Kelley regained her composure and drove to the east side of Hot Springs to comb the streets.

After two hours of fruitless searching, near dusk she was amazed to see Larry's truck—with Adam driving and someone in the passenger seat—pull out from a side street directly in front of her. She stopped beside him at a traffic light and when Adam looked over and saw her, he hit the accelerator and sped through the red light. Kelley glanced left and right and did the same, staying on him as best she could. She pulled over briefly to wait for traffic to clear after Adam wildly swerved across two oncoming lanes to turn down a street. Then she continued the chase.

On a long straightaway, Adam pulled over onto the shoulder, hit the brakes in a cloud of dust, jumped from the truck, and dashed into the woods. Parking behind, Kelley got out and approached the middle-aged man, a "sleazy drug addict," sitting in the passenger seat. She leaned in through the open driver's door and grabbed the keys, then called the Browns on her cell phone, gave Larry the street name, and confirmed that he had his own set of keys.

Ending the call, she told the addict to get out. "Where did he go?" she demanded.

"Hell, lady, I don't know," the man snapped. He stepped out of the truck.

"Where did he go?" Kelley repeated. "I know you know."

The man stood there, shaking his head. "Well, I can take you to where we were going."

"Fine. Hop in my car."

He directed her to a neighborhood not far away, where she parked in front of a run-down house.

"You want me to go in, see if he's there?" the man asked.

"Yes," said Kelley. "Bring him out if he is."

She locked the doors after he left and waited for a few minutes, but feeling increasingly uncomfortable, she called the Browns to let them know she was okay and drove back to Little Rock. At home she kicked off her shoes and fell into bed, exhausted. Staring at the ceiling, she prayed for Adam's safety—she always did on nights like this. This time, however, knowing she was at the end of her patience, she also asked for a favor.

"Lord," she prayed, "if you have something in mind for Adam, maybe you could nudge him a little, because he's having a real hard time finding that path on his own."

Jeff received a phone call at his apartment in Corpus Christi, Texas, the following morning.

"Busch," said Adam, "I'm in trouble again and could really use your help. Can you get me a ticket to come down there? I promise I'll pay you back."

Without further thought, Jeff bought Adam a one-way ticket from Little Rock and picked him up that evening at the airport. Over dinner Adam filled him in on everything that had happened since the wedding, how he'd done something so stupid that Kelley could have been raped or killed. From where Adam was hiding in the woods, he'd watched her leave with the addict in her car. He'd hoofed it to the crackhouse where he'd been headed, searching for her car, but she'd already driven away. Then he walked to a nearby church and spent the night on the front steps, praying.

As much as he loved Kelley, Adam had concluded that he could not continue to endanger her life. The only way to protect her was to disappear, go somewhere far away—like to his buddy's place in Texas. "I owe you," Adam told Jeff. "I had to get out of there, but you gotta promise me: if my parents or Kelley call, you can't tell them I'm here."

About the same time Adam's plane landed in Corpus Christi, a woman who worked at the Steak and Ale phoned Kelley with the news that she'd given Adam a ride to the airport, but she didn't know where he was headed and he had no luggage with him. "I just thought you should know," she said to Kelley. "He didn't look so good."

All of Adam's friends were within driving or hitchhiking distance of Hot Springs—everyone except Jeff, whom Kelley called as soon as she got off work. Jeff had just promised to keep Adam's whereabouts under wraps when the phone rang. Pointing at the receiver he mouthed to Adam, "Kelley."

Adam shook his head adamantly, mouthing back, "I'm not here."

You bastard, Jeff thought. *You're going to make me lie to her, aren't you?*

"Hi, Kelley," he said. "How are things? How's Adam?"

"Jeff, you are such a bad liar," Kelley said, laughing. "I *know* he's there. He got on a plane and flew there this morning. I checked the flight. Let me talk to him."

"Okay," he said, handing the phone to Adam, who cursed at his friend. "She knows you're here," Jeff whispered. "She checked the flights—dude, she's a travel agent."

But Adam refused to talk to her, so Kelley told Jeff she'd try again in a couple of days. "I'm glad he's safe," she said. "I'll let his parents know he's with you."

When Jeff returned home from flight school around ten the following night, he heard loud music in the apartment complex. His neighbors were young families, professionals, and officers in the military, and there was Adam on the second-floor balcony, music blaring and a can of beer in his hand. "Busch!" he shouted.

Infuriated, Jeff rushed into his apartment. He pushed aside the cold beer Adam offered him, shut off the stereo, closed the door to the balcony, and said, "Adam, this isn't gonna cut it, man. You cannot be doing this."

"Busch," Adam said, "I don't know what else to do. I sat here all day thinking maybe I'll go work on an oil rig, make some money, pay my parents back, the Whiteds, you. But what then? I can't go back and work for my dad; I don't want to either. I don't want to go back to Teen Challenge. I'm praying every single day, but it's not getting any easier. I'm a loser."

"You're not a loser," Jeff replied, sitting across from Adam at the kitchen table. He had a sudden thought. "What about enlisting in the Navy?"

"With my record?"

"My dad could probably help with that and find out if it's even possible."

Jeff knew the Navy—he'd spent a lifetime listening to his father talk about what it had to offer—and he knew Adam, so he considered the possible jobs that might fit Adam's personality. Something elite, but not out of reach. Says Jeff, "Most people didn't think of Adam as smart because he was always acting like a dumbass, but he was super intelligent, a thinker; also fearless and a little crazy."

"You could be an EOD guy," he told Adam. "Explosive Ordnance Disposal. You know, disarm bombs and blow things up."

"That'd be fun," said Adam, nodding. "But how about a SEAL? Your dad always said they're the best."

"I don't know, Adam. They *are* the best, but man, their training is tough, real tough. And they do most of their training in the water. You have to be a good swimmer and diver."

"I can swim."

"You can keep yourself from sinking," said Jeff, to which Adam laughed. "But it's not just the training; you have to be a really good swimmer. And I'm not talking Lake Hamilton; I'm talking about the *ocean*."

If Adam did qualify for general enlistment, he'd be four or five years older than most of the other recruits in boot camp; it would be tough to keep up with the guys fresh out of high school. The boot camp standouts would get the good positions, and Jeff didn't want Adam to end up a fleet sailor, assigned to a ship on tours lasting nine months and sometimes more than a year. So he kept pushing Adam toward EOD. It wasn't popular, for obvious reasons, but it was elite and important.

By the end of their discussion, Jeff saw some of the spark return to the eyes of his old buddy, who shook his hand and thanked him.

The next day Adam called Kelley to apologize. He told her that he'd run from the woods and tried to chase her car down when she'd driven off with the addict. "I knew nothing about that guy," he said. "He could have been a serial killer, you could have been killed, and it would have been all my fault. I'm not good for you; that's why I left. I don't want you to keep chasing after me."

"Do you really want me to stop?" Kelley asked. "In your heart?"

"No," said Adam. "In my heart I love you, but that's why I need to let you go."

Kelley told Adam how she'd been praying, and praying hard, asking God for guidance, asking him directly if she should abandon the relationship. "Adam," she said, "God has not told me to leave. I love you. My heart says stay and see this through."

"You are *stubborn*. How can I argue against that?"

She laughed, then warned him that she wouldn't be stubborn forever. It was time for him to make a plan, a real plan that he would stick to.

Adam said that Jeff was encouraging him to join the Navy and aim for EOD, "but ever since I saw that movie *Navy SEALs* in high school, I've wanted to be a SEAL. Do you think I can do it?"

"Of course you can," Kelley said without hesitation, even though she had only the most basic idea of what a Navy SEAL did.

There was a long silence before Adam spoke again. "This is what I need to do," he said. "I can feel it in my heart. I need to get out of Hot Springs. But the only way I'm going to do it is if you marry me. I want you with me. Will you marry me, Kelley?"

So many times she had prayed about whether she should leave Adam or stay, and "God never told me to leave—not once." Still, it was a leap of faith when she said, "Okay, Adam. I'll marry you. But there are going to be some rules."

The following day, July 19, 1998, Adam returned home to Hot Springs and married Kelley in front of a justice of the peace. They didn't tell a soul, nor did they celebrate with a special dinner or even a date. While she loved Adam dearly, this marriage was almost a business arrangement. "He knew I was committed," Kelley says. "Now he had to prove *he* was committed. I had to play it tough and couldn't let my guard down yet."

The day after, Kelley went to work and Adam called Ryan Whited, who was now married and living in Hot Springs. Adam shared his plan to join the Navy. "If this is what you feel like you need to do, I'm behind you a hundred percent," Ryan replied. "But you need to make real sure, because a military prison is going to be awful. And that's what's going to happen if you slip up."

"I'm certain," Adam said.

Ryan agreed to take him to the local recruiting office, and on the drive there, Adam said that he planned to be completely honest. "Well, you might not want to volunteer that you smoked crack," Ryan replied. "If you do, I can promise you that you're not getting into the military. Just wait and see what they ask."

"If I can't be honest, then maybe it's not what God has planned for me," said Adam.

Inside the spartan office were two large framed photographs: president Bill Clinton and a highly decorated Naval officer. "Check it out," Adam whispered to Ryan. "There's Mr. Buschmann."

"Hey, guys, what's going on?" asked the recruiter.

"Hello, sir," Adam said. "I'd like to join the Navy. I want to be a SEAL."

"Great! Have a seat."

While they talked, Ryan listened in and paced around the office, examining the posters of aircraft carriers, battleships, and the camouflage-painted face of a SEAL rising out of dark waters. Adam filled out forms, and the recruiter explained that some standard questions would need to be answered and that Adam would be fingerprinted and have to sign under oath. Lying under oath was subject to a fine and possible imprisonment, "so traffic tickets, stuff like that, are okay, but if you've ever been arrested or anything like that, tell us up front."

"Yes sir, I have."

The recruiter nodded and said, "Okay. For what?"

"I had eleven felonies, mostly stealing, nothing violent, but I don't think you'll find them on my record because I went to a drug treatment program after jail."

"Are you clean now?"

"Well, sir, I'm not sure how long it stays in your system, but I have smoked crack. But I'm done with that. It's not going to happen again."

The recruiter leaned in on the table and shook his head. "Adam, I really appreciate your honesty," he said. "I do, but do you *really* think you can join the Navy? This isn't a joke?"

Adam pointed to the photograph of Captain Roger Buschmann, Commodore of U.S. Navy Recruiting Command Area Three—the highest-ranking officer in all the Navy recruiting districts in the southeastern United States and the boss of this recruiter's boss. "Call and ask him."

"You're serious?" the recruiter said.

"I'm serious. Maybe he can help. Give him a call. He'll at least vouch for me."

In his office in Macon, Georgia, Captain Buschmann received a call from the recruiter in Hot Springs. "Sir," he said, "I'm really sorry to bother you, but do you know a young man by the name of Adam Brown?"

"I sure do," said Captain Buschmann.

"He wants to join the Navy. He says he wants to be a SEAL, but he's…well, sir, are you aware he's got a record a mile long? He's had some drug issues, and just a *lot* of issues. I was going to send him out the door, but then he asked me to call you."

A wave of positive memories washed over Captain Buschmann. Adam Brown was the boy he'd considered most likely to succeed, the boy who had always followed the rules, even when it wasn't cool, even when nobody was looking. Months earlier, Jeff had filled him in on Adam's problems, so he knew about the drugs; he wasn't aware, however, of Adam's arrest—or of the laundry list of offenses the recruiter read to him. He couldn't fathom any of it, because it was so out of character for the Adam he knew. And if there was one thing Captain Buschmann had an eye for, it was character.

"I'll vouch for him," he said.

"Sir?"

"Use whatever waivers he needs," Captain Buschmann confirmed. "Treat him like he is my own son."

After Adam signed the required stack of waivers, it was official: he was a Navy recruit. The newlyweds took Ryan and his wife up on their offer to stay with them until boot camp began in three weeks, then decided that they should start their life together properly by getting married in a church—God's house. They discussed whether to invite their parents, but Kelley was certain her dad would not be pleased. And Adam thought his parents would conclude that he and Kelley had acted rashly and try to talk them out of it.

"We'll just have to prove to them that it was the right thing to do," said Kelley.

They explained their situation to Ryan, who introduced them to his pastor, and that Sunday, July 26, he called them to the front of his church. Before the congregation Adam and Kelley said their vows and

Brown family archives

Newlyweds Adam and Kelley, during the period
Adam was training for boot camp.

were married for a second time. The pastor then asked his congregation to bow their heads. "God," he said, "we pray for a miracle in the lives of this young couple."

Adam called home the next day.

"Dad," he said, "I have some things I need to tell you and Mom."

"Okay," said Larry. "I'm ready."

"Kelley and I got married."

"Well, your mom and I love Kelley and we would like to have been there—but that's okay."

"There's something else. I joined the Navy."

8

Rising Up

"THOSE THREE WEEKS BEFORE HE LEFT for boot camp, there was something different about Adam I hadn't seen before," says Kelley. "There was an intensity. A focus."

In the evenings while she watched television or read, Adam was on the living room floor cranking out push-ups and sit-ups. During the day, every overhanging tree branch and playground monkey bar he passed gave the opportunity for as many pull-ups and chin-ups as his arms could muster.

When Kelley went to work at the travel agency, Adam swam laps at the YMCA or drove to Wolf Stadium—six years after graduating from Lake Hamilton High—and jogged the track and ran the bleachers. "I could smell the crack sweating out of me," he told SEAL buddy Kevin Houston years later. "I ran those steps, just like in high school, singing 'Eye of the Tiger' in my head—*'Risin' up, back on the street, did my time, took my chances'*—I love that song."

One morning Adam parked his truck on the eastern side of the 70 West bridge and walked down the trail to the shore. He waded into Lake Hamilton, swam the quarter mile to the western shore, hoofed it up one of the trails he'd used as a kid, and tried to run back to the truck he'd borrowed from Larry. By the time he got there he was stumbling and nearly collapsed.

Angry at his weakness, Adam returned the next morning to do it again.

The second week of August 1998, Adam reported to the Naval training center in Great Lakes, Illinois—more than a thousand miles from the nearest ocean. Jeff Buschmann had called him right before he left for the airport to wish him luck. "And hey," he'd said, "if you think you're going to screw this up, go AWOL to smoke dope or something, don't do it. Because my dad really put his ass on the line for you."

The following day, twenty-four-year-old Seaman Recruit Brown lined up with a hundred some eighteen- and nineteen-year-olds in his division to get his hair buzzed off, his uniforms issued, and his bunk assigned. Then he had two minutes to use the phone—long enough for him to call Kelley and sing out, "Hey, baby. I'm in the Navy now! I'll call you again in three weeks."

Back in Little Rock, where she had moved in with her father, the new Mrs. Brown was "a nervous wreck." She knew Adam had what it took to make it through boot camp, but she also knew the likelihood for relapse. Every time the idea of failure weaseled its way into her mind, she prayed for Adam to have strength against his addiction. "That was the only thing that would stop him," she says. "I couldn't forget how Adam would tell me, every time he messed up, 'It calls my name.'"

It gave her hope that all he was allowed to bring with him to boot camp were the clothes on his back, his identification, and five dollars.

Kelley had nixed the five dollars. With money in hand, an addict can find drugs anywhere.

Over dinner with Janice and Larry one night, Kelley could sense their reservations, despite the optimism they conveyed—exactly what she was experiencing. "We didn't get our hopes up," says Janice, who had continued to pray that Adam was finding his path. Sometimes the worry consumed her, and then she'd call her now close friend Helen Webb. "Don't you worry," Helen told her during one such call. "We are surrounding your Adam with the Holy Spirit. There's a hedge of protection around him. Those fiery darts of Satan won't penetrate."

Her words gave Janice chills—she could physically *feel* something like an electrical charge. Her faith was renewed.

If Adam made it through boot camp, Kelley knew she would be moving to Great Lakes to be by his side on the long journey to become a Navy SEAL.

Completing eight weeks of boot camp was only the first hurdle. In addition to the normal duties of learning how to march, salute, fold your clothes, and make your bed the Navy way, recruits interested in becoming SEALs held a SEAL Challenge Contract, which gave them three opportunities to pass the SEAL Physical Screening Test (PST):

- Five-hundred-yard swim, using breaststroke or sidestroke, in no more than twelve minutes and thirty seconds. Ten-minute rest period.
- Forty-two perfect push-ups in no more than two minutes. Two-minute rest period.
- Fifty sit-ups in no more than two minutes. Two-minute rest period.

- At least six pull-ups from a dead-hang position, with no time limit. Ten-minute rest period.
- One-and-a-half-mile run in boots and long pants in eleven minutes and thirty seconds or less.

If Adam passed the SEAL PST and graduated from boot camp, his next hurdle would be A-School to earn a Naval Rating. He had chosen Fireman, Interior Communications Electrician Striker (ICFN), the career path recommended by the recruiter because of Adam's experience as an electrician and that involved almost six months of intense classroom and field training at Great Lakes. He would have to graduate with satisfactory grades before heading to a twelve-day BUD/S—Basic Underwater Demolition/SEAL—indoctrination course on Coronado Island, across the bay from San Diego, California. This would determine who would attend what was arguably the toughest military school on the planet, the 173-day BUD/S course. Only then would Adam be assigned to a SEAL team. But he wouldn't truly be a SEAL until six to nine months later, when he had completed advanced SEAL training and earned his Trident—the gold insignia pin worn only by fully trained SEALs.

More than two years of training were required to become a qualified Navy SEAL. Getting to that goal required that Adam remain completely drug free. The waivers he'd signed made it clear: one drug infraction and he was gone—out of the Navy and perhaps into a military prison. Statistics were also against his chances of success: only about 20 percent of candidates complete BUD/S; those who don't are assigned to a ship in the fleet.

All this information made Kelley's head spin, but it also gave her focus. In the weeks Adam was away, she came to realize how much of her life, her emotional being, she was devoting to him. She herself had been somewhat lost before she'd met him, and Adam, baggage and all, gave her direction.

———

"An angel sent from heaven" was how Janice and Larry described their new daughter-in-law. "There was no question," says Janice, "that she was going to stand by Adam's side no matter what." When they prayed for Adam, they wanted him to succeed as much for Kelley as for himself, because they knew she was in it for the long haul. Currently, Kelley was in limbo, poised between her old life as Adam's girlfriend/cheerleader/baby-sitter and her new life as a Navy wife—which, Janice and Larry joked with her, would be the same as before but with more ironing.

In Adam's fourth week of boot camp Kelley received a letter with great news: he had passed the SEAL Physical Screening Test. He didn't let on how well everything was really going. His year at Teen Challenge had prepared him for the seemingly endless string of rules and regulations, and what the Navy dished out physically wasn't much worse than the sweltering two-a-day summer football practices with the Lake Hamilton Wolves.

At twenty-four he was the "old man" of his division, but on the runs he was always near the front of the pack, right there with the recent high school graduates. Adam never took the yelling and berating from the recruit division commander personally, unlike many of the younger guys, who felt the full stinging disparagement of these verbal beat-downs. Being Adam, he'd wait for opportune moments to build his fellow recruits back up, demonstrating the leadership that had been MIA all those years.

On October 16, Kelley, Larry, Janice, and Heath Vance gathered at the Naval Service Training Command center to watch Adam—who had been named Honor Recruit of his division—graduate. The whole world got a little brighter for the Brown family that day, especially when the commanding officer read aloud from his commendation letter to Adam:

By virtue of your demonstrated attention to duty, military conduct, responsiveness to orders, cooperation, loyalty and comradeship, you have been selected by your shipmates as Honor Recruit
for Division 401.

I take great pleasure in commending you for your fine
performance, which has earned you the admiration and respect
of your shipmates and extend to you a 'well done' for your
impressive achievement.

"I love you, Adam," Kelley told her husband when she finally got the
chance to wrap her arms around him. "I'm so proud of you."

When Adam carried Kelley over the threshold of the on-base apartment,
secured for them by Captain Buschmann and their first home as newlyweds, she was twenty-two and he was twenty-four. A few days after graduation, as the couple settled into the military community of Naval Station
Great Lakes, Adam made some phone calls. The first was to Captain
Buschmann. "Thank you for believing in me, sir," he said.

"I had no doubts," said Captain Buschmann. "None."

Adam called Kelley's father, then Richard Williams and his father,
Curtis Williams, as well as Ryan Whited, Grandma Brown, and of course
Manda, whose tough-love approach had been the softest. She had rarely
distanced herself from Adam, and now she congratulated her brother and
thanked Kelley for the unconditional love she had shown him.

But a call to Shawn, Adam's original hero and moral mentor, meant
the most. Even though they had put the past behind them, Shawn had
remained understandably skeptical throughout Adam's attempts at sobriety and had withheld any accolades—until now. "Mom and Dad are so
proud of you," he said. "And so am I."

Kelley and Adam, holding his diploma
and Honor Recruit commendation
letter at boot camp graduation.

The praise Adam received from his family was like rocket fuel as he headed into an intense blur of classes and fieldwork for the next six months. On the first day of A-School, the coffee maker began brewing a few minutes before Kelley and Adam's alarm clock went off at 4:00 a.m. She made him breakfast, then hopped back into bed while he hurried off to SEAL PT—what would become their routine each weekday.

At 5:00 a.m. every morning, some 150 prospective SEALs would queue up outside on a slab of concrete the size of a basketball court, or in the gym if there was a blizzard, or at the pool on swim days. Standing atop a small wooden block, the "motivator" was an active-duty SEAL whose goal was to physically prepare these boot camp graduates for the wet and sandy hell of BUD/S. "A couple of hours a day a few days a week is not enough time to prepare you for what I promise will be the longest twenty-seven weeks of your life," yelled the motivator. "What we'll be doing here is *fun*. If you're not having fun, you're in the wrong place—better go and pick out a ship, 'cause that's where you're heading."

The temperature, like the original number of 150 men, dropped significantly as fall merged into winter. Two-mile runs in the rain became five-mile runs in hail and then eight-mile runs in snow, as the Great Lakes region dished out storm after storm, rivaled in intensity by whatever the motivator could concoct for that day's session—after the run. It might be an hourlong crab walk, five hundred push-ups, or a buddy-carry through knee-deep snow.

On one particularly miserable morning, the motivator decided the students should do nothing but sit-ups for an entire hour, with a goal of a thousand. No one but the motivator could actually do that many, but they grunted and jerked their bodies through the motions till their backs were bleeding.

Then there was swimming. Miles and miles of swimming, sometimes underwater, sometimes with fins, sometimes with clothes on, other times with rocks in their pockets. "Just a little taste of what you'll face at BUD/S," said the motivator.

After the two-hour PT, Adam would rush home, his lips blue and his cheeks red and windburned, but with a smile on his face. "I can't wait for San Diego," he'd say to Kelley, not a doubt in his mind that was where they were heading.

He would take a quick shower, change into the uniform of the day, and find a full breakfast waiting for him that he'd gobble down before running to his A-School classes at 8:00 a.m. Kelley would walk Sidney, then head off to her job at the base travel agency. Dinner was ready or in the oven when he got home by 6:00 that evening. Then he would study, Kelley quizzing him with flashcards.

"I babied him," says Kelley, who finished each night by drawing Adam a hot bath complete with mountains of bubbles, just the way he liked it. "I wanted to give him every advantage because I knew, with that drug calling his name, he was fighting something none of the other guys were. 'Stay in bed; it's cold and dark,' he'd tell me when he got up. He never took it for granted. We were broke, but he treated me like a princess. Every day he'd tell me how pretty I was or how lucky he was. We saved our change in a bucket, and on weekends we went to the MWR [the base's Morale, Welfare, and Recreation center] and had Pac-Man wars for hours, till our quarters ran out. When he wasn't at school and I wasn't at work, we were attached at the hip. A-School was our honeymoon."

On April 6, 1999, Adam—one of only a few dozen students who had stuck it out through SEAL PT—was chosen as a Distinguished Military Graduate from the A-School course. His commanding officer praised him in his commendation letter:

> …exemplary performance in military decorum, appearance, respect for authority, and leadership in your peer group in addition to your outstanding academic record. These achievements are significant and have distinguished you as a "top performer" and "team player."
>
> This superb performance demonstrates your self-motivation and sets an outstanding example for your peers. You are encouraged to sustain this level of performance…not only will you benefit from it, your example will encourage others to carry out their duties in the proud traditions of the Naval service.

Kelley was ecstatic when she read the letter. "You're on a roll, baby! Remember where you came from, and look where you are. You need to call your parents. Good job!"

Kelley and Adam drove cross country in a big Ryder truck, her Pontiac Grand Am parked inside the back, surrounded by boxes, and Sidney in the cab with them. Each day brought them closer to the home they'd rented online in the town of El Cajon, twenty miles northeast of Coronado Island. Each state line they crossed brought Adam nearer to twenty-seven weeks of the most torturous military training ever devised.

At the same time, former SEAL Dick Couch was gaining clearance from the Navy to observe and document what Adam was about to undergo, "a process," he would write in *The Warrior Elite*, "that transforms young men into warriors…a distillation of the human spirit, a tradition-bound ordeal that seeks to find men with character, courage, and the burning desire to win at all costs, men who would rather die than quit."

Adam wore his dress whites when he checked in at the Naval Special Warfare Center on the Naval Amphibious Base in Coronado, California, at the beginning of May—one of 145 men in SEAL Class 226. The class proctor outlined the course and told them that only 20 percent of them would remain at graduation. He explained the DOR (drop on request) option that any of them could use at any time, a "get out of hell free" card where one need only ring a bell, a public announcement that said, "I'm not good enough to be a Navy SEAL."

"The reputation you forge here will follow you to the teams," the proctor said. "Your reputation here will define you."

"Hooyah!" was the response.

And so began the punishing rite of passage. Most candidates admit being a little awestruck and a tad intimidated when they first encounter the jaw-dropping male specimens who show up for BUD/S to strut their stuff. Then there was Adam. "He was nothing special," says Christian Taylor, at twenty-nine one of the few guys older than Adam. Christian was *not* going to ring that bell, and he made it a game to predict who would. "I didn't take him seriously," Christian continues, "that southern accent and all. He seemed too friendly to be tough."

But boot camp and A-School had awakened in Adam the "psycho" who never quit. On top of that, as he told Kelley many times, his ace in the hole was his faith, which gave him a refuge to go to and a shield of strength. Quoting the verse Pastor Smith had shared with him in jail—"I can do all things through Christ who strengthens me" (Philippians 4:13)—he said he had complete confidence. Not in himself, but in the One who lived within him.

If innate mental and physical toughness was his armor and faith his ace in the hole, Kelley was Adam's secret weapon. As he began the first phase of BUD/S, Kelley charged into her own grueling routine. Once again she'd found a job at a travel agency, and every day at 5:00 p.m., she'd get off work and hurry home to take Sidney for a quick walk before driving the half hour to the BUD/S compound. Arriving around 6:00, she'd park and read her Bible or another book until Adam showed up, anywhere from 6:00 to 10:00. Perhaps his boat team (or even the entire class) had been pegged by the instructors as requiring some extra "motivation" in the form of a four-mile run, some log PT, or an hour of push-ups and sit-ups. Occasionally, she'd pick him up as late as midnight if there had been a night-specific exercise.

While Kelley drove, Adam would strip off his wet, sandy cammies and T-shirt. At home he'd hose off outside, then jump in the shower while she shook the sand out of his clothes and tossed them in the washer. She'd make dinner, and he'd practically fall asleep in his food before flopping into bed, already snoring when she put his clothes in the dryer, then "boxed his cover" (shaped and creased his hat), and, if it was a scheduled inspection day, shined his boots, touched up the paint on his helmet and polished it, and starched and ironed his camouflage uniform. Only after laying out his boots and still-warm-from-the-dryer PT clothes—long pants, T-shirt, and socks—would she crawl into bed next to him.

At 3:30 a.m. Kelley would rise and make a breakfast of scrambled eggs, toast, and bacon or ham and wake Adam up at 3:45 with a cup of coffee. He'd wolf down the food, pull his clothes on, and they'd be on the road by 4:00, Adam snoozing with his head on Kelley's shoulder. She'd wake him up when they arrived at the gate between 4:30 and 4:45, and he'd push her nose like a button, kiss her on the lips and forehead, and say, "Bye, Itty Bitty." He'd drop off his duffel of sparkling clean clothes in his room (everybody was assigned a room, even those who lived off base) and line up on the concrete meeting area called the grinder, ready for PT at 5:00 a.m.

By the time Kelley was back on the freeway heading east, Adam was already either sweating from a combination of push-ups, sit-ups, dips, and pull-ups; wet and cold from a trip into the Pacific; or enduring being a "sugar cookie"—jumping into the ocean and then rolling around in the sand. After running anywhere from two to six miles, he'd eat a second breakfast with the single guys, who stayed on base. "You cannot eat enough" is a BUD/S instructor's mantra; it's impossible to replace the calories burned on a daily basis.

Unable to go back to sleep, Kelley would spend the hours before going to work prepping for dinner, cleaning the house, and taking Sidney for a longer walk. Weekends were for recovery for both Adam and Kelley. On Saturdays they'd sleep in late and watch movies, and on Sundays they'd regain their spiritual strength for the upcoming week by attending church.

———

Kelley came home for lunch one day, after three weeks of this schedule, feeling unusually exhausted. She sat on the couch, closed her eyes, and woke up after an hour. In the past, she couldn't nap if she tried, but the following day the same thing happened. "Maybe you're pregnant," a co-worker suggested.

"No," said Kelley. "Of course not."

But after dropping Adam off the next morning, she bought a pregnancy test at a pharmacy and rushed home to take it. Positive.

"Oh, Lord," she said aloud. "Really?"

Returning to the pharmacy, she bought two more tests; both were positive. *Right now? Right at the start of BUD/S?* she thought. Beyond the shocking reality of impending parenthood, she was worried about putting Adam into a tailspin. *Okay, how am I going to tell him?* she asked herself.

That evening she didn't say a word about the pregnancy during the drive, just got Adam home and put him in a bubble bath. Then she sent Sidney into the bathroom, her collar hooked up to a balloon that read, in big letters, "Congratulations! You're having a baby!"

Standing outside the door, Kelley waited for a reaction but none came. Finally she walked in, saw that Adam hadn't noticed the dog or the balloon, and handed him a small plastic stick.

"Honey," he said, "I'm fine. I feel fine."

"No, no, no," said Kelley. "It's not a thermometer. See this?" She pointed to the pink line and then the balloon and said, "It's a pregnancy test, baby. I'm pregnant."

They stared at each other, for a minute or more.

"Okay, this just makes it even more important," said Adam. "I *have* to get through BUD/S."

9

Pays to Be a Winner

As a new father-to-be, Adam tackled the gauntlet headfirst. On his boat team he chose the front-left paddling position, next to Christian on front-right—arguably the two toughest positions. Together they dug deep with their oars, first to crash through the cresting waves that broke over them as they paddled out through the surf, racing the other boat teams and battling painful "ice cream" headaches brought on by water temperatures in the high fifties.

During the long, rigorous paddle, his boat crew would try to rotate out with him but Adam routinely refused. "'Ah got it,' he'd say in that deep Arkansas twang," says Christian. "I would get so mad, because if *he* wasn't going to switch, *I* wasn't going to switch. And I was getting smoked—he could suck it up more than anybody.

"Competitively, Adam was my nemesis. I'd push it as hard as I could, and we were neck and neck running, neck and neck on the obstacle course, same with swimming, and it just annoyed me. In surf-torture they'd make us lie down and link arms in the sand, freezing cold waves splashing over us, our teeth chattering like we're running a jackhammer, and I'd look over at Adam next to me, and he was blue from the cold and grinning, like he was loving it. I remember thinking, *What is driving this guy?*"

With Hell Week about to begin, Adam stood before the performance review board. He had passed the fifty-meter underwater swim, under-water knot-tying test, and drown-proofing test. He had finished the twelve-hundred-meter pool swim with fins in under forty-five minutes; one-mile bay swim with fins in under fifty minutes; one-mile ocean swim with fins in under fifty minutes; one-and-a-half-mile ocean swim with fins in less than seventy minutes; two-mile ocean swim with fins in under ninety-five minutes; obstacle course in less than fifteen minutes; and four-mile run in boots and pants in less than thirty-two minutes.

But he needed to work on his swimming times, the review board told him. He'd barely made the two-mile ocean swim within the ninety-five-minute time constraint, and the next two-mile swim had to be finished within eighty-five minutes, with the final two-mile swim in phase three in under seventy-five minutes. The fact that the board was coaching Adam, not reprimanding him, meant the instructors liked him. He had continu-ally exhibited the teamwork and can-do attitude they were looking for.

Ninety-eight students entered Hell Week: five days of relentless, round-the-clock physical and mental hazing with only four to five hours of sleep the entire time. At its end, Minnesota governor Jesse Ventura made a guest appearance, calling out the ceremonial "Hell Week is se-cured!" to Adam, Christian, and the sixty-three other students who re-mained. Ventura, whose real name is James Janos, had graduated from BUD/S Class 58 in 1970 and served during the Vietnam era on Under-water Demolition Team (UDT) TWELVE. He shook hands with the men and told them they were one step closer to being part of the greatest fraternity in the world. "Don't give up," he said.

Later, the soft-spoken base chaplain Bob Freiberg gave a personalized Bible to each of the sixty-five, letting them know that they didn't have to read it "or even keep it."

After thanking the chaplain, Adam opened the book and read the inscription:

ICFN Brown,

    Congrats on completing Hell Week 25–30 July 1999. Class
226—God Bless!

    Chaplain Freiberg

Adam knew exactly what he was going to do with his camouflage-covered Bible—but first he had to make it through the rest of BUD/S.

"You're beautiful!" was the first thing Adam said to Kelley as he stumbled to the car—the first time he'd seen her since the start of Hell Week.

"You're delirious," she said with a laugh. "How you feeling?"

"I'm just fine. How are *you* feeling? Everything okay? How's our little baby?" He rubbed Kelley's belly, which didn't yet show any sign of being pregnant, and she said, "Hungry."

"Me too," he said. "Let's eat."

Adam was asleep before they reached the freeway, and at home Kelley got him bathed, fed, and into bed, where he slept for another fifteen hours. "I have to cut ten minutes off my time or it's done," he said to her as soon as he awoke, referring to the two-mile ocean swim. "I'll get rolled or they'll drop me."

A student who couldn't pass all the requirements could be dropped completely from the course or, if instructors saw potential, rolled into the following course during any of the three phases of BUD/S. This meant that if Adam couldn't pass the two-mile ocean swim, the instructors could roll him into Class 227 at phase two. While waiting for his new class to get to the second phase—which would take about two months—he would have to maintain his fitness level and assist the instructors.

He had three weeks to improve his time, and he knew he'd already given his all just to make the ninety-five-minute cutoff. With rigorous training he had improved his strokes and bettered his time by the final week of phase one, but not by enough.

"I got a call from Adam before this big open-ocean swim, and he asked us to pray for him," remembers Larry. "We had the whole church praying for him on that day. I was at a men's prayer breakfast when a friend, Ted Smethers, prayed aloud that Adam would not only qualify, he would beat his best time by so much that it would be evident to everyone that God did it, not Adam."

On the crucial day, Adam came in at under seventy-five minutes. He not only cut twenty minutes off his prior best time, he also beat the required time by a full ten minutes.

The second phase of BUD/S, dive phase, is considered by many to be as difficult as Hell Week. In pool competency, students must perform specific tasks underwater—sometimes with mask, fins, and dive gear; sometimes without—displaying perfect technical procedures without panic while being harassed, to the point of near drowning, by the instructors. It's not uncommon for an unconscious student to be hauled out of the pool, vomiting water. This was most often the case with mentally tough students like Adam who wouldn't give up—students who would rather die than quit.

But no matter how much he tried, Adam could not pass pool comp, and when the review board informed him that he would be rolled to the dive phase of the next class rather than dropped, he was both angry with himself and relieved. He also added up the months in his head: Class 227 would finish very near Kelley's due date.

Twelve students were rolled during pool comp, including Christian, medically rolled for stress fractures in one of his legs. Also rolled was a fellow student five years younger than Adam named Austin Michaels, one of the single guys whom Adam and Kelley invited over for home-cooked meals on weekends.

When Adam said grace before dinner one night, Austin realized that they shared the same religious beliefs, and he was stunned when Adam confided in him about the dark times he and Kelley had gone through. From that point forward the Browns and Austin were family.

Adam and Austin began the second phase of BUD/S for a second time with SEAL Class 227. Christian Taylor was also on the roster and ready to go, his fractures now healed.

"You again," said Christian when he saw Adam, only half joking.

A couple of weeks later Christian and Adam were facing each other in the ice bath, teeth chattering and lips turning blue, after getting in trouble for putting away their dive gear before the instructor told them to.

The ice bath was a trough of freezing cold water, affectionately referred to as a slushy by instructors who used it as a motivational tool. After adding a pitcher of ice cubes to the water Adam and Christian were sitting in, their steel-faced instructor said, "The only way you're getting out of this slushy is to make me laugh. One of you better have a joke or something that is going to make me laugh."

He dumped another pitcher of ice into the trough, crossed his arms, and stood over them like an emotionless robot.

Shivering violently, Adam said, "Hooyah, instructor, I have one for y'all." Class 227 gathered around while Adam relayed a story that had been infamous at Lake Hamilton High, an embarrassing incident at a party that happened to a buddy and the buddy's girlfriend, both of whom drank too much *and* suffered food poisoning. For full effect Adam told the self-deprecating story, detail by detail, as though it had happened to him.

The account included meticulous descriptions of bodily functions occurring simultaneously—to the horror of the poor fellow's girlfriend, who had a front-row seat to it all. By the end, the instructor was laughing so hard that Adam and Christian could barely make out his words: "Pays to be a winner, Brown."

Which meant they could get out of the ice bath.

While "cold, wet, sandy" is the theme for BUD/S, "Pays to be a winner" is the mantra of instructors who demand teamwork—anybody who hasn't pulled his weight is long gone by phase two—yet also create competition by offering rewards, usually rest, to those who finish first. The winning boat team on a course out through the surf, around a buoy, and

Adam overcame a cold, wet, sandy hell—plus his own gnawing demons—to get through BUD/S Hell Week.

back to the beach gets to lounge in the sand while the other boat teams do it again. A poor result on the obstacle course might find an individual running it again that night while the rest of the class eats dinner. Instructors know that every student is exhausted, but "winners" prove they can dig deep when they're at their breaking point, finding that something extra when their bodies tell them nothing is left.

Adam was known among the instructors for two reasons: his wife was expecting a baby, and he was one of only a few throughout the course who never once failed to give his all—and then some. His scores were not the highest, but his determination was unmatched, and that carried him into the third phase of BUD/S.

By the time Adam and the thirty remaining students of Class 227 headed to San Clemente Island—seventy-five miles off the coast of San Diego—for some of the last weeks of their training, he had learned the rudimentary skills of a combat diver. Now the focus was land warfare. Physically, Adam was in the best shape of his life, having completed the obstacle course in ten minutes, the four-mile run in boots in less than thirty minutes, and the two-mile ocean swim with fins in less than seventy-five minutes. He had also finished a grueling fourteen-mile run without stopping and a five-and-a-half-mile ocean swim.

Even though instructors never allowed students to slack off, during third phase they were particularly vigilant because of the use of explosives and live ammunition. Students also learned more advanced patrolling tactics and how to plan and execute realistic missions—firing upon target buildings, calling in close air support, and clearing buildings of the enemy. The men remaining had proven they weren't going to quit; now they had to remain focused and uninjured for one last phase.

One of 227's first training days on the island took the class on a conditioning jog up a steep, rocky rise. At the top the instructor allowed the men to catch their breath before leading them to a small, nearly vertical cliff that dropped down onto another steep, rocky slope. He pointed out a landmark at the bottom of this ankle-twisting obstacle course. Get down to that as fast as you can, he told them, then run back up. "Pays to be a winner," he added.

Immediately, the men began to carefully sideslip and shuffle down the slope, which was "about forty-five degrees, a big giant rock face," says Austin, who was just a few steps into his descent when Adam passed him. "Adam was sprinting a hundred miles an hour. He made it about halfway, his gangly legs and arms just flying, till he lost control and started somersaulting—three or four big flips—crushing him each time on the rocks. Somehow he ended up on his feet, ran to the end, and then sprinted back up. He was back on top before most of us were at the bottom.

"Everything Adam did was a sprint; he didn't know how to hold back. He cared more about his performance and his reputation than his physical body."

The baby was due February 18, 2000. Scheduled to return home from the island on January 31, Adam received permission to check in with Kelley the week before. "Everything's fine, it's all good," Kelley told him. "What's going on with you?" Good, Adam said, but there was a huge weapons practical test that coming Wednesday that had him stressed.

Kelley never let on to Adam that she had been on mandatory bed rest for the past few days due to complications with the pregnancy: pre-eclampsia and intrauterine growth restriction, both of which are potentially dangerous—and even fatal—for mother and baby. The morning after she talked with Adam, she headed to a doctor's appointment for her weekly checkup. "We need to deliver this baby today," the doctor said upon examining her.

When Kelley gave Adam's parents the news, Janice took the next flight to San Diego, arriving at midnight. By then Kelley was already in induced labor and suffering from a literally blinding headache from the magnesium sulfate she'd received to lower her blood pressure. After eighteen hours of painful labor, through which Kelley couldn't see much more than shapes and blurs, Nathan Cole Brown was born on Wednesday, January 26—all four pounds eight ounces of him.

While in recovery Kelley called the BUD/S compound to let them know that Adam Brown was the father of a healthy baby boy. "But do not tell him until *after* he completes the weapons practical this afternoon!" she told the instructor who answered the phone.

"Yes ma'am," he replied. "Understood."

On San Clemente Island, Adam waited nervously for the weapons practical to begin, hoping he wouldn't get called on first.

"Brown!" The instructor broke the silence. "You're up!"

Adam stepped up to the carbine and handgun laid out on a table. When the timer began, he first cleared a jam in each weapon, then began disassembling and reassembling each weapon while the instructors peppered him with questions. "What is the effective firing range of this weapon, Brown?" "What is the purpose of that mechanism, Brown?" "What caliber is the ammunition used in that gun, Brown?" Answering in stride, Adam reassembled both weapons. "Done," he said, clicking the final part into place and raising his hands off the table.

"Good job, Brown. Good job. Now go over to the office and call your wife at this number." The instructor handed him a piece of paper. "She just had a baby. You're a dad. Congratulations."

At the news Adam sprinted to the phone. "Are you okay?!" he asked Kelley. "Nathan is all right?"

"Yes," Kelley said, sounding tired but happy. "He's healthy. He's little, but your mama is here and she said you were little too and that never slowed you down."

"My mom's there?"

"She's staying for graduation, so you get done. Finish up and come meet your baby boy."

The ocean swell picked up and waves started pounding the island, making the conclusion of phase three particularly brutal for Class 227. In one exercise, as students swam through the surf zone with their rucksacks, a wave hammered Christian when he attempted to pull on a fin and he ended up with a broken ankle. He struck a deal that he could graduate from BUD/S if he pushed through the final exercises on crutches.

Before the other students headed back to Coronado and Christian headed into surgery, they celebrated their last day on the island with a barbecue, during which the commanding officer followed tradition by telling them that this was only the beginning of their training. "You'll train for the rest of your careers," he said. "And if you're lucky, you'll get a chance to serve your country and do the real thing."

Kelley and Nathan were released from the hospital and able to drive to the BUD/S compound with Janice when Adam returned from San Clemente Island. The family's reunion was shared by a throng of Adam's classmates, who slapped the new father on the back when Kelley presented him with his swaddled baby boy. "He's so little," said Adam, holding the newborn awkwardly. The baby's head flopped to one side, and Janice jumped forward. "Don't drop him," she said, guiding Adam's hand up to support his son's neck.

That evening Nathan fell asleep cradled in Adam's arms as he sat on the couch of the Browns' El Cajon home. "It's a miracle," he kept saying. "I can't believe it."

Kelley cuddled up beside Adam and together they stared at Nathan as he slept, mesmerized.

At BUD/S graduation a week later, Adam was one of only twenty-six men left, including Austin and Christian, fresh out of surgery. It was an especially moving occasion for the Brown family—including Shawn and his wife, Tina, and Manda and her husband, Jeremy—as they watched proudly. "We knew something extra about Adam," says Shawn. "Nobody there realized what else Adam had been through just to get in the Navy."

During training an instructor had told the men that they would become like brothers, closer than any friends in high school or college. He had encouraged them to embrace that brotherhood and find strength in it, but to never, ever forsake the importance of family. Now, after hugging and thanking every member of his family for having faith in him, Adam presented to his father the Bible that Chaplain Freiberg had given him after Hell Week. Inside the cover, on the page opposite the chaplain's note, Adam had written,

> Dad: Thanks for instilling in me all that I have. Thanks for
> believing in me even when I didn't believe in myself. God
> couldn't of given me a better example of who I want to be
> in life. If I become half of the man you are, I'll be happy of
> who I am. I wish I could express in words the respect I have
> for you. I think you're the greatest dad ever. Thanks for being
> so positive in my life.

10

A SEAL Is Born

THE DOCTOR WHO RECONSTRUCTED Christian Taylor's ankle told him the injury was a game changer. "He told me I'd never be able to do the job," says Christian. "Never be able to jump out of planes or handle the pounding I'd take as a SEAL. But I knew I could. I just had to get some rehab and suck it up.

"When they told us what SEAL teams we were going to go to, there were two things I wanted," he continues. "One was to go to the East Coast, and the other was to *not* be on the same team as Adam. I heard my name and 'Team FOUR,' which was perfect—East Coast team. Then they said, 'Adam Brown, Team FOUR,' and I just shook my head."

Still annoyed that he'd been medically rolled from Class 226 into 227, Christian put the blame for his stress fractures not on the instructors or the curriculum of BUD/S, but on Adam. Adam was the only person to ever push him so hard his body had failed. If they were on the same team, that rivalry was sure to continue, and frankly, he didn't know if he could maintain the pace.

These were some of the thoughts Christian mulled over as he convalesced in Coronado while Adam, Austin (who was also assigned to SEAL Team FOUR), and most of the other graduates headed to Fort Benning, Georgia, for three weeks of airborne training before checking in at their respective teams. Kelley returned to Arkansas with Nathan, planning to bounce back and forth between the Browns' home in Hot Springs and her father's home in Little Rock. One week into airborne training, however, Adam called.

"Itty Bitty," he said, "everything is okay, but…it's calling my name."

"My heart sank when he said that," says Kelley.

Adam had been drug free for a year and seven months, but she'd done her research and learned that relapse was still extremely likely. For Adam the trigger was a glance at a gas station from a man he instantly knew was a dealer—a suggestive look that said, "You need something?"

"You have come too far," Kelley told him. "You are not going to throw all this away. You need to be strong; we've got a family now."

"I know," said Adam.

"We're coming out," she said. "Think about where we can stay, and I need to talk to Austin. Is he there?"

When Adam had filled Austin in on his past, Kelley wasn't so sure it was a good idea, thinking word would get around that Adam was a recovering addict and had been in jail, which couldn't help his reputation in a community where reputation was everything. But now Austin reassured her that he was keeping an eye on Adam and urging him to be careful about whom he shared his story with. Kelley was thankful and relieved that Adam had someone close by watching out for him. "You're a good friend," she said to Austin before hanging up.

Next Kelley informed her father, who had planned to drive with her to Fort Benning in a couple of weeks, that there'd been a change of plans. "Something came up with Adam's training," she said. "We need to leave sooner."

"When?"

"I'll get packing now. Can we leave tomorrow?"

———

Two days later Kelley's father helped her and Nathan move into a one-room vacation cabin that Adam had found on the base. Now, when Adam wasn't in class, in an airplane, or jumping out of one, he was with his family. "I put Nathan in his arms every chance I got," says Kelley. "While he was studying, when we ate dinner. I knew holding Nathan made him strong, reminded him he was a father and why he couldn't give in."

After Adam earned his parachute jump wings, the three drove east to Virginia Beach, where they rented an apartment not far from the Naval Amphibious Base at Little Creek, the East Coast home of Naval Special Warfare Group TWO. On the morning of March 27, 2000, just after Nathan turned two months old, Adam checked in at the SEAL Team FOUR headquarters, a single-story building within a fenced compound at the water's edge of the base. Wearing the required dress whites, Adam approached the main reception area, or "quarterdeck" of the "ship"—what all buildings in the Navy are considered—sticking out like a sore thumb and eliciting scornful comments from the team guys dressed in cammies or PT shorts and T-shirts. "Get your sunglasses, boys," announced one SEAL, shielding his eyes. "There's something bright white and stupid coming on board."

The ridicule began another rite of passage for the new guys, one in which their SEAL Trident pins were prominently displayed in a glass case inside the entrance to the quarterdeck, a continual reminder that they were not yet official U.S. Navy SEALs.

Established in late 1970, the Naval Special Warfare Trident signifies a SEAL's official membership in this exclusive fraternity. The coveted insignia recognizes those who have completed BUD/S training, made it through a six- to nine-month probationary period, and passed advanced SEAL Tactical Training. Only then are SEALs authorized to wear the Trident, as a gold pin on dress uniforms and an embroidered patch on cammies.

There are four components to the Trident: the anchor, symbolizing the Navy; the trident, which represents the SEALs' historical ties to the sea; the cocked pistol, a reminder of SEALs' capabilities on land and their constant state of readiness; and the eagle, which—in addition to being the national emblem of freedom—symbolizes the SEALs' ability to insert from the air. The eagle's head is traditionally held high, but on the Trident, its head is lowered, signifying that a true warrior's strength comes from humility.

The day after Adam checked in, Austin joined Team FOUR and was permitted to wear his Trident—briefly. A master chief pulled it out of the case and pinned it to the wrong side of a black wool vest that the chief made Austin pull on over his dress whites. Looking ridiculous, Austin then had to walk the halls of the building, receiving jeers from the established members of SEAL Team FOUR. Every new guy was at the mercy of whoever happened to be around when he checked in, and endured anything from catcalls about his dress whites to getting his Trident painted blue, the same color as an inert training munition—the derision being that until he was fully trained, that's exactly how he would be regarded: inert, harmless, useless.

So began the probation period for Adam and his classmates from Class 227. They would go through SEAL Tactical Training (STT), the apprentice-to-journeyman stage in learning and absorbing the tactical aspects of the SEAL trade and honing basic war-fighting skills: land warfare, combat swimming, land navigation, weapons skills, and patrolling. At the end of STT they would have to take a three-day final exam, with both written and oral aspects. Those who passed would be "platooned up"—assigned to one of twelve platoons on Team FOUR, each comprising sixteen men: two officers, a chief petty officer, and thirteen enlisted. Then, after a punishing ocean swim, they would be presented with their Trident and deemed SEALs by their brethren.

The next East Coast STT course wasn't set to begin until June, so in the meantime the "mission" of the new guys was to support the Team FOUR platoons. Their ships needed upkeep: floors mopped, walls painted, windows washed, trash taken out. In his first week at Team FOUR, Adam scrubbed garbage cans, unclogged the toilet a few times, and reorganized a storage closet. But he also sat in on a planning meeting for a training exercise, joined a platoon at the firing range, and absorbed the peripheral chatter that gave shape and purpose to the job.

"He attacked whatever task he was given," says a Team FOUR master chief. "Sometimes we'd give the new guys BS tasks, like 'Go do a backflip off the dock.' Some guys rolled their eyes, said okay, and then did whatever it was at half speed, knowing they were getting messed with. But Adam ran down to that dock like he was on an op—no questions, no hesitation— like, 'There must be a higher purpose that I'm doing this backflip with all my clothes on into the ocean.' He was can-do from day one."

During his second week Adam was chosen to support a platoon's training dive. In the dark of night, Adam and five SEALs, all in full dive gear, boarded an inflatable boat and paddled across the Little Creek inlet on the southern shore of Chesapeake Bay to a training area. There they would place limpet mines, magnetic Naval explosives named for their superficial similarity to the limpet mollusk and used since the early 1900s to destroy enemy ships, piers, and bridges.

While the SEALs readied for the dive, Adam slid his brand-new SEAL "pup" knife out of its sheath and attempted to cut through the heavy-duty plastic zip tie holding a dive buoy against the boat. The tie held fast, so with the blade facing him, he used his full might to pull up.

The blade cut through the tie, then continued up to Adam's face, jabbing him above his nose, right between his eyes.

"Ah, man," Adam said, pinching the deep gouge to stop the blood pouring from the wound. When he looked up, the SEALs were shocked to see blood dripping off the end of his nose and streaming down his cheeks.

"What the hell happened?" one said. With his free arm Adam waved off their attempts to get a closer look. They were only a half hour into a four-hour training operation that he didn't want aborted, especially because of him. "Hey, I'm good. I'm okay," he said, squeezing the wound while blood trickled out.

The SEALs gaped at him.

"Carry on!" he said. "Let's do this."

Adam remained in the boat the two hours it took to place the mines. Then the team leader, who because of Adam's injury had no intention of forcing Adam to retrieve them, jokingly said, "Okay, Brown, go get the mines." He gestured with a thumb at the cold, black water.

Without hesitation, Adam flipped backward overboard, the knife wound pouring blood again as he donned his mask and submerged. When he resurfaced, lugging a mine that he tossed into the boat, his mask was a quarter full of blood. He emptied the blood and dived again.

A SEAL started humming the theme from the movie *Jaws* while the team tracked Adam's underwater movement by watching his marker buoy travel from the boat to the bridge pylons and back. On his final trip, the buoy started heading out to sea—the opposite direction from the remaining mine. Assuming that Adam was either visually disoriented from blood in his mask or mentally disoriented from loss of blood, they yanked on the line and tried to redirect him to the boat. But determined to get the job done, Adam refused, instead redirecting himself to the mine, retrieving it, and only then returning to the boat. When he reached for an oar to help paddle back to shore, a SEAL told him to stand down.

"We'll make it to shore, Brown," he said. "You just keep pressure on that wound and try not to bleed to death."

The following morning, more than a hundred SEALs from Team FOUR stood at quarters: the once-a-week gathering where all platoons not deployed or training elsewhere stand in formation and receive official information from the master chiefs. It's also a time for the skipper, at the time Captain Pete Van Hooser, to address the entire team, sometimes giving out awards or highlighting "a dumb new-guy mistake," says Austin, who stood beside Adam that day.

The master chief from the platoon Adam had supported the night before took this opportunity to address some "very serious concerns." He proceeded to give a Cub Scout–level "refresher" on knife safety: never pull the business end of a knife toward your body, especially not toward your face. The men laughed as Adam, stitched up and bandaged, was presented with a rubber knife and a nickname: Blade.

Although Adam had been embarrassed and berated himself the night before, he laughed at the nickname. In spite of the rookie blunder, "he left a solid impression," says Austin. "Everybody knew Adam Brown was not going to let anybody take up his slack, even if he was bleeding."

For long days and longer nights, the SEALs on Team FOUR worked the new guys, integrating them, as Adam had been on the diving exercise, and hammering them with information they must remember. "I hope you're taking notes" was a common admonishment as they jumped from task to task. "It was like drinking water through a fire hose," explains Christian, who had cut short his rehabilitation and joined the team in late April, pins still in his ankle.

At the beginning of May, Christian and Adam were tasked with supporting an Operational Readiness Exercise (ORE), the "final exam" for a SEAL platoon after its twelve-month workup—intense cumulative training exercises that prepare them for deployment into the real world. The ORE consists of a series of war games in which the platoon is pitted against an opposing force of "enemy" soldiers attempting to thwart its mission.

The cadre of instructors orchestrating this particular ORE employed Adam and Christian to role-play as enemy patrolling the area where an American pilot had gone down. Their job was to spot members of the platoon being tested, whose mission was to locate and rescue the pilot undetected.

"I'll drive," Adam said to Christian as soon as they were handed the keys to a pickup truck and told where to go.

"He peeled out, literally burned rubber," says Christian, "then drove like a maniac—drifting around corners, hitting potholes. I thought he was being an ass, trying to scare me, see if I'd tell him to slow down. I just tightened my seat belt and held on. I was not going to give in."

On the third day of the ORE, Adam and Christian had the afternoon off. In their nine months of BUD/S together, they had done little more than compete, never once sitting down to have a conversation.

"We were sitting on a pier watching this guy fishing," says Christian. "No rivalry, nobody yelling at us. For the first time we were relaxed. So we talked. Adam opened up and showed me all the demons from his past—how messed up he'd been on drugs, gone to jail, how his wife would go looking for him in crackhouses, and how becoming a SEAL wasn't a dream for him; it had been his last hope.

"I was awestruck, but I was glad to know he had demons too, because I sure as hell did. Weaknesses make people real, and he let me know his, and that took serious trust. If the wrong people got wind of his past, that could have been bad for him. Something in him trusted me, and so I shared my demons with him, the bad things I'd done in my life. We talked until the sun went down, and when we walked away from that pier, I thought, *This guy is good to go.* I could trust him completely."

Late that night they were awakened by the master chief running the ORE. A large rigid-hulled inflatable boat (RHIB) being used in the exercise had run aground on a sandbar during a beach landing. It was now Adam and Christian's job to rescue it—an important task for a SEAL and unheard of for new guys.

"It was our first mission ever," says Christian, "and the last thing the master chief told us was, 'You'd better not f—ing fail!'"

They sped an hour north to a Coast Guard base, where they jumped aboard a waiting towboat for the two-hour ride to the marooned boat. As they approached the stranded vessel, Adam readied the tow rope; before the anchor dropped he was in the water with the rope, swimming toward the inflatable.

That's when Christian realized that Adam's crazy driving wasn't a personal affront. "It was just Adam's speed," he says. "Everything he did was fast and furious."

Christian joined Adam in the water while a couple of SEALs who had been left on board the marooned boat monitored their progress, offering little more help than "Get it done."

"We free-dove—masks only—and were danger-close to the intakes of revved-up jet engines," says Christian, describing conditions around the RHIB. "There were currents, and we had to fix and refix lines while the towboat pulled. We had to look out for each other, especially when we were clearing the intakes—massive suction going on, the water all churned up—but we got the engines running and got it off that sandbar. For the first time we weren't competing with each other. We were working together as a team."

———

When Adam began SEAL Tactical Training in June, Nathan was a little over four months old, and his parents had weathered the basic training of their new careers and were now honing their skills as warrior and mother. While Adam mastered land navigation through the woods, Kelley memorized grocery store aisles for quick in-and-out missions; as he skillfully blew up an enemy bunker, she deftly changed a "blown-out" diaper; he evaded a mock enemy, while she dodged projectile vomit.

As STT progressed, the training and subsequent real-world scenarios became more complicated—for both of the Browns.

In the STT field classroom: "You've patrolled for five hours through enemy-held terrain, and your platoon has remained undetected." The instructor describes a scenario to Adam and his teammates during the patrolling phase of advanced land warfare training. "*Boom!* The guy in front of you hits a booby trap, his lower leg is blown off, he's screaming, hemorrhaging blood, and guess what? There's an enemy observation post right there, and they open up with heavy machine-gun fire. What's your first priority? What are you gonna do? C'mon, your buddy is dying, you're under attack, there are enemy reinforcements heading your way— what's the call?"

In the Browns' small apartment on base: Nathan has his first cold and is awake most of the night. Kelley needs to go shopping because there is no food in the house and only four diapers. On the drive to the store, Nathan finally falls asleep and snoozes in his car seat. With Nathan still sleeping, Kelley maneuvers the shopping cart through crowds, rushing from aisle to aisle. Throwing in milk and frozen foods at the very end, she rushes to the front of the store only to find long lines at the two open registers. *Boom!* A little old lady bumps her cart into Kelley and apologizes, but Kelley's focus is on Nathan's eyelids. They open and the hungry baby starts to cry, then scream. Everybody around watches, obviously annoyed, as she picks him up. And here comes the snot. Quick rummage through the purse—no tissues. The frozen stuff in the cart is melting. There is no way she's going to breast-feed Nathan standing in a line that she estimates will take fifteen minutes to get through.

In the field: "C'mon, guys!" the instructor yells. "Your buddy is bleeding out and you've got another casualty. What's. The. Order?"

In the grocery store: Kelley starts to cry. She surrenders, lifts the car seat from the shopping cart, and runs to her car.

By the end of STT three months later, Kelley had learned a lot about what it meant to be a Navy SEAL's wife. In the first seven months of Nathan's life, Adam had been with his son only a handful of days. His social life outside the Navy was an extension of the friendships he'd forged within, so it worked out well that Kelley clicked with Christian's wife, Becky—soon to be a new mom herself—and Heidi Ames, the girlfriend of an officer on Team FOUR named Paul Jacobs. As is standard in the military community, the women spent time together and became each other's support group while "the boys" trained.

Paul, a buddy of Adam's from Class 226 who had sailed through BUD/S training without getting rolled, attributed much of his physical endurance and mental focus to being a high school and college wrestler, the same thing Adam said about football. And of course, Adam would not be outdone when the two waxed poetic about their backgrounds. He claimed that his two-a-day summer football conditioning practices in the sweltering humidity of the South rivaled Paul's "steam room" wrestling practices.

This segued into how much better a state Arkansas was than California, where Paul was from. "You got beaches, we got lakes," Adam would say. "California has to import its drinking water, but Arkansas doesn't have to import anything. We could put a bubble over the entire state and we'd be just fine. We have every natural resource. You name it, we have it. Or grow it. Fruits, vegetables, we've even got catfish farms. The soil in Arkansas, the dirt, is richer in minerals—you scoop up a handful, it looks like coffee grounds…"

His Arkansas Bubble Theory, its roots in an eighth-grade history class, would lead back to football and the best high school team in Arkansas, the Lake Hamilton Wolves, then to the best college football team in the country, the University of Arkansas Razorbacks—which always included a rousing rendition of the university's hog call: "Woooo, pig! Sooey!"

"You didn't want to get him started about Arkansas," says Paul. "Everybody knew where Adam Brown was from. He had more pride in his home state than anybody."

While all of Adam's teammates knew he was from Arkansas, they also knew Paul was a wrestler—due to his standing bet during STT that he could pin anybody in thirty seconds or less.

Says Christian, "I thought Adam was going soft when he wasn't the first to take the challenge." But Adam wasn't "going soft"; he was analyzing the problem—and Paul was a big problem. In college he'd wrestled in the 184-pound weight class, and now, after BUD/S, he was in the best shape of his life. Officers, enlisted men, even some of the cadre instructors gave it a go, every one of them ending up flat on their backs and pinned in under thirty seconds.

After a few weeks of this, a crowd gathered on a grassy field to watch Adam finally face off against Paul. At the count of three, a designated timekeeper hit his stopwatch and Adam turned and sprinted, much to the surprise of Paul and the spectators, who started cracking up as they cheered him on. He made it about thirty yards before Paul tackled him, flipped him over, and pinned him—in thirty-five seconds.

"He was the only guy who ever made it past thirty," says Paul. "And I respected him for it. He beat me, and I learned something about Adam that day: he wasn't only tough; he was smart."

On September 5 Adam, along with Austin, Paul, and an expanding list of fellow SEALs who had become brothers in arms, went through a timed series of pass-or-fail tests based on what they'd learned in advanced SEAL Tactical Training. Stations were set up for map reading, weapons handling and maintenance, communications/radio drills, medical procedures, and other skills.

Then each man except Christian—Becky was in the hospital having a baby—stood before the Trident Board for the final oral exam. When Adam's turn came, his superiors presented him with the same earlier scenario of a patrol hitting a booby trap and coming under heavy machine-gun fire. He was ready.

"First thing to do, sir, is win the fight." Adam proceeded to give a rundown on procedure. Returning fire is the first priority, then maneuvering against the enemy while the team leader calls for close air support and casualty evacuation. If the down man is conscious, he is doing self-aid and putting a tourniquet on his leg, but most likely he is unconscious. The fight must be won before helping the down man: "self-aid, buddy aid, and then corpsman aid." As soon as a SEAL can be spared from the fight, he will treat the down man.

The chiefs of SEAL Team FOUR passed Adam, evaluating him as "one of the hardest workers, a role model, and top performer."

"I love what I do," Adam told Kelley once STT was completed. "I love the guys, the brotherhood, and I just love being a SEAL. Thank the Lord for putting me on this path."

Kelley, too, had grown in her role as mother. What had once sent her running out of a store in tears was no longer a big deal after nine months of on-the-job training. Instead of abandoning her cart of groceries, she had learned a trick of the motherhood trade: request an employee to park the cart in the walk-in refrigerator behind the milk and dairy department while she went to the car and fed Nathan.

Representatives from all of Team FOUR's platoons assembled on the sand at Virginia Beach one week later to watch the remaining twenty graduates of STT pair up and make their way out through the rough seas for the Trident swim. "I'll never forget that day because the surf was horrible," says Christian. "Big waves and swell lines out to the horizon. We had to swim a half mile out to get beyond the breakers before we began the three-and-a-half-mile swim up the coast."

A couple dozen SEALs swam with them, but they wore shorts and T-shirts, maybe a wet-suit vest, while the new guys wore cammies and dragged along a sledgehammer and a rucksack stuffed with clothes. Says Christian, "Our strongest swimmer carried the hammer the whole way. The rest of us switched off dragging the rucksack in groups of two—and that thing, when it was wet, was like a lead weight."

They were also accompanied by the commander of Naval Special Warfare Group TWO, as well as the commanding officer of Team FOUR, Captain Pete Van Hooser. Both men were widely respected. Van Hooser had served multiple tours as a Marine in Vietnam, then laterally transferred into the Navy and went through the SEAL program. In a parachuting accident he suffered a compound fracture, shattering his leg so badly that he was told he'd never walk normally, much less run again, if he kept it. Van Hooser chose to have the leg amputated so he might function at the level he wanted and continue his career.

Wearing a prosthetic, he joined his men for their hardest workouts, the Monster Mashes: grueling combinations of back-to-back runs, swims, and paddles. On the Trident swim with Adam and his teammates, his prosthetic was fitted with a fin, so he could swim alongside.

Janice and Larry had flown out from Hot Springs and stood with Kelley and Nathan and dozens of other supporters on the beach near the finish line. All smiles, the men exited the water and gathered in the shallows until everyone had finished. It had been a two-year journey from the day Adam checked in at boot camp until he stood at attention in the surf on the Virginia Beach shore facing Captain Van Hooser as he took the backing off the pushpin of the gold Trident.

He pushed the Trident through the fabric above the upper left pocket of Adam's soaking wet cammie top, and a U.S. Navy SEAL was born—on paper anyway.

The rite of passage for a new SEAL involved one more initiation ceremony for full induction into this fraternity of warriors—an unofficial one. The night after the Trident swim, the newly pinned SEALs were invited to an off-the-record party—attendance not optional—at a Team FOUR member's house. The new guys were called in pairs to the garage and directed to stand with their backs against the wall.

"This was the real pinning," says the SEAL who stood next to Adam as they handed over their Tridents to a senior enlisted SEAL and removed their shirts. "He pulled off the frogs [the pin backing], pushed the pins into our chests so they stuck, then punched them in with his fist."

A line of at least a dozen Team FOUR SEALs followed suit. "One by one they punched the Tridents into our chests. It was hard-core; we were yelling and screaming—not screams of pain, screams of pride. All of our chests were bloody, and when we left that party, the ceremony was complete. We finally had credibility.

"We'd bled together, now we could fight together. We were brothers."

Captain Van Hooser pinning Adam with his Trident
minutes after the three-and-a-half-mile swim.

Brown family archives

The Calling

PICTURE A ONE-YEAR-OLD FLYING through the air, arms and legs flailing like an airborne cat. That was Nathan reentering Earth's atmosphere after Adam had tossed him into orbit.

"Don't throw him so high!" Kelley said.

"Ah, he loves it," said Adam. "Look at him, he's laughing."

"He's laughing because he's petrified. It's a *nervous* laugh."

"It is not. Kids don't know nervous."

"Well, *I'm* petrified," pleaded Kelley. "Please, just—"

Adam sent Nathan sailing again, caught him, then walked over to Kelley and gave her a hug and squeezed her nose. "Have I ever dropped him?" he said. "No. I have not. I will not drop our baby."

It was January 26, 2001, and Adam and Kelley's closest friends in Virginia Beach were at their apartment to celebrate Nathan's first birthday. Says Austin, "I was more comfortable handling explosives. No kidding. Nothing made me more nervous than watching Adam throw Nathan in the air."

Paul was also there with Heidi, now his wife, and Christian and Becky had brought along their baby boy.

It was fortunate that their training cycle allowed them to be in Virginia Beach on Nathan's birthday. For the nearly five months since the

Brown family archives

Adam's daily workout included throwing Nathan into orbit.

men had earned their Tridents, they'd been training with their newly assigned platoons: Golf Platoon for Adam and Paul, and Hotel Platoon for Christian and Austin. These sister platoons trained and deployed together as a single "task unit"—one of six such units on SEAL Team FOUR.

As Golf Platoon's 60-gunner, Adam single-handedly carried the Vietnam-era M60 machine gun, the heaviest weapon on a patrol. In every other unit in the military, the M60 is crew serviced: one man shoulders the twenty-three-pound gun and one hundred rounds of ammo, weighing about seven pounds, and a second man takes four hundred rounds of ammo, about twenty-eight pounds. On SEAL teams one man—in this case, Adam—handles it all solo, almost sixty pounds of weapon and ammo in addition to the rest of his equipment, altogether a total of eighty and often ninety pounds. The only other man in a SEAL platoon whose load rivals the 60-gunner's is the radioman, Christian's job on Hotel Platoon. Though these backbreaking jobs aren't desirable and are routinely assigned to the new guys, Adam and Christian took pride in them, arguing over whose load was heaviest.

"They would go on and on with their man talk," says Kelley. "And they spoke a different language now. It took a while for us girls to catch on—the acronyms and calibers and klicks. We'd just laugh at them, these big tough Navy SEALs talking the talk while drinking fruit punch in tiny paper cups, holding their babies, and wearing *Blue's Clues* party hats.

"We were all pretty naive and innocent back then. We were young military couples, just starting to have kids. We knew what our husbands did, what they were trained for, but it was peacetime. In my mind it was like what they did was in a movie. What they were training for would never really happen."

Thirty-six-year-old Shane Harley, Golf Platoon's chief, had served ten years at the Naval Special Warfare Development Group—DEVGRU— before taking over a platoon at Team FOUR. Even the new guys knew what this meant: he'd been a tier one operator with SEAL Team SIX. On paper, the men who serve at DEVGRU test weapons and equipment being considered for Navy-wide implementation. Indeed, they *are* the Navy's weapons experts—but that is only the cover story.

DEVGRU SEALs are also one of the United States' premier Special Missions Units, capable of executing top-secret missions anywhere in the world. This was the rapidly deployable, highly elite counterterrorism unit the Navy had created as a result of the failed hostage rescue mission in Iran in 1980, when Adam was six years old. DEVGRU operators take orders from the highest levels within the Pentagon or directly from the Oval Office.

Chief Harley was the only member of Golf Platoon who had seen action, and even though the details of that action were classified, he was revered by the men because only a tiny percentage of SEALs are chosen for DEVGRU. First, a SEAL has to be recommended by his commanding officer. Then his mental health and past are meticulously scrutinized for top-secret clearance. Finally, he is given a chance to qualify through a process that—according to those who have passed it—"makes BUD/S look like a cakewalk."

As Team FOUR SEALs, the guys on Golf and Hotel Platoons already represented the alpha males of the U.S. Navy; but compared to the tier one SEALs, "they were playing college ball," says Harley. "DEVGRU is the NFL." His DEVGRU experience was the major reason Harley continually reminded the men in his platoon during their twelve-month workup that they were training for the real deal, despite the fact that it was peacetime. Having lost friends both in training and on missions, Harley knew the stakes were high.

"At the end of the day, this job has huge rewards," he told the platoon as they rested in the dirt after a particularly brutal patrol exercise, "but you also pay a huge price for failure. Pro football players like to compare what they do to the warrior mentality, being at war, going to battle. Well, if you lose the Super Bowl, yeah, you're going to be pissed, you may shed a tear, you may go home and kick the dog, but the next morning you're going to wake up, eat breakfast with your wife and kids, and life goes on.

"The difference between Joe Quarterback and you is if you make a mistake and lose, you may be coming home in a body bag. You're not waking up the next morning, your wife's not going to have a husband, your kids aren't going to have a father. So when we're out here shooting blanks, you work hard and pray that if you make a mistake it only costs *you* something and you don't have to have another teammate pay that price for you."

Early on in the workup it became clear who had their sights set on DEVGRU. Adam was one of the first to take Harley aside, asking, "Chief, how do I get over there? What's my best route?"

"Keep doing what you're doing," Harley said. "If you continue to be a top performer, the top one percent, you will get the opportunity to go over there. Be a sponge, keep soaking up that knowledge like you're doing right now. I don't believe in luck, but I do believe in opportunity, preparedness, and hard work. You prepare yourself with hard work, and when that opportunity comes, take advantage of it."

When training took place locally, Adam was home with Kelley and Nathan in Virginia Beach—about a third of the yearlong workup. The other eight months were spent at military bases across the United States and in the jungles of South America and the Caribbean.

"He'd come home after being away for a couple of weeks," says Kelley, "and he'd be bruised up from some fall, his hands callused and cut up, his feet a mess, and within a few hours, a day tops, of being home, he would tell me, 'Itty Bitty, your job is so much harder than mine.'"

Although Adam avoided dirty diapers at all costs, Kelley knew he didn't take what she did for granted. Every minute he was home he devoted to his family, making up for lost time and taking care of things around the house. "He'd turn that 'work switch' off," says Kelley, "and turn that 'daddy and husband switch' on."

At the end of the week they would go to Atlantic Shores Baptist Church with Austin and his wife, Michelle, who had become Kelley's good friend. Kelley and Michelle volunteered their time in the church's nursery, a program that allowed parents to attend services and Bible study classes while their children were looked after. When Austin and Adam were home they also helped in the nursery, playing with the babies.

"Austin and I were the newlyweds," says Michelle, "but Adam and Kelley were still on their honeymoon. In church I'd look over and they'd be holding hands. He'd have the Bible with one hand and she'd turn the pages. We'd go over to watch a movie and they'd be on the couch planted side by side, cuddling."

And at the end of each day they spent together, Kelley and Adam would read aloud from the Bible, a ritual they wanted to be a part of Nathan's life. They prayed for their families back in Arkansas and thanked God for the "simple little life" they were living together, one they hoped would someday return them to Arkansas. No matter how dark Adam's experiences in his hometown had been, they never blotted out the good memories he cherished.

While taking long strolls with Nathan, he and Kelley talked about the home they'd have in Hot Springs, one with wood floors, a nice big kitchen, and a yard where Nathan and a sibling or three could "grow up right," running and playing outside. If it was God's plan for them to return, that's where they would go after Adam served at least ten years in the Navy. In the meantime, they would keep saving what they could from his paychecks and buy a house in Virginia Beach.

Regardless of what they were doing separately or together, "Adam still wrote me love notes and bought me flowers," says Kelley. "He never once missed my birthday or an anniversary. Even if he was gone, roses would show up, or a card, or something."

After Nathan's birthday, the boys geared up for winter warfare training, and the Browns were able to go out on a date, splurging with a restaurant dinner. It had been more than three years since they'd met, and "I still felt that deep, almost nervous love I felt in the beginning," says Kelley. "The military life pulls a lot of couples apart, but for me, it kept it new. Every time he'd leave, I couldn't get enough of him—I could never get enough of my Adam."

Adam Brown, a.k.a. Blade, was a funny guy. That's what Chief Harley kept hearing from his platoon—not only the stories Adam told and what he said, but the funny things that happened to him. "When you're out in

Brown family archives

Austin Michaels and Adam living the dream as fully
armed and dangerous U.S. Navy SEALs.

a crummy situation," says Harley, "and in our line of work that's most of the time—it's freezing cold or hot as sin, you're working your butt off rucking all over the mountains, whatever—the guy you're with can either bring you down or boost you up. However he accomplishes it, if he can make you laugh in those dismal situations and still get the job done, he'll go far."

Harley experienced Blade's celebrity firsthand when he paired up with Adam for winter warfare training in Virginia as well as some one-on-one mentoring. They were dropped off in a field in the middle of nowhere one early February morning with loads approaching ninety pounds, a map, a compass, and a directive: reach a specified location the following evening without discovery by the enemy force on patrol. Their route might include old logging roads, thickly vegetated wilderness, or steep, wooded mountains. Structures along the way—barns, sheds, hunters' cabins—were considered risky but usable shelter.

Harley and Adam chose a route that took them over nearly fifteen miles of brutal wilderness, during which rain turned to freezing rain and then, as night approached, to snow. A summer cabin that was as cold inside as out acted as a "layup" point where they could find shelter and sleep for a few hours.

"Chief," said Adam, his teeth chattering, "would it be tactically okay, since it's after dark, to build a small fire in here?"

"Hell, yeah," Harley said. "We've got wood, we've got a fireplace, we're hypothermic. Definitely light a fire."

Bringing in a pile of wet wood, Adam built a small teepee in the fireplace, then asked what they should light it with.

"I didn't know Adam could be, well, a little clumsy," says Harley. "And with frozen fingers and hands that weren't working so well from the cold, maybe I should have thought it through more, but I didn't. I told him, 'Just take some of that white gas we have for our stoves and throw it on there and then throw a match. It should light right up.'"

Wearing his glove liners, Adam followed Harley's instructions, and "Whooof!" says Harley. "It flamed right up, and Adam stepped back and was looking at the fire, his hands at his sides...burning."

"Brown!" yelled Harley. "Your gloves are on fire!"

"Aw, *damn*," said Adam and clapped his hands together, but the gloves kept burning. He pulled them off and stomped the flames out.

"Adam!" said Harley. "Your hands are still on fire!"

Eventually, Adam was able to smother the flames under his jacket. "Chief, I'm good," he said.

"Let me see your hands," Harley said, expecting to see second- or third-degree burns.

"Naw, naw, Chief, I'm good."

"No, Adam, let me see your hands."

Adam relented, holding out his hands, which Harley was amazed to find were only slightly red. The flames had been residual gas burning off and never reached Adam's skin.

During the weeklong exercise, Harley accumulated story after story. Says Harley, "Adam kept me entertained till the end of that miserable training," including the final night, when they had to follow a road in order to make their linkup point on time.

"So here's the deal," Harley told Adam. "We'll walk down this road. If you see headlights coming, just step off the side about ten or fifteen feet, lie down, and they'll never see you."

Fifteen minutes later, a car approached and they shuffled off the road. As Harley flattened out on his stomach, he heard *Thud! Thud! Bang! Crunch!* coming from Adam's direction. The car passed by, and Harley hurried over to where Adam had been, finding a drop-off into a massive drainage ditch lined with big, jagged rocks.

"He was lying on top of these rocks in a slump at the bottom," describes Harley, who for a second thought he was looking at a dead body. "I called down, 'Brown, you okay?'"

The body stirred and peered up at Harley. "Chief," Adam said, "I fall a lot, but I don't get hurt."

Adam's task unit—Golf and Hotel Platoons—headed to Mississippi at the beginning of September for their ORE. The thickly vegetated, hot, humid, jungle-like environment of Stennis was the setting for react-to-contact drills performed in a realistic exercise, complete with explosions going off, blanks being fired, and a motivated opposing force attempting to "kill" them.

Between drills, the men of Golf Platoon were resting in some shade when Adam and teammate Mark Kramer noticed nine or ten guys from Hotel Platoon gathered in a circle.

"What's going on?" Mark yelled over.

"We got a pool going," one of the SEALs shouted back. "Twenty bucks a man for whoever is crazy enough to set their balls on this fire ant nest for thirty seconds."

"A second later Adam had his pants down to his ankles," says Austin. "'Where is it?' he said. 'I'll do it.'"

"Whoa, wait, hold on a second," said another SEAL from Hotel. "There're some rules. Your balls have to be *on* the anthill for thirty seconds; they cannot lift up for one second, they have to be on it the entire time. Otherwise you don't get the money."

By now both platoons had formed a large circle around the anthill, then "all the head shed, all the leaders, came over," says Mark. "You'd think they'd say, 'This is stupid, don't do it.' Nope. They were all over it. 'Okay, we'll put in twenty bucks too,' they said. Same with the corpsmen, the medics—no concerns about anaphylactic shock or anything. In

Naval Special Warfare, I've found the corpsmen are the most sadistic of our bunch."

With six hundred dollars in the pot from some thirty takers, Adam shuffled over and got into position, his bare behind hovering above the anthill while a stopwatch was set and Christian stirred up the nest with a stick. As Adam squatted down slowly, the angry, swarming ants rose up to meet his anatomy, climbing on top of each other into a pyramid of defense. The second Adam touched the nest, three SEALs, including Mark, jumped on him and held him down.

"Adam screamed like a little girl," recalls Christian.

"I will never forget his expression," says Mark. "His face conveyed such acute agony, while everyone else was cheering."

"Time!" shouted the SEAL holding the stopwatch, and Adam exploded off the nest, swatting himself furiously. "Get them off!" he shrieked. "Get them all off!"

Looking Adam over, the medics counted almost four hundred bites around his groin, "but it was hard to tell, because there were bites on top of bites," explains Mark. "Over the course of the day, there was massive swelling. In terms of fruit, think cantaloupes. Small watermelons."

"All those stories—the burning gloves, the blade incident, the anthill—are all funny, and they all help us understand the man Adam was," says Chief Harley, who contributed his own twenty dollars to the pot, "but without a doubt, they should *never, ever* diminish his abilities, his personality as a warrior, as a SEAL. He could flip that switch from having this stuff happen, these funny moments, and the next minute we could be downrange and be in harm's way and he would be the ultimate professional, operator, warrior that you'd want. Adam had that rare ability to go from looking in the mirror and laughing at himself to being the cool-headed professional, the one person I'd choose to have beside me if I was surrounded by enemy and running out of ammunition."

———

Adam was granted the rest of the day in the aid station by the corpsmen, who propped his amply spread legs with pillows, iced his groin, put him on an IV, and shot him up with an antihistamine to counteract the venom from the fire ants. The cash poured in. A couple of men who hadn't even been present gave Adam a twenty just because they'd heard the story.

By September 9 Adam felt good enough to waddle his way through the next evolution of training. On the night of September 10, Golf Platoon was tasked with a combat search-and-rescue operation that took them into the morning hours of September 11. The SEALs returned to their camp around four in the morning and were snoring within moments of hitting their bunks.

"A plane just crashed into the World Trade Center!" shouted the officer in charge as he ran into their tent a few hours later. In a flurry Golf Platoon pulled on pants and boots and ran to the communications tent, where men were stacked like human bleachers—seated, kneeling, and standing around a small television set, watching in solemn disbelief.

As horror upon horror was broadcast, there was "shock, worry, tears, and anger in that tent," says Harley, "but mainly, there was resolve. There wasn't a guy in there—Adam included—who didn't want a pound-of-flesh vengeance for what they were witnessing. They knew we were going to war, and more than anything, these guys wanted to be a part of it."

"During peacetime, pre-9/11, it wasn't a popular decision to join the military to protect your country," says Mark Kramer, "so my decision was sort of validated that day. Adam and I were going around trying to find coverage to call home, and he was right with me, saying, 'Get us out there—let's get some payback.' Adam had this intense love for his hometown and state, which is really what patriotism is. We had both been competitive in sports, talked about the frustration of watching a game from the sideline, so we were hoping and praying that the powers that be would let us go out and do what we were trained to do."

Kelley, just back from an early morning trip to Wal-Mart for diapers, was holding Nathan tight and watching the news when Adam finally got through.

"It's horrible," she said.

"I know," said Adam. "Pray for all these poor people who are suffering and scared, and you and Nathan stay home. Stay away from the base. Don't do anything, and I'll call you when I can."

"What does this mean for you?" Kelley asked.

"I'm not certain," said Adam, "but I know now why God led me to do what I'm doing."

He called her again that evening, and then once a day while he completed the final week of the ORE. During these talks Kelley sensed a shift in Adam's being, "like, *clunk,* he found the right gear," she says. "He had always been a proud American, but his patriotism definitely started defining him and who he was going to be. Those attacks really brought out the old Adam, before all the junk. He started to emerge again."

On the day Golf and Hotel Platoons passed their final ORE drills and were officially ready to deploy, Chief Harley stood before his men. "They all wanted to go join the fight that they knew was being planned for Afghanistan," says Harley, "but their stated area of focus was South and Central America. That was where they were going for a six-month deployment.

"So I told them, 'We don't know where the front lines are going to be in this war against terrorism, and as part of the big-picture military, it's our job to cover our zone. Before last week nobody was thinking about

Chief Harley congratulating Adam for his
advancement to an E5-ranked SEAL.

Afghanistan, and you know what? That's too bad. We aren't going to
make that mistake and abandon the rest of the field; we're going to do our
job, and it's an important job, and I know you will do your country and
your families proud. Don't spend your time home bitching and moaning.
Enjoy them and this life and the freedoms we have. That's what you'll be
fighting to protect soon enough. Mark my words, gentlemen.'"

One of the first things Adam did when he returned to Virginia Beach was
go to a jewelry store he and Kelley had walked by months before. She had
stopped to admire a platinum-and-diamond necklace, completely outside
their budget, which Adam now paid for with a stack of twenties.

"I love it, Adam," Kelley said when he presented it to her as an early twenty-sixth-birthday gift. "I absolutely love it, but we can't afford this. We need to return it."

Adam then revealed the ant bites, starting at his torso and on down to the heart of the matter. "There's a little money left over," he said. "We can put it in savings. I just want you to have the very best." Adam's words and what came to be known as the Ant Necklace brought Kelley to tears.

"You are crazy," she told him as she hugged him. "I love you."

Not one to boast or brag, Kelley made an exception with the Ant Necklace and wore it proudly to dinner with their friends later that week. While Michelle, Heidi, and Becky admired it, their husbands recounted the event, starting with the dare, continuing with Christian stirring up the nest, and ending with Adam "screaming like a little girl."

Laughter soon turned to soft talking among the women, who shot glances at Christian, Paul, and Austin.

"What's wrong?" Austin finally asked.

"I was just wondering why it was Adam and not you that took the dare," said Michelle, gesturing toward Kelley's necklace.

"You would have wanted me to?" said Austin.

"Oh yeah," she said, Heidi and Becky nodding their agreement. "Definitely."

Adam had expected to be somewhere in South or Central America for Christmas 2001, but an initiative known as Force XXI—a massive re-organization of the United States military—had prompted the Navy's top brass to rethink the SEAL teams' areas of focus, organizational struc-ture, and deployment schedules. Currently, an entire team consisting of six task units each focused on a geographic region. With the new plan, only one task unit on Team FOUR would focus on South and Central America. Another task unit would cover Eastern Europe, another the

Middle East and Central Asia, another Africa, and around the globe. In other words, each SEAL team could now cover the entire world.

Adam's task unit was transferred to SEAL Team TWO, also based at Little Creek—a highly unusual move since a SEAL would generally remain on the same numbered team for the duration of his career. Led by Chief Harley, Golf and Hotel Platoons became Team TWO's South and Central American task unit, a reorganization that postponed their deployment and added six more months of training.

This meant that Janice and Larry Brown would have all their children and grandchildren (Nathan; Josie, Shawn and Tina's little girl, nine months younger than Nathan; and Maddy, Manda and Jeremy's four-month-old baby girl) home for Christmas. Following family tradition, they went to church on Christmas Eve and, between visiting and eating, watched National Lampoon's *Christmas Vacation* and *The Outlaw Josey Wales.*

As usual, Shawn and Adam ended up outside tossing a football back and forth, their breath hanging in the cold like smoke, chatting about the world, the Razorbacks, and fatherhood. "I'd like to coach Nathan when he gets older," said Adam. "If it works out, God willing, we'll be back here in time for him to play ball for the Wolves."

Says Shawn, "Adam started talking about moving back to Hot Springs early on as a SEAL. After 9/11 it was a blur, but I remember Adam saying that he was going to be fighting for us, for our way of life. Not 'us' as in our family, but 'us' as in America."

Since October, Green Berets had been on the ground in Afghanistan, as well as some SEAL teams conducting reconnaissance missions in advance of two raids by Special Operations Forces: an airfield seizure in southern Afghanistan and a raid on one of Mullah Omar's compounds. The hunt for Osama bin Laden had begun, and while Adam assured his family that his first deployment would be to South America, he didn't hide his enthusiasm for getting into the fight in Afghanistan as soon as possible.

"I was in awe," says Manda, "because Adam was just Adam all over again—but in a different uniform. He was my hero as this crazy football player who loved Lake Hamilton High; now he was a SEAL, and his team was our entire country. But he wasn't loud about it, like he'd been before. He'd matured and was more quiet and humble, and that to me made him more powerful."

"I was so proud," Janice says. "Think of those months after September 11 and all the American flags that were going up everywhere. We put one up, a big one. And when I saw a flag, I think, like any military mother, there was a little something extra. In fact, I was getting used to being proud of Adam instead of worrying about him, but 9/11 changed all that, and there I was worrying about him again, worried that he was going to war."

Larry felt the same conflicting emotions, but trusted that God had a plan and that Adam's part in it would be revealed. "He told me it was his calling," says Larry, who remembers that particular Christmas as the first time he'd discussed politics with his son. There was no need for debate; they were both on the same page. "People were arguing back and forth about whether or not this was a holy war, and Adam and I couldn't figure out why," says Larry. "For the terrorists, it wasn't anything *but* a holy war, stated clearly by them. There was no doubt in our minds that they were waging a holy war, and Adam—as an American, as a warrior, and as a Christian—was not going to stand for it."

12

War

On April 3, 2002, Kelley drove Adam, now Petty Officer Second Class Brown, to the SEAL Team TWO compound at Little Creek to see him off on his first deployment. She watched as Adam held Nathan, now two years old, tightly against his chest, then tossed him in the air until the toddler was laughing.

"More, Daddy!" Nathan shouted.

"That's it, little buddy," Adam said, holding him in one arm while he wrapped his other around Kelley and kissed her nose and Nathan's, back and forth a few times. "Don't y'all grow too much while I'm away," he told Nathan.

He stooped to put his son in the car, then stepped back and threw him in the air one last time before strapping him into the seat. Adam gave Kelley a long hug and kiss and rubbed her stomach, which was barely showing a bump; the baby was due at the end of Adam's deployment. "You drive safely," he said to her, "and take care of our babies."

While Adam flew south with his task unit toward Puerto Rico, Kelley and Nathan drove west to Arkansas where, in order to save money, they would split their time between her dad's house in Little Rock and the Browns' place in Hot Springs. "Once the water warms up," Adam had said to Kelley, "be sure you take Nathan swimming in Lake Hamilton."

———

Nearly six months later Adam flew into Hot Springs in time to witness his daughter, Savannah Nicole Brown, enter the world on September 24, 2002.

Tough in every other aspect of his life, Adam was overprotective of Kelley and downright squeamish when it came to childbirth. "He attended to me," says Kelley. "Wouldn't let me lift things, like a box of detergent or whatever, and I'd say, 'How do you think I've survived all these months you're away?' But I loved it, and how he'd get real quiet if I started talking about an ultrasound or something going on down there after I saw the gynecologist. He'd get this glazed look, like he did *not* want to be hearing this. There were times he thanked God that he was a male. When Savannah was born he was there, and his eyes got a little teary and he called her 'My Little Baby' right off the bat—and that stuck. She had his heart."

Adam brought Nathan into the hospital room to meet his baby sister later that day, and "Nathan's little outfit did not match," says Kelley. "I bit my tongue, but inside I laughed because when it came to stuff like that, Adam was a fish out of water. Put him in the jungle, the desert, mountains, ocean, whatever, and he'd maneuver his way to wherever he needed to be, but he'd get lost in the kids' sock drawer."

Everyone who came by Janice and Larry's to congratulate the family of four also wanted to hear about what Adam had done while deployed. He remained the consummate, quiet professional. "We just kind of did our thing," he said to Manda's husband, Jeremy. One of the more exciting tasks he'd been assigned was assisting a sailor who had been injured in the jungle, Adam said, but he wouldn't elaborate on the story, simply saying that he "helped with the medevac."

Even Kelley had a hard time getting the full story from her husband because "he underplayed everything," she explains. Months later she learned that Adam had been awarded his *third* Navy and Marine Corps Achievement Medal for his actions. When she asked what the other two medals were for, he replied, "It was no big deal; just doing my job."

The commendation certificate, stuffed by Adam into a file in a desk drawer, read,

> For professional achievement in the superior performance of his duties while serving as a member of a volunteer rescue team that provided medical assistance and comfort to an injured service member in the El Yunque Rainforest from 5–6 May 2002. Petty Officer Brown demonstrated great foresight by gathering needed medical supplies for the injured man. Displaying impressive courage and skill, he fought through five hours of treacherous river currents and vertical ascents. Once on scene, he expertly assessed the situation and stabilized the patient. He continued to provide vigilant care throughout the night until evacuation was accomplished. Petty Officer Brown's professionalism and devotion to duty reflected great credit upon himself and were in keeping with the highest traditions of the United States Naval Service.

More official praise thickened the U.S. Navy's file that archived Adam's Enlisted Service Record—evaluations that Adam had signed and Kelley never saw. These records documented Chief Harley's assessment that Adam's goofy, sometimes clumsy, laid-back demeanor belied his outstanding professional performance as a SEAL.

In one of Adam's earliest performance evaluations while in Golf Platoon, Harley wrote:

Despite his limited experience, Petty Officer Brown's initiative and determination ensured 100 percent success in his [platoon's] department. A team player who is always willing to lend a hand where needed. Even with an extensive workload, Brown dedicated numerous late night, weekend, and off duty hours to assist his teammates in their departments. His exemplary performance has been a great influence on the junior members of the platoon. He scored OUTSTANDING on the most recent command inspection and SEAL PRT. Brown is on track to become a stand out performer. [He has] unlimited potential and is dedicated to excellence. He is among the top of the Second Class Petty Officers.

A lieutenant who was the officer in charge during Adam's first deployment—which included joint training missions with host-nation military in Puerto Rico, Suriname, and St. Croix, and counterdrug missions in Ecuador—described Adam in his next evaluation as "a hard-charging SEAL operator. This warrior gives 100 percent the first time, every time!"

Providing a glimpse into what Adam's job entailed, that same lieutenant wrote,

His absolute dedication ensured 100 percent accountability and maintenance of over 300K of parachutes and associated mission essential equipment [while he] served as lead instructor and established standard operating procedures for a vital week of interoperability training with the 160th Special Operations Air Regiment. Professionally instructed his sixteen-man platoon in every facet of helicopter insertion and extraction techniques with HH-60 and MH-47 helicopters. Served as the jump master during 40 high-risk air insertions and extractions, ensuring the safe control of over 75 SEALs in jump, rappel, fast rope, and helicopter cast operations, and 150 hours of live-fire demolition and field craft exercises. Brown implemented an innovative re-directing braking system that improved safety of rappel operations. This dedication to his teammates is his trademark.

Two weeks after Savannah was born, the Brown family returned to Virginia Beach, renting a house with a yard in a suburban neighborhood. While Adam began the twelve- to eighteen-month workup for his second platoon, Kelley figured out the logistics of raising two children.

In Afghanistan, the oppressive Taliban government that provided a safe haven to Osama bin Laden and his fellow al Qaeda terrorists had surrendered ten months earlier, on December 5, 2001, after just two months of war. While SEALs, Marines, and Army Rangers played a role in the beginning of Operation Enduring Freedom, it was fought predominantly by fewer than a hundred Special Forces Green Berets, working with the CIA and a handful of Air Force combat air controllers. They joined forces with the Northern Alliance in the north of Afghanistan and a ragtag militia in the south led by a Pashtun tribal leader named Hamid Karzai, who would become the first president of Afghanistan.

The swift victory against the Taliban regime then shifted to a counterinsurgency mission of fighting hard-line Taliban insurgents and their allies—foreign jihadists pouring in from Pakistan and Iran. They sought to overthrow the fledgling Afghan government and oust the American-led coalition forces, whom they considered invaders and infidels.

In addition to fighting these insurgents and jihadists and providing security for the newly formed Afghan government, the U.S. military's priority mission remained the manhunt for Osama bin Laden, the archi-

tect of the September 11 attacks on American soil. He was at the top of
the list, followed by Mullah Mohammed Omar, the Taliban's founding
father, and a laundry list of Taliban and terrorist leaders on the run in
Afghanistan and around the globe.

War planners realized almost immediately after the surrender of the
Taliban that this was merely the beginning of combat operations in Afghanistan. Then, while Afghanistan's post-Taliban government and national police and army were still under construction, another war was
being planned in the Middle East. U.S. intelligence, military leadership,
and ultimately Commander in Chief and President George W. Bush
deemed Iraq—more specifically, Iraqi president Saddam Hussein—the
gravest threat to national security.

On March 17, 2003, President Bush demanded that Hussein and his
sons, Uday and Qusay, surrender and leave Iraq within forty-eight hours.
When that time line was not met, the "shock and awe" bombing of Iraq
began. Two days later, about forty-five minutes after the first bombs struck
military targets outside Baghdad, President Bush addressed the nation
and outlined the objectives of what would be a military invasion of Iraq:

> ...to disarm Iraq, to free its people, and to defend the world from
> grave danger.... The people of the United States and our friends
> and allies will not live at the mercy of an outlaw regime that
> threatens the peace with weapons of mass murder. We will meet
> that threat now, with our Army, Air Force, Navy, Coast Guard,
> and Marines, so that we do not have to meet it later with armies
> of firefighters and police and doctors on the streets of our cities.

That week, as the bombing campaign continued in Iraq, the master
chiefs of SEAL Team TWO conducted an annual closed-door meeting

in which they discussed, evaluated, and graded all the enlisted SEALs under their command. They ranked Adam Brown five out of thirty-two second class petty officers.

Adam's superior, another lieutenant, noted in his March 25 evaluation that Adam was a "proven, tactically proficient operator" and that he had been selected as "operator of the quarter" due to his performance while deployed. Again, Adam was recognized as "always the first to volunteer for the hard jobs and the last to leave. Leads, mentors, and sets the example—The Definition of a Team Player: Advance to First Class."

Now six months into his second platoon's workup, with war being waged on two fronts, Adam was virtually guaranteed deployment to a combat zone of a war he fervently believed in.

"Adam trusted our leadership, the checks and balances of our Constitution, and felt it was his duty to go where he was ordered to go," says Larry. "Beyond that, he believed in his heart that what we were doing was the right thing. He educated himself so he'd have an informed opinion. Going after bin Laden was a no-brainer; the Taliban, the atrocities they committed, they needed to be removed. Their treatment of women and children was always a big deal for Adam; that got to him. And in Iraq Adam remembered this photo of a Kurdish girl lying dead on the street, eyes open, after Saddam Hussein had gassed her whole town. All this argument about whether or not they had weapons of mass destruction— that was proof enough for Adam that they not only had them but that Saddam Hussein had used them against his own people. He was evil, he was a bully, and to stand by and watch that and not do something about it was unacceptable to Adam."

Says Kelley, "Adam believed in a spiritual battle between good and evil. Reading the Bible was part of his training, really. Just like what was going on in Iraq and Afghanistan, with good people versus bad people, there was good and bad in a spiritual sense, and he wanted to be educated. So he read and read and read—books, the classified reports he could get his hands on—and he watched the news. But more than anything, he couldn't wait to get over there and see for himself, try and do some good wherever he was."

One morning Adam donned a fireman's hat and proceeded to exhibit what Chief Harley says was his "ability to flip a switch and adapt to any situation."

Wearing the bright red hat, he got down on his hands and knees and went to work. He slinked like a leopard, hopped like a rabbit, climbed onto a desk like a monkey, and with accompanying growls, clicks, and howls, he kept a dozen two- and three-year-olds riveted for the entire hour of Kelley and Michelle's Sunday school class.

"He was a great big kid himself," says Kelley. "I had a rule: no climbing on the desks. But I step out for a minute and who's on the desk when I get back to the room? My twenty-nine-year-old husband."

Says Austin, "The fact that Adam taught Sunday school really defines who he was. He'd play and act out the animals on Noah's ark, and he'd tell me that was just the best way he felt he could praise the Lord. He was a human puppet for the kids. They loved Adam."

Since Virginia Beach is a military town, each Sunday the congregation at Atlantic Shores Baptist Church prayed to God to watch over all who were serving, and almost every Sunday they also prayed for the families and souls of those killed the previous week. Michelle and Kelley never verbalized their own fears, but as each month of training brought their husbands closer to war, all it took was a glance during these all-too-frequent prayers for fallen warriors. If the wives' eyes met, they knew they were both experiencing the same sense of dread that only a military spouse can feel when a loved one is bound for war.

—

While the wars waged on, Adam quietly continued to fight the personal battle that had begun the first time he'd smoked crack some eight years earlier. His faith, family, and determination had kept him drug free for almost five years, but his body and brain had been altered by the drug and they would seek that pleasure forever. He had a one-beer limit, a tough maximum to adhere to in a community where "if you don't go out drinking with the boys," says one SEAL, "you're not really one of the boys; it's the reality of the job. But there are exceptions, and Adam was one of them. Austin was another. Both solid operators who didn't get obliterated. They'd either limit themselves or sometimes I'd look over and realize Austin was drinking water. They were a good influence, and most of the guys respected them for it."

But Adam was human and would push his own self-imposed limits. On a Friday in late June, Adam and Kelley went out for a night of pizza and bowling with Christian, Paul, Austin, their wives—all of whom had been pregnant during the South American deployment—and children ranging in age from a few months to Nathan, the oldest at three. The Browns returned home to a neighborhood get-together that Kelley encouraged Adam to attend while she put the kids to bed.

After two hours Kelley glanced out the window and saw that the lights were off at the neighbor's house. Then she realized that their car was gone. She called Adam's cell phone throughout the night, but he wouldn't pick up, and by the next morning Kelley knew without a doubt what had happened. She was both crushed and furious.

According to the neighbor, Adam had left with another neighbor to have a beer at a bar, and Kelley surmised that one beer led to another and another. Somewhere in there, with his willpower weakened by the alcohol, Adam had searched out the drug or maybe somebody had offered it.

Either way, he'd done it.

Kelley asked Christian if he would go out and search for Adam, and together with Paul, the two SEALs spent all of Saturday driving around the worst neighborhoods of Norfolk and Portsmouth. "When we couldn't find him, I was devastated," says Christian. "Kelley was really troubled, and I felt like I was letting them both down. They were family."

"Thank you," Kelley told Christian that evening. "He'll be home tomorrow. This is the last time this is going to happen."

For Kelley it bordered on miraculous that Adam had lasted this long without a relapse, because "it was the devil to him. Toward the end of his dark time he'd come home and say, 'I can't believe I let him get me. He paints this pretty picture, but I *know* it's wrong and I don't want to lose y'all.'"

Kelley had spent that day and evening playing with the kids and praying, not overly concerned that something bad had happened to Adam. No doubt he was hiding somewhere, afraid to return home because he was ashamed and angry at himself for giving in to the voice he had overpowered for so long. She believed this was another test, another hurdle put before her, and while God had never told her to leave Adam before, this time she felt guided to do just that. "I wanted to shock him," she says.

Kelley filled Janice and Larry in on what was going on, receiving their full support to go forward with her plan. When Adam finally walked in the door Sunday morning, his head was hung low. Quietly, so Nathan, who was playing in the living room, could not hear, she said with all the venom she could muster, "How dare you. You have a family. How *dare* you!"

He shook his head and appeared "beat down and ashamed," says Kelley. He began to speak.

"No," she said. "I've heard it all before."

Studying his eyes, Kelley could tell that Adam was no longer under the influence of the drug, so she placed nine-month-old Savannah in his arms, picked up the suitcase she'd packed the night before, walked out the door, and drove away. While she completely trusted Adam with the children, it took all her willpower to leave her family and camp out for the next twenty-four hours in a room at the Navy Lodge at Little Creek. She read her Bible, watched television, and walked around the base for hours, listening to the ringing of her cell phone as its message box filled with Adam's apologies and promises.

In addition to apologizing to Kelley, Adam was apologizing to God for being weak. And he prayed that Kelley would give him one more chance. He was also handling all the things Kelley usually did for their children—mixing formula for Savannah, changing diapers, preparing meals, bathing them. At bedtime, Adam held Savannah and sang to Nathan the happy song that he and Kelley had been lulling him to sleep with for almost a year. But tonight, for Adam, it was just plain sad:

I love you, you love me,
We're a happy family...

Kelley returned home on Monday morning having not answered even one of Adam's calls. She wanted him to understand what it felt like to have a spouse, the parent of your children, disappear.

"Please forgive me," he said as she passed him by and went straight to Nathan and Savannah and hugged them. "I'm sorry."

"Get to work," Kelley replied. "We'll talk about a few things when you get home."

For the first time in his Navy career, Adam was late for his job that morning. In the afternoon, at Christian's request, he headed to a Village Inn restaurant.

Christian was already seated when Adam showed up, looking "like a beat dog—you know, when a dog knows they did something wrong, just guilty. I take this job seriously, and I knew he did too. But we all have weaknesses and that makes people real, and controlling those weaknesses makes people strong."

"I really messed up," Adam said.

"I know," said Christian, and then he let Adam have it. "I am beyond disappointed; I am pissed. There is no room for that in this job. No way. We train at high levels, shooting real bullets. There is no room for error. I mean, seriously? We are Navy SEALs! I have to be able to trust you, man. We're going to war soon. You have to be the guy that's got my back when we go in and we're on target."

"I know," said Adam. "You're right."

"And you're letting your family down," Christian went on. "Kelley is an angel putting up with this. What the hell! I have to be able to trust that you've got my back, and if you're thinking about doing something else, thinking about doing crack and not protecting me or anybody when we're doing our job... I need to know where your mind is when we go into a room and we need to shoot and make decisions."

"That's it. I swear I'm never going to do it again."

"All right then," said Christian. "I trust you. We're done here."

That evening Kelley informed Adam that there would be no more chances; the next time it happened, she and the kids would be gone for good. "It was tough talk," says Kelley. "He believed it, I said it so he'd believe it, but I can't honestly say I really would have left him if he did it again. We prayed that night, we read the Bible, the verses on strength, and I told him he was letting God down too."

———

A month and a half later, Team TWO was training in a MOUT (military operations on urban terrain) village on a base in Alabama. Defending the buildings within this setting were an opposing force of SEALs armed with M4 rifles and 9mm simulation rounds—actual bullets with liquid, paint-filled tips, advertised as nonlethal for training purposes. Often referred to as paintballs on steroids, they are painful and can penetrate the skin. Protective gear for the neck and eyes is mandatory.

Adam was moving up a stairway when he came under intense fire and was hit in the chest. He lifted his arms to signal that he was "dead" and began to walk down the steps to "reset" the assault by regrouping with his team to try again. At the instant he turned, a final round aimed at his head slipped past his wraparound sunglasses and hit him in the right eye. He trotted outside the building, where his team was waiting. "Man, I got dinged," he said to Austin, then pulled off his glasses. "How does it look?"

The outer corner of his right eye to the center was covered with blue paint. Near the tear duct, it was blood red.

"Can you see out of it?" asked Austin.

"Naw, everything's blurry," Adam replied calmly.

After being treated at a local hospital's emergency room, Adam called Kelley. "Baby, I've got a problem," he said. "I'm okay, but I got shot in the eye with a sim round. Just grazed it, but I'm coming home. It'll be late; I'll get a ride."

From the way Adam downplayed it, Kelley assumed that his injury was probably a black eye. But when he came home—the bandage off because of pain and his eye swollen to a squint—"my heart nearly fell out of my chest," she says, remembering the bloody tears that streamed down his cheek. "It was mangled, just trashed."

"Are you going to lose your eye?" she asked, hugging him tight.

"I don't think so," he said. "I'm scheduled for surgery in the morning."

———

At Portsmouth Naval Hospital, Adam and Kelley were told the bullet that had glanced off Adam's eyeball had all but destroyed his cornea, as well as damaged the lens, surrounding nerves, and muscles. Adam was now eligible for a medical discharge as a disabled veteran, at a level of disability that would pay a significant sum each month for the rest of his life. He refused to even consider the option. "One, I'm not disabled, and two, I'm not a veteran," he said. "I haven't even fought for my country yet." The doctors explained that he was still considered a veteran for having served in the military.

"That didn't count, as far as Adam was concerned," says Kelley. "End of discussion. There wasn't an ounce of quit in him. What we did do was move out of our house into a smaller apartment, to save a little more money in case this was a career-ending injury."

For the next few months, which Adam spent alternating between doctors' appointments and his ongoing training cycles, the ophthalmology staff fought to restore the sight in his injured dominant eye. He could see shadows and detect movement peripherally, but beyond that the eye was essentially blind. In addition, there was severe swelling of the eyeball, which the doctors had a difficult time getting under control.

"The pressure was painful," says Kelley, "but he wouldn't let on. I'd see him grimace when he didn't know I was looking." Furthermore, Adam had come to believe that what appeared to be a freak accident "was actually God tapping him on the shoulder, letting him know he wasn't happy that Adam had succumbed to that voice," says Kelley. "He was so depressed for a few weeks, and then he decided it was just another challenge, another lightning bolt God was throwing at him, to see if he'd get up or stay down."

The ongoing prescription was for steroid drops and an eye patch that

Brown family archives

For as long as Savannah could remember, Daddy wore an eye patch and gave her nose a pinch every chance he could sneak one in.

delighted three-year-old Nathan. "Arrrrgggh, matey," Adam would say, donning a pirate hat. He'd sword fight with his son and draw maps that would lead them to treasure he buried in the sand at a nearby playground. "If he had to be home recovering after a procedure," says Kelley, "he was going to play with the kids as much as he could."

Adam's task unit was scheduled to deploy to Iraq in April 2004. This gave him seven months to both heal his eye as much as possible and re-train himself to work around the injury. Even with limited vision he was able to excel in—and successfully complete—a highly competitive one-month Naval Special Warfare Assault Breacher Course. The "breacher" is the SEAL who gains access to a building or compound during a raid so the rest of the assault team can enter the target structure. He is the first to sneak up to an objective while the rest of the team holds security from a distance. As an explosives expert, the breacher can also safely implode whatever stands between the SEALs and the enemy: a door, a gate, or a wall.

In addition, Adam taught himself to shoot using his nondominant left eye. This didn't affect how he held a handgun, but aiming an M4 carbine required that he turn his head and lean out over the stock for accuracy.

Once the platoon workup was finished, Adam was cleared by Medical, having exhibited proficiency in SEAL tasks, but with the notation that he was doing so with limited vision in his dominant eye. He flew to Baghdad for a six-month deployment, and upon his arrival, Adam's superiors decided that his limited vision was a liability. They would not allow Adam to participate with his platoon in direct-action combat missions on the ground.

This had been a possibility, he knew, but he'd thought it was a slim one, especially considering his most recent evaluation, based significantly on the training he'd taken part in *after* his eye injury. In the evaluation the master chief had stated that Adam was his "FIRST CHOICE for the toughest jobs." He'd gone even further and recommended Adam for "NSW DEVGRU."

Instead, Adam was given a job working with intelligence as part of a reconnaissance-focused task unit. As a team player, he dealt positively with his disappointment. "He thought he'd work hard and prove himself and then persuade leadership to clear him for direct action," says one of his Team TWO teammates. "That was his plan."

For the first few weeks in Iraq, while Adam's teammates were conducting special reconnaissance, sniper missions, and raids—capturing or killing insurgents, clearing houses, and gathering intelligence—Adam tirelessly performed a myriad of support tasks while based in the northern city of Mosul. He constructed the C4 charges his team used for explosive entry; he took aerial photographs of target buildings and neighborhoods from airplanes and helicopters; he participated in the interrogation of captured insurgents; and most importantly, he pored over intelligence and played a lead role in planning missions.

Knowing how SEALs operate and with a keen sense for strategy, he "developed a systematic approach for intelligence and operations fusion," wrote his commanding officer in evaluating Adam's performance after the deployment. "His techniques were used to positively identify follow-on targets within 24–48 hours and facilitated an accelerated targeting cycle that resulted in the capture of 36 known anticoalition fighters in less than two months of combat operations."

"He was making huge contributions, doing really important work," says Austin. "They just would not let him do all of what we were doing because of his eye." Adam continued to feel sidelined and "it drove him crazy. He didn't realize he was probably working harder than anybody on the team."

Back in Hot Springs, Kelley had no idea what Adam or any of the SEALs were contributing to the war effort, and to preserve operational security, Adam couldn't tell her in his e-mails and phone calls. She could only trust in his training and pray for his—and the entire unit's—safe return. Janice and Larry liked to keep abreast of what was going on in the war by watching the daily news, but Kelley would often walk away from the television. Not only did it escalate her worry, it also infuriated her whenever the U.S. military was portrayed in a negative light. She was livid at the soldiers who had taken part in the Abu Ghraib prison scandal. "It reflected poorly on all the military," says Kelley. "It reflected poorly on my Adam."

It was so important to her that their children understand their father's efforts in the war that Kelley had given Adam a journal before he deployed and made him promise to write about his experiences. "When Nathan and Savannah are older," explains Kelley, "I want them to understand the war—not from the media or their school history books, but from the perspective of their daddy, who fought in it."

After only six weeks in Iraq, in spite of the limitations placed on him by his superiors, Adam had a firm grasp on how this war was being fought, especially how intelligence was gathered and "extracted" from prisoners. On May 10, the same day the *New Yorker* magazine reported "numerous instances of 'sadistic, blatant, and wanton criminal abuses'" in its cover story, "Torture at Abu Ghraib," Adam sat down on his bunk at the end of a fifteen-hour workday in Mosul. He picked up the stuffed toy duck Savannah had sent with him and wrote about how he could still smell his Little Baby on it; he pushed around the toy #24 race car from Nathan. Then he wrote them a letter:

Dear Nathan and Savannah,

Let it be known that if it weren't for you kids, I'd be sleeping right now, but I promised your mom I'd write in this journal for you. I want you to know, as you read opinions and history in school about 2004, that going to this war was right. No matter what you hear 20 years from now by elite media and historians, things get distorted.... Just like Vietnam, I fear OIF (Operation Iraqi Freedom) will be abused in the same way. Just as you hear more about American soldiers in Vietnam raping women and children and shooting unarmed men, today the media is focused about this detainee debacle for two weeks solid, in contrast to American Soldiers being dragged in the streets and dismembered, which was covered for less than 72 hours.

I am part of the Special Operations Forces elite. Our detention center is for the sole purpose of obtaining evidence as quickly as possible for rounding up more terrorists. We are harder than anyone at these detention centers and let me tell you, we treat these guys with the utmost professionalism. We do not hit them, we don't humiliate them or cause them any bodily harm for the purpose of entertainment. This is WAR and treated very seriously. People are being killed and it is our job to get information.

Honestly, it is the hardest thing I have ever done. I fight for people's freedoms, not to take [them] away. The humanity in me wants to warm them, tell them their family is okay, feed them, and even embrace them in a loving way. As a Christian, one assumes great compassion. Most, even in my stature, feel the same way. This is the American Soldier.

As for the punks that have humiliated our country and our sovereignty, I show them no pity and insist they are in the deepest minority of American professionals. What they did was not to gain intel, only to elevate their weak and pathetic lives to a status for some reason they have only dreamed of.

My hand hurts and I can only imagine what my sleepiness has caused me to write on this paper. You kids, Nathan and Savannah, y'all are so precious to me. I get chills thinking about watching you grow. You are both already so big. If your mom and I ever teach you anything, I pray it is at least to show all people courtesy and respect. The truly courageous and powerful never have to prove it. It is always shown in their actions.

I love you dearly,

Daddy

13

Something Important

LATE IN MAY 2004 ADAM WAS RECRUITED by the CIA—for a few hours, anyway—when a case officer learned he was good with electronics. A local resident's vehicle, to be used for drive-by reconnaissance missions in Mosul, needed to have installed a discreet surveillance system with its own power source. The system also had to be remotely activated. "I used parts from a bomb maker's house that we did a hit on earlier this week," Adam wrote in his journal. "He's giving back and doing his part to fight terrorism and doesn't even know it."

While lending a hand to the CIA, Adam met a seasoned DEVGRU operator named Dale who had worked with Chief Harley. They discussed Operation Red Dawn, which had led to the capture of Saddam Hussein on December 13, 2003, near Tikrit, as well as Osama bin Laden and how Dale hoped to be the guy who took bin Laden out when the time came. That was, to Dale, the ultimate mission, the "Big Mish."

The conversation segued to Adam's recommendation for Green Team, the seven-month proving ground/selection course for those seeking to move up to DEVGRU. "He was really humble about it," says Dale. "Adam was smart about how he got information. Some guys are annoying with their questions or come off as cocky, but Adam was so genuine, you wanted to give him all you could. And one question he asked me was why I chose to go to that next level.

"I explained it to Adam like this," he continues. "Guys will say they're going to get out and do something else, but honestly, the reason guys don't go, the *only* reason a SEAL from the regular teams won't go to Green Team, is because he's afraid of failing. Because if you fail out of Green Team, then you're automatically ranked in the SEAL teams as not good enough to be at DEVGRU—and, some of us might say, not good enough to be a SEAL. If you don't go, then you're never ranked. Oh, you can still think you're a hotshot at the regular team level, but that's only because you've never been tested at the next level.

"The big thing for a SEAL is how many platoons you've done. Like this guy did seven platoons; he's a badass. I told Adam, 'I don't care if you did a hundred platoons'—I'm kind of a snob that way, and a lot of guys are—'if you don't at least try for DEVGRU, then I really don't want to talk to you. Not to be a dick, but I'm just saying, why wouldn't you? Who they gonna call first when the Big Mish goes down?'"

After two months in northern Iraq, Adam's unit was assigned the mission of protecting top Iraqi government leaders, including the Iraqi president and prime minister. His platoon would relocate to Baghdad immediately.

As a member of the support team for Team TWO in Mosul, Adam had planned nearly a dozen successful direct-action raids and missions that resulted in the capture or killing of numerous insurgents. But not once had he been allowed to participate himself. Now he was informed that he also would not be allowed to take part in the security detail protecting the Iraqi leaders, and was given the option of going home.

"We all talked about it," says Austin. "He didn't want to leave us, but we agreed: go home, try to get your vision back with surgery, and gear up for the next deployment. He had to take a step back to take a step forward, and that wasn't easy for Adam, who was always in fifth gear. But he did it."

Kelley was still in Hot Springs with Nathan and Savannah the first week in June when Adam called her from Virginia Beach. "They benched me," he said, explaining how he'd been held back because of his eye. Then he told her he wanted to screen for Green Team, the selection course for DEVGRU.

According to documentation, fewer than 15 percent of more than two thousand SEALs on active duty at the time had successfully "screened" for the course—that is, been approved to participate in it. Those who actually pass are considered the top 1 percent of the SEAL community—the absolute best of the best. "He was fired up," says Kelley, "and I was thinking, *Wait a minute, you just told me in that last sentence that you got benched.*"

"Baby," she interjected, "you have only one good eye, and the doctor says that's probably not going to change."

"That's why I want to screen for Green Team," Adam said. "If I don't pass the screening, then I'll know. Then we'll have to think about what's next. If I'm not going to get to do my job, I don't want to be strung along."

While Adam had accepted that the bad choices he'd made—quitting football in college, the drugs, the crimes—had led him to where he was now, he still regretted them. That regret strengthened his resolve this time to push through until he could push no further.

"Itty Bitty, remember when you prayed about us back when I seemed hopeless, and God never once told you to leave? Well, I've been praying too, and all I'm getting, all I'm feeling in my heart, is that I'm not done. I've still got a lot of fight in me. I want to do something *I* can be proud of. I want to do something that's going to make a difference, and I have *not* had the chance to do it yet."

"All right then," Kelley said. "Let's keep praying about it. If you get in, it's God. If not, we'll figure it out."

With Adam back in the United States, Kelley wanted to return to Virginia Beach as soon as possible, but it was summer and rentals were hard to come by—at least in their price range. Even with a recent promotion to the E6 pay grade, Adam's net income as a SEAL (including some extra cash he made cutting down trees in residential neighborhoods) was about three thousand dollars a month. Still, with two kids, three maxed-out credit cards, a car payment, and life and auto insurance, they had managed to save twenty-five hundred dollars for a down payment on a house of their own.

After a couple of weeks in Virginia Beach, during which Adam stayed in the bachelor barracks for free, Kelley said to him, "I'll do anything to be there with you. We'll camp if we have to until we can find a place."

That's exactly what they ended up doing: buying the cheapest tent and air mattresses on the shelf at Wal-Mart and camping in the midsummer heat as a family at the Little Creek base campground.

"It was insane," says Kelley. "I do not know what I was thinking. We were slipping and sliding in our own sweat, the sheets were soaking wet, and that was at night, when it was only in the nineties, with 90 percent humidity. During the day it topped a hundred. Both of the kids had heat rash, and little Savannah was getting potty trained, so you can imagine changing diapers with a flashlight in what felt like a steam bath inside that tent."

When Adam went to work each morning, Kelley piled the kids in the car and drove, blasting the AC and searching for a place to live as well as spending hours in stores, malls, the library, anywhere there was air conditioning. They were all trying to sleep one night when Nathan spoke up. "Daddy," he said, "are we in hell? 'Cause I think hell's hot like this."

"I was at my rope's end by the end of our first week of camping," says Kelley. "Then one of the guys on Team TWO who was about to deploy offered to let us stay in his condo, his *air-conditioned* condo, and we jumped on it."

They moved into the SEAL's place the following day, and it was "truly a bachelor pad," says Kelley. "Nathan went exploring and showed me a poster on the wall and asked, 'Mommy, why are those two girls naked and hugging?' And I told him, 'Well, they must be sisters and they love each other. They're cuddling.'"

She sat him down in the living room, then walked through the condo removing X-rated posters and magazines and toning it down to a family-friendly G. Then she tackled the bathroom, which she suspected had not been cleaned that century. "Don't get me wrong," notes Kelley. "I was so grateful to be staying there; it just shows how the SEALs take care of each other. But for that bathroom I wore gloves—there were things growing in there science couldn't identify. I needed a chisel for the bathtub."

Two weeks later the Browns were able to rent a little house, complete with picket fence, in the Virginia Beach suburbs, and Adam began the screening process for Green Team, along with Austin and Christian. On the questionnaire Adam stated his reasons for entering BUD/S and the SEAL community: "To serve this country in the highest possible manner. To do things that others cannot." To the question "Do you have any past or present injuries or physical condition which detracts from your physical capabilities?" he answered, "I was shot in the eye with a sim round. Temporary. I expect a full recovery."

This was followed by an oral board review and written and oral psychological testing, a phase that approximately half the applicants fail.

Adam, Austin, and Christian passed, with Austin and Christian placed on the roster for the next Green Team selection course, scheduled to begin in mid-2005. On his doctor's advice, Adam chose to postpone Green Team for another year: once he was screened, his slot was reserved for a future class of his choosing.

In the entire history of Naval Special Warfare Development Group, nobody had ever attempted, much less passed, the stringent Green Team qualifications with good vision in only one eye—especially Close Quarters Battle (CQB), where peripheral vision and split-second reaction times are critical. The deferral meant further experience as a SEAL, another platoon, another deployment, and more time for Adam to either regain his sight fully or adapt to living and working with near blindness in his right eye. In the interim he planned at least one more surgery to improve his vision.

The surgery was not a success. "In fact," says Kelley, "the eye seemed to get worse."

What movement Adam could make out with his right eye became even blurrier. Kelley tested him by waving her hand around. "He'd say, 'I can see what you're doing there,'" explains Kelley, "but he couldn't see how many fingers I would hold up or anything like that. He caught flashes of light and movement, but that was about it. He couldn't read a stop sign out of that eye if he was three feet away."

Realizing that his vision was not going to improve, Adam decided the best training for the DEVGRU selection process would be qualifying for and attending the Naval Special Warfare Sniper School, arguably the most difficult advanced combat course in the Navy—outside of Green Team. "By far the hardest school I ever went through," says Christian. "I was more relieved to finish that than BUD/S. Tons of pressure every day, and I had *both* of my eyes to rely on."

Adam had attempted Sniper School once before, in 2002 when both eyes were functioning, but had failed the attritional "stalking" portion of the course (as did nearly half his class), which drove him even harder to complete the three-month course now. To do that he needed to master stealth, patience, and camouflage. He had to judge distances with absolute accuracy, anticipate the wind's effect on a bullet's trajectory, and learn a new language universal to Navy snipers. "But really," says Christian, "the root of the course is teaching us to be silent hunters who can stalk our prey.

"Imagine a field full of sniper students," he continues, "who have been given four hours to move over a thousand yards, set up a 'hide site' within a hundred fifty to two hundred fifty meters of the target without being detected—and there's at least five guys with spotting scopes sitting on a truck trying to bust you. All they have to do is see you, identify you in the landscape. They did not cut us any breaks at all; it was a huge deal to be an NSW sniper, and they weren't gonna hand it out to just anybody."

Between January and April 2005, Adam not only completed the three segments of the course—Photo Image Capture, Scout, and Sniper— he also excelled in them. It was a punishing pace: thirteen- to fifteen-hour days six days a week, divided between Little Creek, Virginia, and Camp Atterbury, Indiana. Students endured daily physical training and weekly Monster Mash workouts that rivaled professional triathlons. They had to master one-thousand-meter stalks with a two-hour time limit; photographing or "killing" moving, stationary, and pop-up targets ranging from one hundred to twelve hundred yards out; and building ghillie suits that matched the environment. Since snipers work in teams of two, students must learn both shooter and spotter skills and know their weapons inside and out.

"You learn how to be invisible with your partner in any terrain," says Brad Westin, a fellow SEAL who became friends with Adam during the course. "And then you must either take a clear photograph or put a bullet through the head of a target."

The final exam is built into a brutal "ruck march," where each student, shouldering a weapon plus a sixty-pound rucksack, is tested at intervals along a fourteen-mile course through urban areas, mountainous terrain, and seemingly flat-as-a-pancake fields on which he must find minuscule rises to hide behind. All the skills learned during the previous months, including steady, accurate shots, must be performed while students are exhausted.

To master this demanding curriculum, Adam completely changed his shooting stance, learning to shoot left-handed so as to best accommodate his nondominant eye. He passed Sniper School on April 8, a feat that Brad, a lifelong hunter, considers "next to godly."

"There was Someone out there," says Brad, "who was just like, 'Adam, you will make it,' and Adam was like, 'Okay, got it.' I can't explain it any other way. To lose vision in your good eye within a year prior to that class and say 'Screw it, I'm going to Sniper School—oh, and by the way, I'll do it all left-handed,' that's hard-core. I don't think it's ever been done in the history of sniper schools in the world."

Graduating from Sniper School was a huge confidence boost for Adam, and with Nathan starting kindergarten in the fall, he and Kelley decided to invest their small savings in a first home. Navy financing helped keep the mortgage about par with their current rent payment, and in April they purchased a three-bedroom house in the Virginia Beach suburbs.

As Adam dived into the workup for his next deployment with Team TWO, Christian and Austin sweated out the Green Team selection process. One weekend in early June, the three SEALs and their families

Brown family archives

Shawn and Larry with Adam just before Sniper School graduation.

went swimming at Becky and Christian's condo. Staying cool by wading around the shallow end of the pool, Christian and Austin swapped stories about some of the mind-boggling scenarios they'd faced in the three months they'd been powering through the course. When they moved inside, Kelley noticed that Adam was subdued. "This is so hard for Adam," she quietly told Christian. "He just wants to be there with you guys so bad."

Christian and Austin dropped the subject, but it became the elephant in the room. Finally, Christian threw his arm around Adam and said, "You will crush it next year, buddy."

At the end of the month, Adam was in the Team TWO building when he heard the terrible news: nineteen Americans—eleven SEALs and eight pilots and crewmen from the 160th Special Operations Aviation

Regiment—had been killed in Afghanistan. Eight of the SEALs, from Team TEN, had been based at Little Creek.

The Team TEN SEALs had been sent out on June 28 as part of a Quick Reaction Force to aid a four-man SEAL reconnaissance team that was outnumbered, out-positioned, and pinned down by anticoalition insurgents in a fierce firefight in the mountainous Kunar Province. An enemy rocket-propelled grenade had struck their helicopter, and the resulting explosion and impact killed everyone on board.

At Little Creek ten days later, Adam stood at attention during a memorial service for the fallen SEALs; it had been the worst single-day loss of life in the history of Naval Special Warfare.

Captain Pete Van Hooser, who had pinned Adam with his Trident and was now the commander of Naval Special Warfare Group TWO, nodded toward Adam and the other uniformed SEALs in the crowd, but his focus in his moving remarks was on the photos of those who had given their lives, as well as on their family members—in particular, the wives and children of the fallen.

"I am always humbled in the presence of warriors," Van Hooser said to the hushed crowd of thousands. "We have been in sustained combat for over three years—things have changed.

"I find myself speaking in public a lot more than I would like, but I always start by thanking four groups of people. The first are our warriors who have fallen; the second, those who have guaranteed that those who have fallen will not be left behind. Some with their bravery, others with their lives. I thank those who have selflessly pulled themselves off the line to train the next warriors to go forward—so that they may surpass the prowess of those currently engaged. And I am thankful for the families that nurture such men."

"Take care of Sissy and Mommy," Adam said to Nathan on October 5, giving a discreet wink to Kelley. "You're the man of the house while I'm away."

"I will, Daddy," said the five-year-old. "Don't you worry."

Kelley put her hand on her heart, watching as Adam picked up three-year-old Savannah and hugged her tightly. It was both sweet and terrifying to think of the burden her little boy had taken on so bravely and naively. For this deployment, Adam's third and his second to a combat zone, he had been cleared for direct action, having proven that his virtually blind eye was not a liability.

"Six months," Adam told Kelley when they finally hugged.

"Christmas will be the hardest," she replied, feeling a lump in her throat.

She and Michelle had talked about and prayed for the widows of the men killed in June, and though she didn't know any of them personally, the SEAL community was an extended family, so she felt a bond with and a deep sadness for the families. Beyond the sadness, they also represented her greatest fear.

Kelley swallowed the lump and slammed the door shut on her emotions. She'd vowed to be strong for Nathan and Savannah, who had grown accustomed to Adam's trips. That was all this was to the children—a longer one than usual, but still just a trip.

Adam knew exactly what Kelley was feeling. "Don't worry about me," he said. "You've got the toughest job. Mine's easy."

A kiss and he was off.

The minute the family returned home from saying good-bye to Daddy, Nathan went upstairs to his bathroom and moved his toothbrush into his parents' master bathroom.

"Mommy," he said, "y'all let me know if you need me to do anything."

Then he went about his business, which at the moment was building Legos.

The following morning Kelley opened the sugar bowl to make sweet tea and found a little scrap of paper within. It read,

> You are so special.
> Love, Adam

Every day she'd find another note. In the cookie jar: *I miss you today. Love, Adam.* In a dresser drawer: *I wish for a kiss. Love, Adam.* Inside the egg carton: *Give yourself a hug & pretend it's me. Love, Adam.*

Cherishing each discovery, Kelley refrained from searching for all the notes at once. She kept them in her wallet and reread them whenever she needed a lift—and by the end of Adam's first month of deployment, the once crisp papers were like those in their family Bible, worn and soft. They sustained her.

At the memorial service for the fallen SEALs, Captain Van Hooser had defined what coalition forces were up against in the landlocked country where Adam was deployed:

> The enemy we face in Afghanistan is as hard and tough as the
> land they inhabit. They come from a long line of warriors who
> have prevailed in the face of many armies for centuries. It is their
> intimate knowledge of every inch of the most rugged terrain on
> earth that is matched against our skill, cunning, and technology.
> They are worthy adversaries and our intelligence confirms that
> they fear and respect us. They have learned to carefully choose
> their fights because SEALs will answer the bell every time.

Indeed, Adam respected the land he surveyed from Bagram Airfield, where he and his task unit were initially based. As a SEAL, he knew to "never underestimate the enemy" but he also "rejoiced," according to his journal, when he saw children playing in a field with a soccer ball as he patrolled in and around the ancient city of Bagram.

Adam continued the journal entry to his children:

From everything I've read, seeing these kids, including girls, playing, tells me we are doing right here. I have not gotten a single sour face from any of the locals, and I don't see fear in their eyes. I'm sure I will learn more over time. They are poor; y'all cannot believe what little they have, Nathan and Savannah, but we have restored their dignity, and their lives…the Taliban had taken that away. (Read Marri's letter in book *Sewing Circles of Herat*.) Kids, I am proud to be here doing what we are doing.

During his personal quest to learn about Afghanistan, Adam had read a book titled *The Sewing Circles of Herat: A Personal Voyage Through Afghanistan* by Christina Lamb. The letter he referred to was sent to Lamb by a secretly educated young Afghan woman named Marri.

Dear Christina,
    …I hope this will help you outside understand the feelings of an educated Afghan female who must now live under a burqa.…

For two pages the letter described Marri's background and various anecdotes of life before and after the Taliban, ending with,

Life here is very miserable. We have no rights at all and we have asked many times other countries of the world for help but they have been silent. Now we heard about this attack on the towers in America with many people dead and my father says the Americans will come and remove the Taliban but we do not dare hope.…

I do not know what you want me to write to you. If I start writing I will fill all the paper and my eyes will fill with tears because in these seven years of Taliban no one has asked us to write about our lives. In my mind I make a picture of you and your family. I wonder if you drive a car, if you go out with friends to the cinema and restaurants and dance at parties. Do you play loud music and swim in lakes? One day I would like to see and I would also like to show you a beautiful place in my country with mountains and streams but not now while we must be hidden. Maybe our worlds will always be too far apart.

Marri

For the first few weeks in-country, Adam and his task unit flew from Bagram to outlying villages. Their living quarters were eight-foot-by-eight-foot plywood rooms with a blanket for a door, a bunk, and some shelves in a building built by Army engineers when the Taliban had surrendered four years before. Adam's missions were with a team of doctors who provided care to the locals, and in many cases their animals, while the SEALs provided security.

After a month of supporting this MEDCAP/VETCAP (Medical Civic Action Program / Veterinarian Civic Action Program) mission, winning the hearts and minds of the indigenous population, the task unit was ordered to relocate. Adam was preparing his gear for the move when his buddy, FBI agent Billy White, who had been accompanying the SEALs on the mission, stopped by his room, the walls of which were covered in graffiti from its many different residents. One message was, "Life is not a journey to the grave with the intention of arriving safely in a pretty and preserved body, but rather to skid in broadside, thoroughly used up, totally worn out, and loudly proclaiming, 'Wow...what a ride.'"

Billy liked it so much he jotted it down in his journal. Then he noticed Adam's Bible, the cover bent, pages marked, and it sparked a conversation about their shared Christian faith—and how they both believed God had led them to fight in this war.

"Neither of us had seen actual combat at that point," says Billy, "and we talked of being warriors and Christians, and mentally dealing with killing. Specifically, we talked about how the Bible says thou shalt not murder; it does not say thou shalt not kill. There is a time to kill, to protect your home, your family, your freedom. And when I said that to Adam he replied, 'Amen, brother.'"

The following morning Adam and Billy were in a vehicle heading south from Bagram, part of the relocation convoy of five Humvees. They rounded a corner and saw an International Security Assistance Force (ISAF) convoy coming from the opposite direction, barreling down the middle of the narrow two-lane blacktop at sixty to seventy miles an hour, roughly the same speed as Adam's convoy. The lead vehicles in both convoys edged over into their own lanes, but in doing so dropped their outer tires into the powdery dirt, instantly creating a large dust cloud.

Adam was riding in the front passenger seat of the second Humvee, his right hand holding on to the upper frame of the open window, when the wall of dust appeared. Their driver barely had time to tap the vehicle's brakes before it was swallowed by the blinding cloud, and an instant later the left front bumper impacted with the second vehicle in the ISAF convoy, causing a glancing head-on collision. Adam's Humvee flipped three times while cartwheeling down the blacktop.

The dust cleared and Dave Cain—a SEAL in the undamaged lead

Compliments of Billy White

Adam was seated in the front right seat of this Humvee when it was involved in an accident on the road to Kandahar.

vehicle—saw Adam leaning into the backseat of the smashed Humvee, administering aid to somebody who was "howling like a dog that got run over by a car," says Dave.

Billy was pinned between the caved-in roof, a piece of which had speared through his left quadriceps muscle, and the seat and floorboard. His lower left leg was crushed, and a bone protruded through his calf muscle from a compound fracture. The left side of Billy's head and his ear were torn open, his left wrist was disfigured and broken, and his M4 carbine, which he'd been holding muzzle up between his legs, had been driven through his left armpit into his back so that it could be seen bulging against the skin there. These were only the visible injuries.

"Adam was applying pressure, trying to stop the bleeding on Billy's leg," says Dave. "Billy was screaming. Another guy had gotten thrown out and was in shock, sort of stumbling around. The guy next to Billy thought his back was broken but was still trying to help Adam with Billy. Then a corpsman from the rear of our convoy ran up and Adam yelled at him, 'Give Billy his morphine! Give him his morphine!'"

As Adam helped extract Billy and the other injured men from the mangled vehicle, Dave noticed Adam's right hand: its fingers were dangling by skin and tendons, every digit but the thumb severed. When the Humvee began to flip, the hand that had been gripping the window frame was crushed between it and the road.

"Adam, your hand is messed up," Dave said.

"Yeah, yeah," said Adam. "I'm all right. Focus on these guys."

A corpsman overheard. "Hey, I need to take a look," he told Adam. After examining the injury, the corpsman carefully laid Adam's fingers back into place and bandaged his hand.

Local men, women, and children had begun to gather, watching the scene. A stopped convoy dealing with a medical trauma was a target of opportunity, and the enemy could easily be hidden within the crowd.

"Let's keep these people back!" yelled Adam, standing up and grabbing his M4 with his uninjured hand. Says Dave, "He balanced the stock on the forearm above his bandages and started holding security. I told him, 'Adam! Sit down, man. We got it. Relax.' But Adam shook his head and kept pushing people away from the wreckage.

"When the helicopter landed, there was Adam, still holding security for his own medevac, refusing to get loaded until all the others were tended to and on board. Only then did he lower his weapon and join them."

14

Green Team

KELLEY WAS DRIVING NORTH, APPROACHING the Hampton Roads Bridge-Tunnel, when her cell phone rang. From the forlorn tone of Adam's voice, she knew instantly something was wrong.

"I'm coming home, baby," he said.

"Oh, Adam. What happened? Are you okay? Talk fast, I'm coming up on the tunnel."

"Well," he said, "I got in an accident."

Unable to pull over, Kelley entered the tunnel and lost the call. Once she was on the other side, Adam called back and filled her in—somewhat. "He was so casual about these horrible injuries," Kelley says. "He was in the hospital and was like, 'I hurt my hand pretty bad, my fingers got cut off, but I got 'em sewn back on.' He was most worried about his friend who was in surgery and in critical condition, lucky to be alive."

Adam asked her to call his parents. "And Itty Bitty," he said, "have everybody we know pray for a guy named Billy White."

Initial surgeries for both Adam and Billy were performed the day of the accident in the Heathe N. Craig Joint Theater Hospital at Bagram Airfield. The following morning they flew together to Landstuhl Regional

Medical Center in Germany, where Billy was operated on more extensively. Adam remained with Billy so he could accompany him home three days later. When they returned to the States, Billy went to Walter Reed Army Medical Center in Washington DC, and Adam was driven home for reconstructive hand surgery at Portsmouth Naval Hospital in Virginia Beach.

"It wasn't until he got home that night," says Kelley, "that I saw his fingers hadn't just been cut off; they'd been *crushed* off between the Humvee and the road. It looked so painful."

The next day Adam checked in at the hospital and insisted on a local anesthetic so he could watch the procedure. "He chatted with the surgeons with his hand laid open on the table," says Kelley. "He watched them work on his nerves, muscles, tendons. Every cut, stitch, screw, and pin, he saw it all."

Janice and Larry had monitored Adam's situation from Hot Springs since the accident. "Kelley always kept us informed," says Larry, who would then pass the information on to Shawn and Manda. "We'd known he was going to Green Team after this deployment. And with his eye, he'd already dealt with so much. I was scared to ask what this injury meant; we just prayed. God knew Adam real well by then. I turned to Romans 8:28: 'And we know that all things work together for good to those who love God, to those who are the called according to His purpose.' That became a theme when Adam got hurt. I'd ask 'Why?' and that was my answer."

Over the next four weeks Kelley cleaned and debrided Adam's hand. Twice a day she would unwrap the ointment-saturated surgical gauze from around each finger, pulling away the dead flesh. "There was pus and blood and goo," she says. "I was lightheaded the first few times, but I got

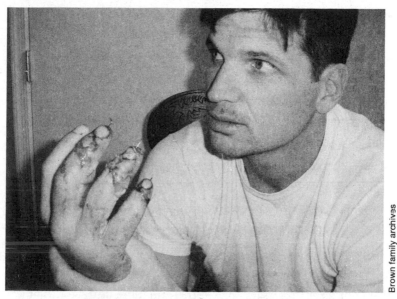

Adam's hand looking remarkably good with his fingers reattached.

used to it. His index finger had an exposed nerve, and we'd save that one for last because when I unwrapped and rewrapped it, it shot a jolt, like an electrical shock, through him that nearly knocked him down."

The pins and screws were surgically removed the second week in December. Green Team was scheduled to begin in June 2006—less than six months away—and "Adam's biggest concern wasn't if he'd ever be able to use his hand for *normal* things, like holding a fork or writing with a pencil," says Kelley. "He was thinking pull-ups." Would he be able to hold on to the bar and do fifteen, the minimum requirement? Would he be able to draw his pistol, pull with his trigger finger, assemble his weapons? "He went down the list, everything he knew he'd have to do to qualify and what he'd have to work on. Because now both his dominant eye *and* his dominant hand were a mess."

While Adam's grip gained strength in rehabilitation, his overall dexterity and fine motor skills weren't the same. A month after the surgery, he began to retrain himself to shoot—both pistol and carbine—with his left hand. This was far more difficult than what he'd done in Sniper School, where single shots were patiently set up, the rifle steadied, if not by its own tripod, then atop a tree stump, log, or whatever was available. And even though he had used both his nondominant eye and his left hand, pulling the trigger as a sniper was a slow, deliberate move, unlike what he would need to do when faced with split-second decisions in the realistic combat testing of Green Team.

Adam's biggest concern was the Close Quarters Battle (CQB) portion of the course, in which he would have to clear rooms, search houses, react to bad guys: tough shooting exercises that require both lightning-fast reactions and pinpoint accuracy. "This doesn't even compare to what Adam was up against," says one Green Team cadre instructor, "but let's say you're right-handed and somebody tells you to start writing left-handed. You have to retrain yourself to write fast, you can't drop below the line with your letters, the letters have to be perfect, and you've got to know and write down the answers to do-or-die questions almost simultaneously. And do all this with bad guys shooting at you. Adam had to re-wire his brain to react 'left' when his whole life he'd reacted 'right,' in a course where half of the very best guys who have two good eyes and two good hands still fail."

By January Adam was drawing his pistol and making consistently accurate shots. "Almost like he had been ambidextrous and didn't know it," says Jack Elliot, an armorer who helped maintain weapons for the SEALs. "We teach our guys to shoot with their off hand in case their good one is injured in battle, so I've seen a lot of guys try and shoot nondominant hand. Adam was smooth. I'd joke with him: 'C'mon, come clean, you're a Jedi, right?' And he'd say, 'Naw, I just pray a lot.'"

With only a couple of weeks of shooting left-handed under his belt and his fingers barely healed, Adam volunteered for what was presented as "an extremely challenging counternarcotics mission" in South America. As the leading petty officer, he headed a twelve-man SEAL unit tasked with creating a premier maritime fighting force from the ranks of Colombia's marines.

When he arrived in Colombia and met the forty marines who had been chosen for training in a variety of ocean-borne tactics and procedures, Adam found one overwhelming problem: only about ten knew how to swim. So, for the first three weeks of the tight two-month schedule, some of the most elite warriors in the world got into a murky swimming pool and, according to one of the SEALs present, coaxed the anxious Colombian marines into the water. Once they mastered dog-paddling, they eventually achieved success at what another SEAL had first considered a "hopeless task." Adam's evaluation read,

> Selected to head a highly successful Counter Narcotics Training mission in Colombia. Created and implemented an aggressive training schedule in which 40 Marines and twenty Colombian helicopter pilots were trained in high-risk helicopter boat and fast-rope insertion methods. He successfully conducted the first ever helicopter "K-duck" boat insertions in Colombian special forces history.

Back home in April, Adam was awarded a gold star, representing his fourth Navy and Marine Corps Achievement Medal for his accomplishments in Colombia. The following month, as he prepared for his transfer to Green Team, the SEALs from Team TWO presented him with a wooden paddle that had a brass plaque on the blade engraved with "The Ballad of Adam Brown."

SEAL Team FOUR was where you made your debut,
Stabbing your face on a dive would be nothing new.
At Stennis you proved insects were a menace,
First bees and then ants breached your defenses.

Arkansas's finest, PTs never wearied,
But who would believe your crazy bubble theory?
Stanardsville taught you Escape and Evasion,
Save your burning gloves, it was a vacation.

A Sim fight in Alabama proved you had no fear,
But a stray round caused more than a tear.
It kept you from combat, this cruel fate,
But showed your true character, your lack of hate.

Afghanistan should have been your time to shine,
I think God was saving you from a land mine.
He took a few fingers, but then gave them back,
You shrugged it off, it didn't mean jack.

So it's off to Green Team, a fate long deserved,
A place at the table for you is reserved.
Any SEAL will agree when they get in the mix,
All would be honored to have you watching their six.

Fair Winds and Following Seas
From the Warriors of SEAL Team TWO.

Two weeks before his move to Green Team, Adam was clearing out
his locker at Team TWO when his chief stopped by to deliver the bad

news: Adam had been medically disqualified from the course. "His file was reviewed," says another instructor. "And even though he'd been cleared and was on the roster, somebody went back in and reconsidered, figured there is no way he will pass without perfect vision, and because it's a dangerous course—lots of live ammunition, explosives—they did not want that liability."

Adam got in his car and drove home. "He was furious and in disbelief," says Kelley. "Adam was a man of his word, and he couldn't stand that they were going back and forth. He knew he could do the job and was determined to make it happen."

They explored every angle to appeal the decision, and they prayed. "He said he would leave the Navy and return to school if that was his path," Kelley says. "He said he would even shoulder the humility of not succeeding at DEVGRU, but still be the best SEAL he could be. He'd go to bed disappointed, but he'd wake up fired up, saying, 'I'm not done.'"

After a week of hitting brick walls with every appeal, Adam seemed out of options. Then one day, as he drove to work on the base at Little Creek, he noticed the familiar gait of a runner on a trail next to the road. Pulling alongside Captain Van Hooser, his former commander, Adam called out through the window, "Good morning, sir! Can I interrupt your run for a minute?"

Despite having commanded thousands of SEALs over the years, Van Hooser knew exactly who Adam was. He remembered the blade incident, and how Adam had not interrupted the training dive in spite of his wound. He was impressed by the way Adam had described being shot in the eye as merely a "ding" and was aware that he had passed Sniper School—just missing being the honor graduate—while shooting left-handed with his nondominant eye.

Adam gave Van Hooser a rundown of his current predicament and said, "Sir, my injuries are no big deal. I can do this. Let me try to qualify, that's all I'm asking. If there is anything you can do to go to bat for me, I won't let you down. I just need the chance."

Van Hooser, a by-the-book Navy man, normally did not interfere with the service's qualification systems. "That was my protocol," he says. But like every other SEAL, he'd learned the rules so he would understand if there was ever a time to bend or break them.

"Let me think about it," he said to Adam. He didn't need to think long. That same afternoon he contacted the command at DEVGRU; a few days after that he called Adam into his office. "They're asking around," Van Hooser told him. "It's under review."

Dozens of SEALs who had trained or served with Adam, from BUD/S onward, received a phone call over the next two weeks as Adam's enlisted record and reputation were scrutinized. The response of one SEAL summarized the overwhelming sentiment: "It doesn't matter if he's missing an eye or has an injured hand. This is Adam Brown you're talking about. Bring him on. Give him a chance."

Days before the Green Team selection process was scheduled to start, Adam was summoned to a meeting with the commanding officer of the training cadre. "You're going to be under a microscope," he said. "No special considerations; you are up against the same qualifications as everybody else. In fact you're probably going to be watched more closely than anybody else. But if you pass Green Team, there will never be another question about your eye or your hand. Never."

Brad Westin, Adam's buddy from Sniper School, along with a few dozen other SEALs from both East Coast and West Coast teams, were sweating— and not just from the humidity. It was the first day of Green Team, and they had gathered at a classified Eastern Seaboard train-ing compound where Brad was amazed to find Adam among those assembled. Because of Adam's eye and severed fingers, "I figured his career as a SEAL was finished," Brad says.

"Adam! Are you in? Really?" he asked.

"I'm in," said Adam. "They told me I get to stay in the Navy if I can make it through Green Team."

Brad slapped him on the back, as did Dave Cain, who had been with Adam in Afghanistan. Only half of the class, which represented the hand-picked best of the best—determined, motivated, and very qualified— would remain by the course's end. And every one of the SEALs had a massive advantage over Adam.

They began the course with a PT test that 99 percent of the world's population would likely fail. First stop: a minimum of fifteen dead-hang pull-ups with no time limit. A candidate must come to a complete hang, elbows straight, before executing the next pull-up, in which the chin must come up and over the top of the bar. Adam completed twenty-two.

Then, with only a few minutes' break, push-ups: all the way down to touch a SEAL's fist under the chest and all the way up to arms straight, with a three-minute time limit for a minimum of eighty push-ups. Adam did one hundred twenty.

Followed immediately by sit-ups: with a partner holding down feet, three minutes to do a minimum of ninety. Adam made it through one hundred thirty.

Another short break, then three miles of blacktop running in 22:30 or less while wearing cammie pants and running shoes. Adam's time was 18:24.

One last short break before the bay swim: an 880-meter (just over a half mile) sidestroke in no more than thirteen minutes. Adam finished in 11:22.

Adam's scores were average to above average among the students, all of whom passed.

After that, the real fun began—six months of rigorous training that would take them to specialized schools and facilities across the United States. There they would either exhibit perfection in or fail out of courses in combat pistol and rifle marksmanship, close quarters battle, military free-fall parachute operations, land warfare, urban warfare, desert warfare, maritime Visit, Board, Search, and Seizure (VBSS) tactics, tactical ground mobility operations, protective security detail training, and various other, classified, classes.

"The whole point of Green Team is to create as much stress and pressure on the student as possible and see if they can deal with it," says an instructor who worked with Adam. "We don't build them up; we break them down." When something doesn't go as planned or expected, "the guys who still perform the task with no mistakes are the guys we're looking for." Says a senior instructor, "You either perform under pressure or you fail, and we are not in the business of failing."

Although the specific qualifications and training tactics of the CQB phase—the crux of Green Team for most SEALs—are classified, "to give you an idea of what Adam had to master, consider where we start them off," says another instructor. "CQB begins with two-man teams doing one-room pistol clearance. They're taught to enter the room exactly as we say, clear their lanes as we've instructed, and if there's a target they engage it or they handle it if it's a noncombatant. In addition to that they can only be within two feet of where we tell them to be inside the room.

"In other words, if we tell them to be X number of feet down their lane, if they're under or over that prescribed distance, they underpenetrated or overpenetrated. And that's important because there are overlapping fields of fire and over-sweeps and all kinds of crazy patterns, sort of like football plays, that we have in a playbook that will essentially teach you to storm into any structure and kill bad guys with guns. If you 'kill' a hostage or a civilian, that's a strike against you, can be grounds for failure."

"What we're grading on," says a different instructor, "is the ability to do what we tell you to do exactly how we tell you to do it. The pressure is piled on—we've got a bunch of cadres hovering over you like vultures while you're doing it, plus you're being filmed. There's one or two guys looking to see if you went down the wall far enough, there's a guy looking at your finger—when it's on the trigger, when it's off—a guy's watching your fields of fire, someone else is watching your eyes, or in Adam's case, eye, assuring that the scenario is being processed, another guy's got a stopwatch, and you've got seconds, split seconds, to engage the right targets. You have friendly personnel mixed in with hostiles, and you have people yelling at you. You have to process it all, under that pressure, and be successful."

Most master the one-room scenario, but then the trainees progress to clearing multiple rooms, or they switch to a rifle, or they begin a raid with a rifle but a situation requires them to draw their pistol. The layout gets harder and harder, with more complicated rooms and multiple levels, and "that's when guys start to fall apart," continues the instructor. "And it only gets harder from there, with more variables added into the equation: complicated entry points, more good guys, more bad guys. The point is you cannot tough it out, you can't grunt through like BUD/S. These are SEALs. We already know they're tough; now we are finding out who's exceptional. We're only interested in the very best."

Says a SEAL from Adam's class, "They put it to you, physically and mentally, but mostly it's mental. The days start at 0'dark thirty with PT, but they aren't trying to torture you, and you aren't deprived of sleep like Hell Week. Some SEALs think BUD/S is fun, but even those guys think Green Team sucks." If a SEAL makes a mistake in the "kill house," the training facility for CQB, for example, a punishment might be extra PT, such as climbing ladders with heavy gear or the tire pull: a tractor tire hooked up to a rope and dragged through a series of wind sprints.

That's where Adam ended up, sent by the cadre to the tire pull after he'd swung around in a room and bashed the side of his head into a pole. "Hit your blind spot, huh?" one of his buddies asked, to which Adam replied, "No, man. Don't tell anybody, but that was the side with my good eye."

According to an instructor, the Green Team selection process is very specific. "Everything is on paper, and you either accomplish what is needed to qualify or you don't. We were skeptical about Adam because you have to use your peripheral vision a lot; you have to clear corners, be aware of movement to alert you to threats." This meant that while most SEALs glanced left and right, Adam had to swing his entire head around, which ate up fractions of seconds. "We're working against an enemy's reaction time and making sure our guys are faster," says the instructor, "so it was amazing—we were all blown away—because he was shooting off-hand with pistol and rifle *and* making accurate shots."

Trainees are allowed mistakes, just not very many of them, and once an issue has been pointed out they must correct it—and quickly. Every time Adam was counseled, at about the same rate as other SEALs, it was something he had to overcome because of his eye; weapon manipulation with his injured hand was flawless. "Adam, you messed up because it's on your weak side," an instructor told him. "Other guys aren't messing that up because they don't have the deficiency like you do. The only way you can overcome that is to not have a weak side. You have to physically turn your head to the point where you can make up for that blind spot with your left eye. You need to have a rubber neck, on a swivel constantly, twice as much as you used to. You've *got* to get used to that."

"Roger that," said Adam. "I'll figure it out. I will get it."

Thereafter, Adam was known as Swivel or Rubberneck by the training cadre in CQB, while continuing to maintain "the best attitude," says one of them. "It was eyes wide open, ears as big as they could be. He was full of just 'Give me the information, give me as much information as you can and I'm going to make it happen; I really, really want to be here.'"

The training cadre knew, as DEVGRU SEALs themselves, that the men they passed would receive the most important and dangerous missions, and that their lives and the lives of their teammates depend on precision and perfection. Passing Adam Brown—the first time a trainee was ever let through CQB virtually blind in one eye (not to mention shooting off-handed)—was a huge decision for the cadre. "We had to set aside our own reservations, knowing Adam could only see half as much as anybody else," says an instructor. "We looked at the standards, and unanimously we agreed: he met them."

During the maritime segment of the course, the Green Team class was on a VBSS ship-boarding exercise when a trainee made an inexcusable blunder. He had left his weapon in his locker.

"It was dark," says a trainee named Frank O'Connor. "The instructors were keeping track of so many details—it's a dangerous exercise, watching for our safety—they didn't notice this guy did not have his M4 slung over his back." When the exercise was completed, some of the students leaked the information to the instructors. "They wanted to get the guy canned for what was a huge mistake."

The following day when the class gathered to review the exercise, an instructor announced that he'd heard a trainee had forgotten his weapon the night before. He waited to see how the class would react, if the guilty party would fess up. Silence. Then Adam stood up.

"This is crap!" he said. "We need to take care of things like this internally. We don't need to be running behind each other's backs to the instructors. That could have happened to any one of us, and we'd be counting our blessings right now if the cadres didn't notice. We are a team."

"Now, I got my own problems," says Frank, who, like everyone else, listened to Adam without saying a word. "In Green Team you do not want to bring attention to yourself, and especially not standing up for an idiot mistake, but Adam—who had more riding against him because of his injuries than any of us—did exactly that. He stood up for what he believed in."

Despite Adam's appeal, the SEAL was cut from the program, but after that, "nobody ever doubted Adam's loyalty," says an instructor. "He was the definition of a team player. And we liked that."

The crux of Green Team for many SEALs is CQB, but the crux for Adam was passing the rigid requirements of the Military Free Fall (MFF) portion. Green Team trainees must flawlessly perform fifteen different tasks while free falling from as high as twenty-five thousand feet—generally a High Altitude, High Opening (HAHO) jump—over the deserts of the Southwest. They get two tries per task, all under the watchful eye of the cadre who free fall alongside, filming the trainees in order to later scrutinize their performance.

It didn't matter that many of the SEALs had already gone through the Army's MFF school, because they all had to complete the tasks. And Adam, who had done only the required static-line jumping where a cord pulls the chute open instantly upon exiting the aircraft, was behind the power curve and starting from square one. Adam had gritted his way through everything that stood before him his entire life, but "in free fall it doesn't matter how tough you are," says Dave Cain. "You have to be graceful and composed, which isn't easy when you're falling toward the earth at terminal velocity. If you fight it, you tumble and you fail."

The most stable way to fall is "belly to earth," the position to be in when the rip cord is pulled to deploy the parachute. That position creates a vortex of air that pulls the chute from the pack and straight up. If a person's body is sideways, upside down, feetfirst—any way but flat, smooth, belly to earth—when the chute is deployed, the situation becomes very dangerous. Cords can tangle around legs, arms, or neck and prohibit the parachute from opening completely. Most free-fall fatalities result from improper chute deployment.

From early on Adam struggled with his ability to fall stable, which was necessary both for safety as well as to complete the other tasks while "flying" in formation with fellow SEALs. As the lead instructor reviewed the video of one of Adam's earliest jumps in front of the class, there was Adam sideways in the air, firmly grasping the rip cord he'd just yanked. The chute was deploying behind and beside him.

"The video does not lie," said the instructor. "Brown! Do you have a f—ing death wish? Everybody else! This is exactly what you do *not* want to do. Flatten out, fall a few more hundred feet, do whatever you need to, but do *not* do this. You're better off hitting the ground than deploying here—then at least you don't take someone else with you."

That stern reprimand set the tone for the next three weeks as Adam tried to embrace gravity, not fight it.

He spent hours in the practice wind tunnel figuring out the aerodynamics of his body, and barely squeaked by each required task. But as he neared the final jump day, he had yet to exhibit immediate stability upon exiting the aircraft. "This is one of the hardest things to grasp in all free fall," says an instructor. "If you're not totally relaxed and accepting of the initial blast of wind, then it will throw you upside down or into a spin. Body position upon exit is crucial."

Adam had completed his other tasks—altitude checks, checking for other jumpers, maintaining a heading—because he could stabilize himself within seconds, but that wasn't fast enough. Dave Cain was also having a hard time, and he and Adam were each summoned to the lead instructor's office the night before the final day of the course.

"Tomorrow is it," said the instructor. "You have two more jumps. That's all I can give you. If you can't nail it, you're out. You need to dig deep and figure out what's wrong and get that done tomorrow, because we won't have this talk tomorrow afternoon. You're either going to pass or you're done."

Back in his hotel room Adam called Kelley and asked her to pray, then dialed Billy White, who, despite continuing to suffer from the injuries incurred nine months earlier, had been able to return to work in the FBI's counterterrorism department. Besides being in the bureau, Billy had been a free-fall instructor for years. When he answered, Adam let out a big sigh.

"Hey, man, I need a pep talk," Adam said. "I'm about to fail MFF. I'm not able to exit and fall stable. If I don't pass, I'm going to action out—no DEVGRU. It's over."

Billy was reassuring. "That happens all the time," he told Adam, "and the reason is something that's easily fixable. This is not your final chapter. God has not brought you from getting your eye shot out and your fingers cut off, passing CQB left-handed and half-blind. He's not brought you all this way to fail you out because you can't fall stable. Let's talk about the stability thing: people who are strong and harder than nails, like yourself, they're rigid, their bodies are fixed, and they're like a propeller. They'll spin and turn and they'll flop. Like a leaf. If you drop a leaf off a tree, it doesn't fall straight."

"So what do I need to do to overcome that?" asked Adam.

"Just relax. If it's truly a stability problem, it can be fixed by relaxing.

And, dude, you've got to know that God's mission is not to fail you out for this. He has greater things in store for you than that."

In the early morning hours of the critical day, Dave stepped out onto the balcony of his second-floor hotel room. "I could not sleep at all," he says. "And there was Adam two doors down, and I could tell he was sweating just like me. He's talking to himself, wringing his hands, leaning hard on that railing. He was looking at the ground, then looking up at the sky, and then back down at the ground. I startled him a little when I said, 'Can't sleep, huh, Adam?' And he was like, 'Let me guess. You can't either?'"

"Nope," said Dave. "Haven't slept all night. I'm totally stressed out."

"Well, I'm praying to God that we don't have to jump in the morning," said Adam. "I need a day off to relax and get my head screwed back on."

"Throw a prayer up for me too. I'll take whatever I can get."

"You got it," said Adam, and they both turned in.

Boom! Adam woke up less than an hour later, thinking he heard the impact of artillery fire. As the rumbling repeated, he opened the heavy window blinds and found a beautiful sky. It looked like doomsday: cloud cover as far as the eye could see, with big clumps of charcoal-gray thunderheads. Lightning flashed, and somebody knocked at his hotel room door.

"Canceled," said Dave when Adam opened it. "The jump is canceled due to weather. We've got a day off!" His grin was so big it barely fit his face.

Lifting both of his arms in the air, Adam shook his fists and looked up toward the heavens. "Thank you!" he said. Then, to Dave, "What do you want to do?"

"Let's just relax. Go to town, grab some food, see a movie, and do nothing."

The following day was clear, calm, and "stable" for Adam and Dave, both of whom made it through to the next phase of Green Team.

Adam called Kelley right after he got the news. "Hey, Itty Bitty, how y'all doin'?"

"Doin'?" Kelley replied with trepidation. "I don't know, Adam. How *am* I doing?"

"You're doing just fine, because your man passed free fall. That's one step closer to DEVGRU, baby. We're almost there!"

15

Top Secret

With only half the trainees remaining, Adam graduated from Green Team in late November 2006, a feat predicted by his chief from SEAL Team TWO six months earlier when he wrote in his final evaluation that Adam was "clearly in the top one percent of the [SEAL] community."

In Virginia Beach Adam enjoyed a quiet celebration with Kelley, Nathan, Savannah, and their closest friends, who understood the need to be discreet about this fabled tier one counterterrorism special mission unit. The trail of publicly accessible military records that began when Adam enlisted on July 24, 1998, ends with a sheet of paper that notes his transfer to the Naval Special Warfare Development Group in November 2006:

> NSWTACDEVRON 3 is a special duty assignment, CNO
> Priority 1 command developing advanced NSW tactics,
> techniques, procedures and equipment and supports a
> classified National Mission. Each member is extensively
> prescreened and among the top performers in the Navy.

From here on, anything pertaining to the newly designated Special Warfare Operator First Class (SEAL) Adam Brown would be stamped TOP SECRET.

—

Behind the barbed-wire-topped walls of the closely guarded DEVGRU compound in Virginia Beach, a draft was in progress among the tactical squadrons of SEAL Team SIX. The squadrons' leadership had reviewed the Green Team graduates' ranks in the class as well as the comments of the cadre. Word of mouth among squadron team members also weighed heavily.

While Adam was not ranked at the top, his personal recommendations were superb, so he was quickly drafted into the same squadron his friend and mentor Chief Harley had been in years before. Brad Westin joined him, while Dave Cain went to another. The previous year Austin and Christian had been drafted into separate squadrons, which meant three different rotational schedules for Adam and his friends, who would all be gone from home eight to nine months of the year. Each had a month of block leave and would be deployed, on standby alert, or training for the remaining eleven months.

Most of their training would be abroad or out of state, but even while on standby alert, these SEALs trained. They were always a private jet ride away from anywhere their services might be urgently required: a hostage situation involving Somali pirates, the disposal of a drug cartel, or an operation intended to kill or capture the most wanted terrorist in the world.

After the draft Adam, Brad, and Dave checked in at their squadrons' "team rooms"—their first glimpse behind the top-secret curtain of DEVGRU, where a classified number of operators work together, with multiple support personnel seeing to their every possible need.

"Think of them like the Knights of the Round Table," says a former DEVGRU SEAL. "The knights had a contingent of support—weapons bearers, two or three attendants to carry their armor, tend to their horse, whatever. While the SEALs don't have those types of personal assistants, the command takes care of everything they need to operate at the highest level—administration, supply, medical, logistics, communications, intelligence, operations, and weapons training. The support team numbers work out to two or three people, both military and civilian, for each operator, and even the support personnel are critically screened and have top-secret clearance.

"It's a team effort, a tight-knit community, and everybody knows if they're working there, they're proud Americans who are trustworthy, motivated, and talented—the best at what they do. They're all patriots."

February 2007 found Adam in a mud hut within the walls of a compound leased from a tribal leader in northern Kunar Province, Afghanistan.

The sharp Hindu Kush peaks to the west were topped with snow. To the east was the bloated Kunar River; Adam could hear the rushing waters as he drifted off to sleep. If he walked the hundred yards from the outstation to the river's edge, he could fling a rock and nearly hit Pakistan on the opposite bank. Considering the location and the fact that Adam was a Naval Special Warfare sniper who had consistently hit targets a mile away, should an opportunity arise, say, across the river, he could engage the target from a lofty crag, camouflaged within the dark shadow of a rock overhang.

As this outstation's assistant team leader, Adam and his boss—a senior DEVGRU operator—were, among other things, a sniper team on a "classified national mission." By definition among the brotherhood, Adam was a "hunter" employed by a unit that did not officially exist, and so it was fitting that his first deployment abroad as a DEVGRU SEAL had landed him in what was described by a teammate as the "vague, mysterious, even shadowy" Kunar Valley, filled with enemy combatants dug into the surrounding mountains, blending among the populace in the villages and using the river valley as a highway from Pakistan to Afghanistan. Impossible to identify ("They don't carry the 'I'm a bad guy' flag," says one SEAL), these hard-line Taliban insurgents, foreign jihadists, aspiring terrorists, and good old-fashioned organized criminals all had the same goal: upset any attempts at regional (thus national) stability for either their own monetary gain or to accomplish Allah's will.

The coalition outstations in northern Kunar and the observation posts (OPs) surrounding them were mortared and shot at almost daily, but that was nothing compared to the Pech River Valley, which was the Wild West, Indian Country, Ambush Alley, and other wartime clichés rolled up into one huge disadvantage if you're the outsider trying to gain a foothold. That's what all the outstations, forward operating bases (FOBs), command outposts (COPs), and observation posts represented: footholds in the uphill battle being waged in Afghanistan seven years after 9/11.

While the presence of Afghan National Army and coalition (predominantly conventional U.S. Army or Marine Corps) forces at these "frontier" outposts was intended to stabilize the regions, they also provided security for regional projects such as building roads, schools, and medical clinics; digging wells; and teaching sustainable farming techniques. In essence, the outposts protected the local population from the neighborhood bullies, who were well armed, motivated, and ruthless in threatening and killing locals who cooperated with coalition forces.

One of the functions of DEVGRU operators was protecting the conventional coalition forces, a job they accomplished by targeting and taking out the "bullies." The outstations in Kunar and across Afghanistan were intelligence depots for the surrounding areas, with operators ascertaining the viability of targets in their sectors, to judge if a certain reportedly "bad guy" really was a bad guy, and if so, how bad. Was he a priority—actively attacking American outposts and placing improvised explosive devices (IEDs) on roads—or was he only talking about it? Was he working alone or with a cell or a neighboring cell? Where was he getting his weapons, and what kinds of weapons did he have? Was he accessible? Could a regular SEAL team, a platoon of Marines, a couple of squads of Army infantrymen get to him? Was this guy a high-level target, meaning he had a résumé of previous attacks against coalition forces? Did intelligence confirm an imminent attack? This would warrant sending a squadron's strike force, the bulk of Adam's teammates based nearby, to go in and get him, but was the risk worth the reward? As operators put it, "Is the juice worth the squeeze?"

Adam had learned early in his deployment that two distinct battles were waging in Afghanistan: One was against the terrorist population, primarily al Qaeda but also a plethora of Islamic extremists, both foreign and domestic. The second battle was against the Taliban insurgency. "Even though there was some overlap at times," says an operator, "we were fighting one to end terrorism and the other to secure Afghanistan as a country."

Punctuating it all, the hunt for Osama bin Laden was "at the front of the back of everybody's mind," says another operator. "We all hoped to stumble upon him, or the clue that would lead us to him, but on a day-to-day basis we had other fish to fry."

In his daily routine Adam reviewed intelligence reports from a range of classified sources, worked out (a favorite being a run with a two-thousand-foot elevation gain up to an observation post), and gained understanding of the terrain in order to plan better operations. He would hike or ride an ATV into the mountains to visit the observation posts manned almost entirely by Afghan army soldiers.

"He would push out farther than anybody," says one OGA (other government agency: for example, CIA, DEA, FBI) operator who frequented

Adam's outstation. "He happened to be visiting an observation post when it got hit. I'd been in the region for years, and we never went into the surrounding mountains to pursue these guys; we just dealt with the attacks and held the ground. But Adam was a JTAC [joint terminal attack controller] and he didn't like getting shot at. He was at the right place at the right time, and called in artillery from a firebase and fast movers [jets], vectored them in on these guys he was tracking visually, killed some of them and had the others on the run. He asked why they'd never done that before, and the Afghans told him he was the first American they'd seen that far out."

In short, Adam came in and, as usual, pushed the limits. "He was

Brown family archives

Adam at a frontier outstation in Kunar Province, Afghanistan.

aggressive," says the OGA. "Loved to talk football and said, 'Sometimes the best defense is a strong offense.' He wanted to overpower them and believed we could. He was definitely the 'glass half full' kind of guy. He believed in what we were doing, and you could tell he wanted to make a difference."

Rarely did Adam leave an observation post without first helping with fortification efforts, such as filling sandbags. He also handed out extra MREs (Meals Ready to Eat) to children in the surrounding villages until he witnessed an Afghan man taking one away from a little girl. From then on he would hand out two to each child: one for the child's family and one for the child to eat right then as he stood guard.

In addition to providing meals, he was known for giving local kids rides on an ATV. "That ATV and his smile were probably Adam's most effective weapons," says the OGA. "Those kids who he put up front and let them drive down the road, they probably don't remember too many of the Americans, but I bet they remember Adam because of those rides. He played with them. That's important. When some AQ [al Qaeda] recruiter tries to tell them Americans are evil and they should be killed, they might think twice because of Adam."

"Coming home to the wife and kids after being over there," says one of Adam's teammates, "is like the space shuttle coming back to Earth from outer space. It's all about reentering the family atmosphere with the proper trajectory, speed, and timing. If you come in too fast, you'll blow up."

Adam was able to ease back into home life more smoothly than many of his teammates, according to Kelley. In fact, he continued to tell her that her job was far more difficult than his, recognizing that for the several months he'd been gone, Kelley had assumed the role of both parents—homemaker, coach, chauffeur, cheerleader—and shouldered single-handedly everything that had gone wrong or right. "He didn't step in and expect to be the boss overnight," she says.

Kelley ran a tight ship, and Adam respected her greatly for it. "The house was always immaculate," says Austin's wife, Michelle. "She'd do things like organize the cupboards. I'd throw my kids a Pop-Tart, and she'd have a snack tray with all the food groups. Her kids were polite. They had a schedule, and she stuck to it. I don't think anybody would disagree that she set the bar pretty high in almost everything, and she was always put together. I'd be like, 'You can look like that *and* bake brownies?'"

No matter the time of day when Adam returned from a deployment, Kelley piled Nathan and Savannah into the car to pick him up at the compound gate. "In the military they'd teach the men how to assimilate back home," says Kelley. "They're supposed to go to their wives before they hold their babies, that kind of thing. But Adam didn't need any schooling. He'd just wrap us all up. Falling into his arms and then watching him lift up the kids was like a blanket. Like I'd been cold while he was away and he warmed me up."

Following Adam's return, there was always one "Daddy Day" each for the kids, such as a day at the mall for Savannah or laser tag for Nathan. There was a date night for Adam and Kelley when they could catch up on all they'd missed out on in each other's lives. Because of operational security, Adam couldn't talk in any detail about what he'd been doing. But if something big had been reported in the news, "like one of the guys on the 'deck of cards' had been captured in Iraq," says Kelley, "or an al Qaeda leader was killed in Afghanistan, I'd mention it and he'd say, 'Hmm, how about that…' That was how I knew he'd been part of it. I'd look into his eyes and see if they were different, like if what he'd seen or done had changed him, but he was still my Adam."

After his most recent deployment to Afghanistan, Adam did "repeat something he'd told me before, something that got reinforced when he

Says Austin, "Adam didn't take the kids to play—he *played* with the kids; there's a difference." Savannah and Nathan with Daddy at a Virginia Beach waterslide.

was over there," says Kelley. "It wasn't bragging; it was just matter-of-fact. He told me, 'I'm not afraid. God gave me this gift—I don't feel fear.'"

"That," says Kelley, "terrified me."

In June 2007, after two weeks with his family, Adam was off again, this time to Holland for training in specialized fighting techniques. He returned to Virginia a month later with a limp, nothing unusual for him, but at the DEVGRU medical center an orthopedic surgeon reviewed his x-rays and pointed out the loose bone fragments in both ankles from years of pounding abuse.

The surgeon was amazed that Adam could walk, much less perform as a SEAL, and told him he would usually recommend ankle-fusion surgery for such battered joints. That would leave Adam with stiff, permanently flexed ankles—a career ender. "Not an option," Adam told the doctor, which left the alternative "Band-Aid" option: removal of all the loose cartilage and bone shards "floating" in and around his ankle joints.

The day after the surgery, Adam showed Kelley what the surgeon had taken out of his right ankle. "This," he said, holding up a jar containing a four-inch-long bone fragment, "was the problem."

Three months later, Christian was getting ready to deploy to Iraq with his squadron when he asked Adam to have a beer with him. "I've got some things I need to tell you," he said.

On his way to meet Christian, Adam noticed a young woman staggering down the sidewalk a few blocks from the bar. He pulled the car over and offered to call her a cab, but she waved him off.

Adam found Christian sitting alone at the bar counter and told him about the drunk woman.

"Unreal," Christian said, meeting Adam's eye. "That's my girlfriend."

"Girlfriend?" asked Adam in disbelief.

"Yeah," said Christian. "It's a long story and I'm not proud of it. I've been cheating on Becky, and I wanted to come clean to you before I deploy. I was going to introduce you to her, but we got in an argument and she stormed out of here." He explained to Adam that he hadn't told him because he didn't want Adam to look down on him. "Becky doesn't know, and you can't let her," he said. "I'm going to tell her after this deployment."

"I won't look down on you," said Adam, "and I won't tell a soul. That's your job."

"Adam kept his word," says Christian. "And even though I took two years to tell him about my affair, I knew that was how he would react. Deep down, the main reason I hadn't before was because I knew he'd tell me to stop, and I wasn't ready—I was getting the best of both worlds. I was a dirt bag, but Adam didn't rub it in.

"He never took the holier-than-thou approach as a Christian either. He wasn't a snob. But he and Austin spent a lot of time trying to convert me. He didn't do that with everybody—he wasn't a Bible thumper—but we were best friends and respected each other and ribbed each other about everything. We exhausted ourselves arguing; every example he had that God existed, I had a comeback of why he didn't. But I was way too much of a wussy to call myself an atheist, and because I wouldn't commit to being a true nonbeliever, Adam saw that as a chink in my armor. He tirelessly tried to get us to go to church and give it a shot. Finally, I promised I'd go…someday."

Planners for DEVGRU don't discount the potential for any type of mission—they can't allow their SEALs to fall into the rut, for example, of only taking down compounds and caves in Iraq and Afghanistan—so training exercises are planned in a variety of places, including major American cities. DEVGRU often partners with business owners or local government officials to use old or condemned buildings as training facilities, turning them into temporary "kill houses" for realistic Close Quarters Battle drills and breaching exercises. In some, these tier one SEALs plan and execute the explosive takedown of an entire building, bridge, or other structure.

Toward the end of September, Adam's squadron visited a professional football stadium. While the city slept, assault and sniper teams worked various scenarios that could present themselves at such a location, say on Super Bowl Sunday.

During a break from drills in which the SEALs would surgically "take out" a gunman in the crowd, Adam set his weapon down, lowered himself over the field railing, and headed for a rack of footballs on the sideline. His teammates followed.

Sometime later a trained ear might have heard the heckling, curses, and quarterback calls one would expect at a sandlot pickup game. One could imagine someone yelling "I'm open!" while charging for the end zone, almost see that someone dive to make the catch. That airborne moment would have made quite a replay: a camouflaged, fully extended Navy SEAL snagging the ball in a spectacular grab. The *pop* of a knee giving out upon landing—not so much. But as would be officially cited, the cause of Adam's crushed tibial plateau was a slip on the stadium stairs while bearing the full weight of his kit and body armor.

The following morning, a phone call: "Hey there, Itty Bitty, guess what? I'm coming home."

"You have *got* to be kidding! What now?"

"I broke my leg."

"Really? Really, Adam? How did it happen?"

"Training accident."

"They were endless," Kelley says about Adam's injuries. "But I would get so mad when the guys would say he was accident prone. I'd tell them, 'No, he isn't—he just puts out harder than anybody. He doesn't know how to hold back, so of course he's going to get injured.'"

When Kelley picked Adam up at the airport, she sensed that he was behaving strangely on the drive to the DEVGRU medical center, not really answering her questions about how the injury occurred. Before heading home, Adam had told his teammates that he was more frightened of Kelley's response than he was of the doctor's diagnosis.

Word travels fast at DEVGRU, and two SEALs in the waiting room spilled the beans when they asked Adam what it felt like to play ball on an

NFL field. Adam was shaking his head, waving his hands, doing everything he could to shut them up.

"You were playing football?" Kelley said. "*That's* how this happened?"

"We did play a little catch, and I did have a fall," he said, sounding like a kid trying to explain why his hand was in the cookie jar. "But that only tweaked it. The stairs are what *broke* it."

Adam's tibial plateau—the upper surface of the tibia, the shinbone—had "caved in, shattered," according to the doctor who saw Adam. He underwent reconstructive surgery two days later at Portsmouth Naval Hospital, and was given a set of crutches and strict instructions to bear no weight on that leg for at least four months. "I can't believe I'm pushing you in a wheelchair," Kelley said to him as they left the hospital.

"Adam was thirty-three years old and had arthritis," she says. "He had serious ankle problems, back problems, constant pain in his eye—always taking drops to relieve the pressure—and he never complained about it, never whined about it once. But I felt the burden of it. I felt sorry for him. I would make jokes when I was pushing him in the wheelchair, like 'You sure are lazy! You need to get out and walk!' Then I'd break down and tell him, 'You can't do this to yourself, you just can't. You're falling apart, and you're *young*. I want you to be around.'"

A week after Adam's surgery, Savannah broke her leg in gymnastics class; the week after that, Nathan broke his arm playing football. "Neighbors would see us get out of the car," says Kelley, "and I'd smile and wave. They must have thought, *What is that woman doing to her family— beating them?* What else can you do but laugh? It was a rough time, but it got rougher. Come February, I was counting my blessings. We all were."

A few weeks before Adam was injured playing midnight football, the Browns had bought and moved into a house that was closer to work, church, and friends. Perfect for the kids, their new two-story home was on a cul-de-sac and backed a greenbelt. What it didn't have was wood floors.

"How hard could it be?" Adam said to Kelley about installing the dark mahogany flooring they'd bought as an early Christmas present to themselves.

Tossing aside his crutches, Adam began hopping around on his good leg, carrying planks as Kelley repeatedly reminded him, "You're not supposed to be putting any weight on that leg." But Adam's squadron was headed to Iraq in January 2008, and he was determined to both toughen up and heal his broken leg as soon as possible, with the added benefit of getting the floors done.

"And we had so much fun," says Kelley. "After the kids went to bed, we'd start up each night. He'd cut them in the garage, I would help him lay them out. When he got frustrated—cut a piece wrong so it wouldn't fit—he'd let that piece of wood have it with his hammer, so there were dings and little chips if you looked real close, but it sure was pretty. We were proud of that floor."

Adam's squadron deployed without him in mid-January. He hoped to join them in the middle of February; in the meantime he acted as his squadron's operations chief, a position that some describe as a lifeline between the deployed squadron and headquarters, supporting everything from the mission abroad to urgent family matters. It was a job usually reserved for more senior operators, but Adam accepted the challenge with "Can do, sir. I got it."

At home he continued to work on the floors, which were nearly done on February 3, when Austin and Michelle came over to watch the Super Bowl.

If they were in Virginia Beach at the same time, the four couples—the Browns, Michaelses, Jacobses, and Taylors—had always gathered for the big game. But in 2008 Paul Jacobs was deployed, and Christian and Becky Taylor had separated after Becky pieced together the affair and moved his belongings into storage; neither was feeling particularly social. Taking full responsibility for their family problems and the breakup of their circle of friends, Christian was in the dumps, his dejection compounded by the recent loss of his good friend Mark Carter, a SEAL in his squadron who had been killed by an IED.

In the fourth quarter of the Super Bowl, at nearly ten o'clock, Adam's beeper went off. He looked at the message and "his face dropped," recalls Kelley. "He showed the message to Austin; they both knew it meant somebody in Adam's squadron had been killed and Adam was to report for duty as part of the notification team."

"I gotta go, Itty Bitty," said Adam. "I'll call you when I can."

The notification team was informed that two SEALs, Nate Hardy and Mike Koch, had been killed on a mission in Iraq. At Adam's suggestion they decided to wait until the next morning to notify Mindi Hardy, reasoning that this new mother with a seven-month-old baby boy should get one last good night of sleep before her world collapsed around her.

Early the next morning, Adam, flanked by two other SEALs and Chaplain Tim Springer, walked up to the Hardy home and rang the doorbell.

"It was the hardest thing I've ever had to do," Adam later told Kelley. He barely left Mindi's side during the long hours of that first day, then he juggled his time between the Hardy home and the team room, planning everything for his fallen teammate—from the memorial service to the military funeral at Arlington National Cemetery in Washington DC.

Then, three days after Nate and Mike died, Louis Souffront, a twenty-five-year-old explosive ordnance disposal technician attached to Adam's squadron, was also killed in Iraq.

"There was a dark cloud over the command," says Christian, who found Adam alone in his squadron's team room the night of Louis's death, putting together the uniform Nate would be buried in. "Adam was exhausted but determined to make sure everything was perfect."

Beyond the uniform, Adam cross-checked Nate's military service records and made sure all his ribbons, medals, and awards were properly credited and exhibited. With Kelley's help he assembled the wooden shadow boxes that held Nate's photos, awards, unit patches, and a folded American flag that he would present to Mindi and Nate's parents from the DEVGRU command.

Adam was a pillar of strength during those difficult early days, according to Mindi. "There was a calm about him," she says, "like he was a chaplain himself. His arms were open and warm, and he took care of me and watched over me."

But whenever Adam hurried home for a shower and hugs from his own wife and children, "he cried," says Kelley. "I never saw him so vulnerable. Telling Mindi that horrible news while she was holding her little baby crushed him."

Throughout this sad ordeal, Adam sought moments of refuge, comradeship, and ultimately spiritual strength from Chaplain Springer. He told the chaplain the only thing that comforted him was the story of Christ's resurrection. Springer said he wholeheartedly agreed.

On February 13, just as Adam was confirming the final funeral arrangements for Nate, Christian informed him that Master Chief Tommy Valentine, a highly decorated war veteran from another squadron, had been killed in a high-risk free-fall parachute accident. "When it rains it pours," Christian said, shaking his head.

Two days later, Kelley joined Adam as he oversaw the side-by-side burials of Chief Petty Officers Nathan H. Hardy and Michael E. Koch, both twenty-nine years old, at Arlington National Cemetery.

A few days after Nate and Mike were killed, a letter written by someone calling himself The Angry American began to circulate around the Internet. Adam printed it out and hung it up in his squadron's team room:

Last Sunday while most of America was enjoying the Super Bowl, several members of our Task Force were commencing an assault on a terrorist stronghold in Iraq. During the assault two of our brothers from the Navy were shot and killed while clearing a building that was occupied by terrorist insurgents. Ultimately, the building was reduced and all of the terrorists in it were destroyed by the assault force.

Remember these names, Mike and Nate. They were good men doing honorable work in the name of freedom. The terrorists they sought to destroy were responsible for unspeakable acts of evil including the construction of improvised explosive devices and explosives to equip homicide bombers. For those of you who may not understand the enemy we face out here let me remind you that the previous week this group of terrorists took two innocent and unwitting women who had Downs Syndrome, rigged them with explosive vests and detonated them 20 minutes apart in a crowded market causing several deaths and hundreds of injuries. These terrorists used innocent people as unwitting vehicles to destroy more innocent lives. There is good and there is evil in this world. The enemy we face is evil. Mike and Nate were fighting on the side of good to prevent further acts of evil that would result in the loss of more innocent lives....

Their work is done here now, but there are many of us who will honor their sacrifice by continuing the fight against evil terrorists. They will be remembered through our actions.

For any of you out there who doubt the validity of this war and the evil that resides in our enemy I ask you to study your history again. Over the last 20+ years dating back to the bombing of the Marine Corps Barracks in Lebanon, various factions of radical Islamic Terrorists have been committing heinous acts of terrorism against the free world. We are fighting the same enemy here. The brethren of an evil ideology that spawned the terrorist attacks of September 11, 2001 claiming almost 3,000 innocent lives....

While the American media strives daily to erase the memory of the terrorist attacks of September 11, 2001, and paint this war as an unjust occupation of a sovereign nation, men like Mike and Nate are out here hunting down and destroying the enemies of the very freedom that allows our media to try and discredit us. Terrorism is real, evil is real, this war is real and real men and women are in this fight because righteousness and freedom are worth fighting for....

Sincerely,
The Angry American

Five days after the funeral, Adam arrived by helicopter at a remote forward operating base in Diyala Province, Iraq. That night he slept in the bunk that had been Nate's.

The death toll in Iraq was pushing four thousand American lives lost, more than 70 percent to IEDs planted on roads that coalition forces traveled daily. Adam's squadron was focused on eradicating the IED and suicide bombing networks prevalent across the country, a mission of "dire importance," according to the Joint Improvised Explosive Device Defeat Organization. To destroy the bombing networks, American forces created an extensive intelligence network. Once the identities of dozens of the highest-level leaders—a mixture of foreign terrorists and domestic insurgents—were identified and confirmed, the DEVGRU SEALs were tasked with either killing or capturing them in their homes and safe houses, almost always under cover of darkness.

"When you blow a door open, it is just smoke, a black hole," describes Adam's teammate Heath Robinson. "At some point, you have to commit to going into that dark void and taking care of business—ready for anything. It could be a guy attacking you with a knife or grenade to somebody shooting at you to somebody being right in your face who you need to immediately disarm. Or, in that same proximity, it could be a woman or a child or an old man. Or it could be one of your own guys who entered from a different breach.

"I use the volume knob to describe the levels of intensity. When you go through that black hole, you are spun up to ten. You come around the corner and you cave in some guy's head who is shooting at you, then you come around the next corner and there is a woman on the ground with two kids on her lap crying, and bullets are still flying, but you have to lower the volume back down to about a three. You turn down the amps and you calm down the mother, let them know you aren't there for them, then scoop up the kids and put them outside, then you dial up to ten and go back in and finish the job."

Known for his compassion, Adam was always the first to do something like break open a light stick for a baby to play with or give a candy bar to a terrified child. But he wasn't the only one. In a group of men whose business is killing, the fury they release upon the enemy is rivaled only by the humanity they display for innocents caught in the crossfire. On one particular assault, "we'd dropped two guys that were directly engaging us, and there was a third guy winging bullets in our general direction," Heath says. "The bullets were hitting the walls and there are these kids who got up out of their beds—because they often sleep in the courtyards—and it's pitch black for them, and they are running around while this guy is spraying bullets all around them. So this huge bear of a guy on our team stops shooting, jumps into the courtyard, grabs these two Afghan kids in one arm, shoots and peels back behind us, and tosses the two kids out of the way."

Another night at another compound, another strike force of SEALs was under fire, and another teammate, "at total risk to himself," says Heath, "jumped down from a wall, where he had perfect cover, and into the line of fire where the enemy was randomly firing shots. He started grabbing women and children—five or ten of them—in the middle of this firefight and throws them over the wall. They got bruised up, but better than getting shot.

"Adam and I talked about how blessed we were to work with the most phenomenal team. Every one of them is unbelievably talented, smart, courageous—every word you can use to describe a true warrior of the highest caliber. *That* is the caliber of the people I work with and the caliber of who Adam was."

A different teammate describes how he and Adam were going after a bomb maker at another objective when they entered the interior room of a residence. "It all happened real fast; this guy was firing at us, we engaged, there was motion to the right, and Adam spun around but didn't fire. It was a bed, with somebody under the covers moving around. It takes a lot of restraint to not open up on something like that, but Adam walked over, pushed back the covers, and there was this two- or three-year-old kid. His father was the bomb maker we had just killed. Adam picked him up in his arms and carried him outside."

Night by night, Adam's squadron continued to dismantle the enemy IED network.

March 22, Adam and his teammates hit two compounds simultaneously near the foothills of the Hamrin Mountains, where enemy combatants were known to enter Iraq from Iran. Two assault teams and a sniper team went to each of the target compounds—containing five to ten military adult males (MAMs) apiece and located about a quarter mile apart—patrolling in on foot from separate helicopter landing zones. With the warming temperatures of the impending spring, many locals were sleeping in their courtyards, which significantly increased the need for stealth.

The SEALs were ready to breach the gates of the two compounds when a startled farm animal made a noise and alerted one compound's militants, who came out of their rooms and began firing blindly into the night.

Stealth no longer an option, the SEALs used interpreters with bullhorns to inform the MAMs they were surrounded by coalition forces and could surrender, an option given whenever possible in these situations. This enemy, however, is often content to die, especially if that means taking "infidels" along, and the firefight continued until every armed insurgent was killed.

Awakened by the gunfire, the insurgents at the other compound had also fought to their deaths. Upon searching the two dwellings, the SEALs discovered a plethora of intelligence that would dispel any lingering

Adam operating with SEAL Team TWO in Iraq.

Brown family archives

doubt that al Qaeda was present in Iraq and that both bomb-making materials and bombers had come from Iran. Seventeen terrorists and insurgents were killed that night. At least six of them were positively identified as suicide bombers because of their shaved bodies, consistent with final preparation for suicide operations.

In the early morning hours, the two groups of SEALs met up at their rally point between the compounds, prepared to fly out together. That's when Dave Cain noticed from the way Adam was walking that he appeared to be in pain. His head was also hanging uncharacteristically low.

"You doing okay, Adam?" he asked.

"Yeah, I'm all right. It's just, you know...it's Easter."

Dave associated the holiday with painted eggs, chocolates, and a bunny. Now Adam told Dave he was troubled that he'd slain men—sent them to hell—on the morning of his Savior's resurrection.

"Man," Dave said, "I don't understand how you can do what we do and be religious."

"One, I'm spiritual, not religious," Adam replied. "And two, I can't believe you can do what we do and *not* be."

The actions of the DEVGRU squadrons, targeting the networks of suicide bombers and IEDs in late 2007 and early 2008, nullified the Hollywood perception that tier one teams are reserved for the occasional high-level mission, training for weeks at a site built to replicate their target before embarking upon that mission.

"These guys are so good at what they do," says an officer who oversaw Adam's squadron, "because they have an op almost every night, sometimes more in a single night than guys did in their whole careers pre-9/11. They never stop training, sure, but nothing compares to on-the-job training."

Between February and April 2008, Adam and his squadron teammates killed 117 enemy combatants and captured 152. For his part Adam
was awarded his first Bronze Star with combat valor. The citation reads,

> For heroic achievement…in combat operations against the
> enemy as an assault team member, [Adam Brown] displayed
> great battlefield courage while conducting multiple direct action
> missions against enemy leadership targets. On 22 February 2008,
> during clearance of a targeted location, the assault force came
> under heavy direct enemy small arms fire. An AC-130 gunship
> engaged the enemy position, but the fighters were well entrenched
> in the structure and close air support had little effect. Special
> Warfare Operator First Class (Sea, Air, and Land) Brown
> maneuvered under intense enemy fire with his assault team and
> engaged the insurgents at close range with accurate small arms
> fire and grenades. By his extraordinary guidance, zealous initia-
> tive, and total dedication to duty, Brown reflected great credit
> upon himself and upheld the highest traditions of the United
> States Naval Service.

Later that year, U.S. Central Command declassified statistics regarding IED attacks in Iraq. According to an *Army Times* article by staff
writer William H. McMichael, posted on September 28, 2008, "The
number of roadside bombs in Iraq that exploded or were discovered and
neutralized tumbled from a high of about 2,600 per month in March
and June of 2007 to 555 in August 2008, a decrease of 79 percent. Coalition casualties fell at a similar rate from August 2006 to August 2008.…
The command says 47 troops were killed by roadside bombs in August
2006, but only seven this past August—an 85 percent decline. And while

384 troops were wounded by roadside bombs two years ago, that figure fell to 52 in August—an 86 percent reduction."

This was one of the greatest victories in the war, but few in the government grasped—and the public did not even realize—that this offensive was executed almost entirely by two squadrons of DEVGRU SEALs. Fewer than one hundred men were responsible for destroying the network, killing in total more than two hundred enemy, and capturing upwards of three hundred. "It's impossible to know how many lives were ultimately saved by eradicating those bombing cells," says one intelligence officer who supported the mission. "But conservative estimates were in the thousands."

"It was a team effort," says a SEAL about the raids. "We lost a few really good guys during the hunt, but we crushed those bastards. Payback was hell for them."

16

Heart of a Warrior

Upon Adam's return from Iraq, Kelley was overwhelmed with relief. "After losing Mike, Mark, Nate, Louis, and Tommy," she says, "seeing him walking toward us in the distance, that unmistakable saunter, I took a moment, thinking, *Okay, we got through another one.*"

She squeezed in "I missed you" and a hug before Nathan and Savannah climbed all over Adam, enveloping him with hugs and kisses. "I sat back and just stared," says Kelley. "My family was whole again."

Having been on a different sleep schedule, Adam was jet-lagged and exhausted, but he pushed through dinner and a game of Sorry! after the kids chanted, "Game night! Game night!" Finally Kelley told them, "Okay. Daddy needs some sleep."

At four in the morning, Adam slipped out of bed. Kelley stirred, then smiled as she heard him turn on the bath water; no doubt he was pouring in Mr. Bubble. Feeling content and safe, she alternated between dozing and listening to the water slosh in the tub.

Click. Kelley jolted awake at the sound of the outside door, located just down the hall, being opened. "My heart nearly stopped," she says. "There had been some home invasions in Virginia Beach, and burglaries; we were always vigilant."

She leapt from the bed and ran toward the bathroom as Adam

"charged out, completely naked, bubbles flying everywhere," she says. "He didn't stop to get a gun; he didn't stop to do anything."

"I'm going to *kill* you for coming into my house!" he shouted, barreling down the hallway.

"He was scary," says Kelley. "I seriously thought he had somebody in our living room and was killing him with his bare hands, because I'd never seen that, ever. Just protection mode, and it was crazy."

"You'd better keep running!" Adam yelled, standing at the partially open door. "If I find you, I'm going to rip your throat out!"

Kelley was frozen, "scared to death," she says. "But then I grabbed our gun real quick while Adam ran upstairs to make sure there was nobody in with the kids." Nathan was sitting up in his bed, eyes wide. Savannah had slept through the whole thing.

The intruder hadn't even gotten a foot in the house before turning tail. Locking the door again, Adam wrapped a towel around himself and hugged Kelley, who was "shaking like a leaf." He was completely calm.

"It's all right, baby," he said. "It's okay. I'm glad I was home."

"Like that," Kelley says, snapping her fingers, "he went from this scary-sounding man back to my cuddly Adam. It gave me a glimpse—just a glimpse—of why he was so good at what he did. Why he was a SEAL."

A week after the intruder incident, the sound of a man shouting snapped Kelley out of sleep in the middle of the night. Kelley says, "It was Adam, beside me in bed cursing and yelling, 'I'm going to kill you!' in his sleep. He was sitting up in bed swinging his arms, his legs were going, he was moving his head around, he was living it." For a minute or two she listened, "and he just kept going. I could tell he was on a mission. He was in Iraq."

Kelley put her hand on his shoulder, gently shaking him while saying, "Adam. Baby. Adam. Adam, are you okay? It's me. Are you okay?"

"Yeah, yeah," Adam finally responded. "What's wrong?"

"Everything's fine," said Kelley. "Go back to sleep."

He slept soundly after that.

The next morning over breakfast, Kelley asked him, "Do you remember last night?"

"No, why?"

"You don't remember your dreams?"

"No. What are you talking about?"

"Look, I know you do some things that I'm sure are very hard to deal with," Kelley replied, "and I know you'll talk about what you can when you're ready. If you never do, that's fine, but I just want you to know that *I* know there are things going on in your head. I'm here for you."

"Thanks, baby," Adam said without elaborating.

The same thing happened the following night, and the night after, and then again—four nights in a row—and Kelley was beginning to worry. She was thinking of urging Adam to speak with a counselor at the command when, on the fifth night, after Nathan and Savannah were asleep, Adam said, "I sure would like to take a bath."

"Do you want me to run you a bath, sweetie?" she asked.

"Well, you know, I feel bad asking, but…"

"That was our routine," says Kelley, "and I loved it. So I got the water just right, poured in the bubbles, lit a candle, and then I did my own thing while waiting for him to ask, real sweet, for a towel."

But Adam stayed in the bath for almost two hours, running the water every few minutes to keep it hot. When he finally called out, it wasn't for a towel.

"He wanted to talk," says Kelley. "I can't share the details—it was private for him—but he told me that he'd killed people and that was the first time he ever even acknowledged that part of his job. I think he felt like he had to tell me, to see if I was okay with it. And I was. What he did had to be done.

"He told me that Easter had been very hard, that a lot of people were killed. Such an important holiday as a Christian—it's about the Resurrection—and here he was taking lives. There wasn't guilt; these people were making bombs that were killing hundreds of people every month. It was his job and he believed in it. However, on Easter? *Really? Really, God?* That got to him and had been haunting him, and I think he had to take the time to soak, to process the whole operation.

"We prayed together, and that night he slept well. Whatever had been eating at him he worked out, and it was done. Never did that happen again."

Three months later, in July 2008, Adam stood beside his mother on the deck of the dream house she and Larry had built on Lake Hamilton, staring out at the amazing view, complete with the 70 West bridge a quarter mile down the shore.

"You could tell his heart was still here," says Janice. "He had been thinking about what he'd do after he got out of the Navy. They came out for a visit every summer, but this time he asked Larry and me to keep an eye out for houses and property for sale. He wanted to price things out, but it *had* to be in the Lake Hamilton School District; that's where he wanted Nathan and Savannah to go to school one day."

In the two-week visit home, Adam spent a lot of time with his children, picking wildflowers with five-year-old Savannah and tossing a football with eight-year-old Nathan on the Wolf Stadium field, imparting fatherly wisdom in the process. Don't pick too many flowers; you want to leave some for others to enjoy, he'd tell Savannah, while he taught Nathan the importance of being tough, not only on the football field but also in life. "When you fall down or get hit, you get up," he would say. "You don't think about it, you just do it."

Together, Adam and Kelley took their family on hikes in the mountains, went canoeing on the creeks, and swam for hours in the lake that was Janice and Larry's backyard—fun-filled days of what Adam called "good, clean Arkansas living." They also looked at lakefront homes they liked but couldn't afford, and land that was more reasonably priced but still had to have a house built on it. One piece of property really called out to them: it was near a small lake, with views of the mountains and lots of open space.

"Plenty of room for the kids to run," Adam said as they stood in the tall grass and dreamed about their future home. "Someday," he told Kelley. "We'll make it happen."

One weekend, Adam and Kelley drove from Hot Springs to Bentonville so Adam could see Sam Walton's original Five & Dime, which had evolved into Wal-Mart—another bit of his Arkansas trivia. As a souvenir Adam bought the "authentic badge holder" that Wal-Mart employees wear.

"I'm going to use it for work," he said to Kelley.

Back in Virginia Beach the following Monday, Adam cleared security at DEVGRU with his ID displayed in his "Hi. My name is Adam" Wal-Mart badge holder hanging on a lanyard around his neck.

"Adam was one of a kind," says teammate Kevin Houston. "We had cover stories if people asked us what we did for a living. I always told people I stocked shelves at Target, and Adam was either a Wal-Mart greeter or a rodeo clown."

Adam and Kevin had been good friends ever since Kevin joined the squadron the year after Adam, and outside work this friendship centered around family: their wives were friends, their kids played together, and recently the Houstons had accepted Adam's invitation to try out the Browns' church. "Kevin was a little rough around the edges," says Kelley with a fond smile. "Meiling [Kevin's wife] and I would cringe when he dropped the F-bomb during service, but he was there, spitting chewing tobacco into a cup, listening in, 'trying to figure this whole Christian thing out,' he'd say."

In addition to being brothers in arms, Adam and Kevin were initially drawn to each other by their ability to talk smack about their athletic prowess in sports ranging from Ping-Pong and darts to football and basketball. In particular, their jockeying for alpha male dominance in basketball had led to the planning of a future one-on-one tournament to settle the score. Kevin knew he would win, and it drove him crazy that Adam wouldn't admit it.

"It didn't matter if he *knew* I was a better player because I'd beaten everybody else in the squadron," Kevin says, "Adam still thought he could take me. If Kobe Bryant was like, 'Hey, let's play one on one,' Adam would seriously think he had a legitimate shot at winning."

While car-pooling to DEVGRU one morning, Kevin told Adam about a friend of his son's who came from a broken home without much money, and how he and Meiling had bought the boy cleats and athletic glasses—setting him up with the proper equipment for the sports he loved and providing some self-esteem in the process.

"Even at our level of military we were on a budget, Adam and I," Kevin explains. "And the first thing he said after I told him about this kid was, 'How can Kelley and I help? Let us buy his pads or help out with his next uniform.'"

This discussion led to an idea: someday, Kevin and Adam decided, they would check out the local football practices and look for "the kid that has nothing," says Kevin. "He's got cleats, but most of them are broken off, his face mask is chipped, his pads are all duct-taped, he's probably a minority, very poor, but he is a freakin' beast on the field, and that is the kid Adam and I would recognize, because he's putting out. He's the kid we're going to size up and buy a brand-new helmet, shoulder pads, cleats—hook him up big time and let him be a rock star. What I'm getting at is I have a soft spot for kids—and so did Adam.

"Best example is 2008. The shoes."

On July 13, 2008, U.S. Army soldiers based at a remote command outpost near the village of Wanat in Nuristan Province, Afghanistan, were surrounded and attacked by an estimated two hundred Taliban insurgents. Nine Americans were killed and twenty-seven wounded in what became known as the Battle of Wanat.

Days later Navy admiral Mike Mullen, chairman of the Joint Chiefs of Staff, spoke to the media, saying that "all involved with operations on the [Pakistan-Afghanistan] border must do a better job of policing the region and eliminating the extremists' safe havens...that are launching pads for attacks on coalition forces."

Three months after the Battle of Wanat, Adam headed to that very same border region, returning to the northern Kunar District where he had targeted extremists on his initial DEVGRU tour in Afghanistan. On Adam's first run up "PT hill," the workout he'd done dozens of times on his previous deployment, a light rain turned to hail near the summit, painting the trail white. A few weeks later, snow flurries announced that winter was coming.

In Virginia Beach the weather was pleasant. Nathan and Savannah were at school, and Kelley was about to head out on a shopping excursion to put together a Thanksgiving care package for Adam when he called, a rarity—generally they e-mailed every few days. She asked Adam what he'd like in the package, but he replied that he needed nothing for himself. "Could you just grab some shoes for the kids here?" he asked. "Smaller sizes, they're little kids. Some shoes and some socks. Instead of anything for me, just mail those."

Adam called Janice and Larry and told them the same thing. Says Kelley, "He'd see the Afghan children walking around barefoot or in flip-flops, and it was starting to snow. He'd say, 'I can't stand it. It makes me think of our kids. It's almost winter, and I haven't seen them wearing anything but sandals. They have got to be freezing.'"

Kelley purchased twenty pairs of shoes from Target; Janice bought another twenty. Both women shared the request with their respective church congregations, who promised more donations.

In the Kunar, the early winter months were accompanied by rocket and mortar attacks that pounded the outstations. This unusually heavy enemy activity—generally reserved for the insurgents' spring offensive—punctuated the ever-present danger of an ambush or an attack.

Says a Green Beret who worked with Adam during the deployment, "Here we are, packing extra ammo and grenades when we went outside the wire, and Adam was stuffing his ruck with shoes, knocking on doors in the villages, keeping track of their sizes on a notepad and telling them all that more were on the way. He's got his weapon slung and he's on his knees in the dirt, helping kids who have never tied a shoe in their life. This is a war zone, and he's passing out shoes."

Ultimately, Adam would distribute over five hundred pairs of shoes (and socks) to the children of Kunar Province.

A decade before, when Adam had shown up at Jeff Buschmann's apartment in Corpus Christi, Jeff would not have believed that his drug-addicted best friend could ever rise to the top of what he considered the most elite fighting force in the world. He also wouldn't have believed that two kids from Hot Springs, Arkansas, would randomly end up at the same remote outpost in the Hindu Kush mountains at Christmastime.

Although Adam had stayed in touch with his friends from Hot Springs by e-mail and phone, he'd missed the Lake Hamilton High School ten-year reunion and it had been years since he and Jeff had seen each other face to face. In early December 2008, Jeff received an assignment to conduct classified intelligence work at an outstation in Kunar Province. He looked at the name of his point of contact and was amazed to see that it was Adam Brown.

Jeff, a lieutenant commander in the Navy, had graduated from flight school near the top of his class, but decided—in part because of Adam's involvement—to also go the Naval Special Warfare route. He did his

Brown family archives

Adam provided the children of Kunar Province, Afghanistan,
with warm socks and winter-worthy shoes during this deployment.

stint in the fleet as a surface warfare officer, then transferred to Special Boat Team TWENTY-TWO as a Special Warfare Combatant-Craft Crewmen (SWCC) before attending Naval Special Warfare post-graduate school and Naval Intelligence School.

In his role as intelligence officer, Jeff arrived in Kunar and spent the week before Christmas tracking a senior al Qaeda agent who had recently popped up on the local radar. His old buddy Adam accompanied him outside the wire, the two riding their ATVs to outlying villages, meeting with locals, verifying reports, and conducting other classified intelligence activities. "When I was with Adam, no matter what we were doing, I always felt completely safe," says Jeff. "He never told me he was worried about me, but I knew he was. He would always double-check my gear, and he would go over anything he thought was important to my safety, so thoroughly you would have thought he was kidding."

On Christmas Eve Jeff pulled out a DVD of the Arkansas High School State Championship—won three weeks earlier by the Lake Hamilton Wolves—that he'd received from a coach. He and Adam had a beer, watched the game, and talked about old times.

"Remember when Richard's dad paddled our rears in front of the cops?" Adam said.

"I'd forgotten that!" Jeff replied with a chuckle. "That wasn't too bright, was it?"

On the drive to school that day in 1990, the boys had pointed wooden rifles, props for a school play, out their windows at pedestrians, drivers, essentially anything that moved. As soon as Jeff and Adam entered the school, Principal Williams called them to his office, where two sheriff's deputies, who had responded to numerous complaints about the two punks pointing guns at people, waited.

"I know both their fathers," Principal Williams told the deputies, doing his best to keep the boys out of big trouble. "How about you watch me beat their asses? Will that suffice as punishment?"

Both Jeff and Adam remembered the look on one of the deputy's faces when he grinned and said, "Yeah, let's do that." And they could still feel the sting on their rears as they endured Principal Williams's wooden paddle.

While both men laughed at the memory, Jeff reflected on how, for Adam, this had been only a temporary reprieve from the Garland County jail. He felt fortunate to have witnessed his friend's rise from darkness to the top tier of the American military, where he performed a crucial job. Jeff was proud of Adam, thought he was an inspiration, and loved him like a brother, but he didn't have to say any of that. "Adam always knew what I was thinking," says Jeff. "We didn't need words."

Christmas morning was celebrated with a run to the top of PT hill, where Adam and Jeff posed for photos while holding American and Arkansas flags. "It was cold, but dry—no snow. We did some target practice and worked out with weights later in the day," remembers Jeff. "Adam talked about how much he loved the seasons back home, how pleasant the woods are in the fall and how he'd rather just go for a run on an old logging road or trail than be cooped up in a gym."

Christmas morning in Hot Springs "just wasn't the same without Adam," says Janice, "even though we felt blessed that Kelley and the kids and Shawn and Manda's families were all here. We knew we'd been lucky all these years Adam had been home for Christmas; guess we got spoiled. Plus I was always worried when he deployed. He'd tell me, 'Mom, we are so well trained.' But I knew he was at some remote location just like the one we'd heard about on the news that had gotten overrun. So yeah, I was worried. And a little sad."

Jeff Buschmann and Adam flying their state colors at an observation post a stone's throw from the Pakistan border.

Brown family archives

Once all the grandchildren had opened their stockings, Larry read aloud the e-mail he'd received from Adam that morning. The subject was "Family."

I just wanted to say Merry Christmas!

The week we come home to Arkansas in December is the week I live for every year. It is my favorite time of the year and my favorite thing to do. I love getting to hang out with all of you and I never take a day of it for granted. I can feel how cold it is there right now and I can picture the view [of] the lake and the 70 West bridge and the hills behind it. I can picture Shawn looking miserable, wondering when will it ever end, Dad reading something real boring, and my ears hurt from how loud the TV is right now. I am sure Reese and Luke are both plotting something against the other, and Josie and Maddy have something ridiculously cute on right now. I love that my kids are there getting to see what the America that I believe in is all about, it's YOU.

How blessed we are to have what we have. I hope everyone realizes how fortunate our large united family is. Meeting the hundreds of people I meet reminds me of it all the time. Don't be sad for me this time of the year because you are all right here with me, you are the people I believe in, the ones I look up to, and you guys are never far away.

I love you all,

Adam

When Adam returned home in February 2009, he was in excruciating pain. "He had been getting these little blisters on his eye for about a year," says Kelley. "It was like it was boiling from the pressure. They'd pop up and then rupture, and it hurt so bad it would knock him down for a couple of days."

The condition was bullous keratopathy, a swelling and blistering of the cornea, and the dry air of the Afghan mountains had compounded what had already been diagnosed as a "severe case." The cells of Adam's cornea could not maintain the fluid balance, causing the cornea to retain water and bulge, pushing against the eyelid. Blinking and movement created blisters that burst.

Adam could have returned from his deployment at any time, says Kelley, "but the man would just not quit. When his leg was broken and his eye would blister up, he'd limp around, and I'd ask, 'How's your eye?' and he'd say, 'It's keeping my mind off my leg.'"

Because of the severe trauma from the paint bullet five and a half years earlier, the doctor told Adam he wasn't a candidate for a corneal transplant. The only option was lubricating the eye and controlling the swelling with drops. "Or," said the doctor, "we can remove your eye."

With less than two years remaining in his contract, Adam was thinking seriously about leaving the Navy but kept it under wraps to everyone except his closest friends and Kelley. "Talking about retiring and actually retiring are two totally different things," says Christian, who advised Adam to really consider the decision. "You don't want to hang up your guns too early," he told him.

Given Adam's service-related injuries and nearly eleven years of service, a medical retirement with disability benefits would have provided him with a nice package at any time; he didn't even have to wait for his contract to be up. "Adam would still not consider it," says Kelley. "He was going to push through his commitment, through 2010. He said they had trained him to do a job and he wasn't going to do it halfway. He was going to finish and retire with an honorable discharge."

Between his last deployment and the next one scheduled for the beginning of 2010, Adam added another commitment to his already full plate: college. Determined to earn his bachelor's degree, he began taking one course a month in an online university program, with the long-term goal of attending business school. He would not let this new commitment interfere with family or work. "He barely slept," says Kelley. "I'd wake up and he'd have snuck out of bed after I fell asleep and be at our desk in the bedroom, working on a paper or studying for a test, a crumpled-up Kleenex where he was dabbing his eye because it never stopped watering.

"He wanted to get an MBA," she says. "And I didn't doubt it. He had conquered his drug addiction—my Adam did not fail. You know where he was going to go? He didn't say he was going to *apply*; he said he was going to *go* to Harvard. Case closed."

———

Adam's eye was surgically removed on July 27, 2009. In simplified terms, it was scooped out and the muscles were left intact for use with a prosthetic eye. As with his hand, the two-plus-month healing process was slow, painful, and "disgusting," says Kelley, who had a difficult time placing the prescribed drops into his empty eye socket.

Though he suffered a life-threatening post-op complication—a medication-induced drop in blood pressure that landed him in the hospital—a week following the surgery, Adam was back to studying for his college courses. Now, however, instead of tears he had to dab at the bloody fluid draining from the socket.

After two months he was fitted with a prosthetic eye. Outwardly, Adam made light of it, joking with Nathan and Savannah by holding it in his hand and "peeking" in their rooms, saying, "You'd better be good—I've got my eye on you." But "quietly, he was insecure," says Kelley. "He'd look in the mirror a lot and always asked me if it looked okay. If it was daytime, he wore sunglasses and not always for the sun."

Indeed, the first eye Adam was fitted with "looked like they'd colored it with crayon," she says. "I went down there and had them make him another one we were both happy with."

Shortly after Adam had gotten his new eye, he and Kelley were teaching the second-grade Sunday school class when a boy said, "Mr. Adam, are you looking at me? Because your eye is not."

"He can take it out," seven-year-old Savannah piped up proudly.

"Really?" another boy asked. "You can take that thing out?"

"Sure," Savannah answered. "It's so cool. He can take it out and he can spin it all around."

"You want me to do it?" asked Adam.

"No!" Kelley jumped in. She walked Adam away from the children and "straightened" his eye with her finger so that it was tracking properly. Then she firmly whispered, "Do *not* take your eye out—you'll traumatize these kids."

The chanting began: "Take it out! Take it out! Take it out!"

"It was hilarious," says Kelley. "One of Adam's biggest concerns about getting the eye removed was that it might freak the kids out, and here it was, a novelty. But I didn't let him take it out, not without their parents' permission."

As 2009 played out, Adam knocked off college course after college course, racing against the clock before his next—what he planned to be his final—deployment in February 2010. Yet he still managed to volunteer as a coach for ten-year-old Nathan's football season. "I loved it," says Nathan. "Best coach ever. He taught us to do things we didn't think we could. I like that. And if we complained because we had to run around the goalpost, he'd run with us, and when he got there he jumped up and did pull-ups. My other coaches would watch us run; my daddy ran *with* us."

History repeated itself that fall when Jeff transferred to a local Naval base in Virginia, and Adam, in addition to insisting that Jeff stay at his home, proceeded to introduce "Busch" to his SEAL buddies. Adam made it a point to brag about Jeff as he recounted stories from their youth. "Making me feel good about myself," says Jeff, "which showed me Adam had not changed in all those years. He was still the same humble kid who knew it was important to be nice to people."

One afternoon Adam received special clearance to bring Jeff along when he went to DEVGRU's shooting range to test out some experimental weapons. After shooting a box of ammo, Adam turned to the attendant and said, "Hey, you want to try this gun?" The attendant was taken aback by the unusual request. "Most of these guys work hard and it goes unnoticed," says Jeff, "but Adam, being who he was, insisted the attendant shoot an entire box of ammo, and we all had a blast."

Respect for others—no matter their rank or social standing—was a theme throughout Adam's life. When fellow SEAL Brian Bill first joined DEVGRU, he was tasked with a new-guy job of emptying the trash cans around the squadron's team room. "Let me get that," Adam told him at one point, taking the can from Brian.

"At first I thought, okay, this guy is messing with me," says Brian. "He's gonna take the trash can and turn it upside down and ask me why I dumped all the trash on the floor. It was *that* weird to have a senior guy like Adam helping a new guy with the trash. But Adam never degraded the new guys—he mentored them. He mentored me."

Two days before Christmas 2009, the Browns hit the road for Hot Springs, driving through a massive snowstorm on the way. They stopped off at a restaurant with Internet service long enough for Adam to fire off a final college paper that Kelley had proofread in the car. Adam was only two classes away from his bachelor's degree, and with two months left before his deployment, it looked as if he would reach his goal.

The family of four arrived at Janice and Larry's home on Christmas Eve, Adam decked out in his finest attire: tight black pants and an even tighter white V-neck polyester sweater covering a black dickey. Complete with hair slicked back and holding a glass shaped like a moose head, he had become Cousin Eddie from National Lampoon's *Christmas Vacation*.

He rapped loudly on the door before heading inside to the living room, where he announced to Janice, Larry, Shawn, and Manda, "You surprised to see us, Clark?"

"Oh, Eddie," Manda and Shawn recited in unison the next line from the movie they'd all watched together every Christmas for over a decade, "if I woke up tomorrow with my head sewn to the carpet, I wouldn't be more surprised than I am now!"

"The house was full of laughter," says Janice. "Everything was perfect, with *our* kids, and *their* kids, and the laughter, and the stories. I remember thinking how blessed we were as a family. Adam was heading to Afghanistan soon, and he'd told me, as he'd told me before, 'Momma, don't worry. We are so well trained, we just go in and do our job, and come out...'

"I don't like to think about that, though. I'd rather just think of that Christmas."

17

Objective Lake James

I<small>T WAS</small> F<small>EBRUARY</small> 5, 2010, and Nathan and Savannah were giggling as Adam blew out all thirty-six candles on his favorite cake, cookies and cream. "What are y'all laughing at?" he asked, grinning, and they pushed a present in front of him.

Soon Adam was laughing too at the adult-size black-and-yellow Batman briefs he'd unwrapped. Pulling them on over his pants, he paraded around the kitchen, striking superhero poses. "I love them," he said, which made Kelley and the kids laugh even harder.

"I'm serious." He got down face to face with Nathan and Savannah. "I'm going to make y'all a promise: I promise these are going to be my undercover underwear. I'm going to wear them on every op I go out on, and"—he lowered his voice to a whisper—"nobody will ever know my superhero capabilities. The bad guys will never know it's really Batman showing up."

"You dork," said Kelley, and the kids cracked up again.

"They were just eating it up," she says. "Daddy's job wasn't real back then. They knew Navy SEALs killed pirates because it had been on the news, and they knew they hunted bad guys—but it was like make-believe."

"Really, Daddy?" Savannah said. "You'll wear them?"

"I will," said Adam. "I promise."

Adam promised Nathan and Savannah he would wear this
superhero underwear they gave him on every mission.

—

On February 26, Kelley and Adam dropped Nathan and Savannah at
school, then drove around town picking up last-minute odds and ends for
his deployment—which included an encyclopedia-size study guide for the
GMAT exam, the initial step toward gaining acceptance into Harvard's
MBA program. In spite of a hectic training and pre-deployment schedule,
Adam had earned his bachelor's degree.

At noon they lunched with the kids in the school cafeteria and Adam
shot hoops with them on the playground. After school let out, the family
headed to Adam's choice of Chili's and his favorite queso dip appetizer.

Kelley watched Nathan's and Savannah's little hands digging into
the chips alongside their daddy's, all three laughing as they jockeyed for
the biggest chips. If Adam landed on one, he would immediately turn it
over to Savannah. Though savoring this sweet moment of family life,
Kelley picked at her own food. She had no appetite.

From dinner they went straight to the base, where Adam flashed his ID, still in the Wal-Mart badge holder. They drove through the main gate, then along the familiar tree-lined stretch of woods. They skirted the chain-link fences, the manicured lawns, and a system of interior gates and finally stopped alongside a curb where a few other families were saying their good-byes, respectfully distanced from each other. While Adam piled his gear on the sidewalk, Nathan and Savannah—even as they tried mightily to be strong—began to cry.

Adam picked Nathan up first, and Kelley remembered vividly those first deployments when Nathan was so small; now his legs were long and lanky. He sobbed on his daddy's shoulder, and Adam closed his eyes and squeezed him tight. Then he pulled back and looked Nathan in the eye. "This is the last time, buddy," he said, a tear trickling down his cheek. "Last time."

When Adam turned to Savannah and lifted her into a hug, he knew she could see his tears. "Bye, Little Baby, it's all fine," he said to reassure her. He held her for a long time, gave her a big daddy squeeze, and pushed her nose as he set her down.

"Beeeep," she responded instantly.

"I love you, Little Baby," he said and walked over to Kelley, who held his face in her hands.

"You come home," she said.

"I promise," Adam replied, and they kissed—long and sweet and perfect. "But different," says Kelley. "I can't explain; it was just different than the other times." The second they pulled apart, Kelley touched her lips, as if pressing on them would keep Adam's kiss there longer.

"Let's get this done," she said to Adam, attempting to sound strong. "Get home."

Right before Adam carried his gear through the gate into DEVGRU,

Kelley felt compelled to ask the guard to snap a photo of the family together, there in the twilight—something they'd never done before. A
final wave from Adam and he was gone.

Saying good-bye was hard on all the SEALs and their loved ones, but
even more poignant for the family men on the team, the ones with children. Inside DEVGRU's restricted zone, Adam and his teammate Heath
Robinson, also a father, met up with each other, the sadness apparent on
both their faces. Side by side they walked.

"Well, that sucked," said Adam.

"Always does," replied Heath, who slapped Adam's shoulder, then
gave it a squeeze—meant to convey both strength and compassion. It was
time to put their game faces on.

Recently Heath had shared with Adam a conversation he'd had with
a longtime civilian buddy. "How do you do it?" the friend had asked him.
"How do you shoot people, kill people, and then come back home, sometimes just hours later, and hang out with your family?"

"There're a couple of books that discuss this," Heath said to his
friend. "*On Killing* [by Dave Grossman] is a good one. He writes about
cops, and he discusses troops from the Civil War all the way up to now.
He talks about mentally, how different people are able to do their jobs
and how some people can't. Why PTSD is so prominent in some people
and why it's not in others.

"And he talks about the 5 percent, which is Special Operations guys,
and how, clinically, we're all borderline sociopaths. But in *my* mind we're
not the ones that are messed up; it's the other 95 percent of the population. We run *toward* the sound of gunfire. Like the fireman who, when
everybody else is running this way, is running into the flames. A cop,

Brown family archives

Before Adam deployed for his final rotation in Afghanistan,
Kelley asked a gate guard at the base to snap this family photo.

anyone who does that sort of work, is in that 5 percent, that personality that we need to get that job done. And be able to do that job and rationalize it, religiously or country or however you deal with it, say, 'Okay, that was my job, that's why I did that. But now I'm back and I'm fine.'"

Heath's friend replied with a fitting analogy for the SEALs. "His wife and daughter have horses," Heath had told Adam, "and they *love* to ride horses, so that's what they're all about. Nothing makes his wife and his daughter happier. Well, horses take a lot of work, they're dirty animals, so every weekend he puts on his waders, goes out in the barn, and shovels the manure, and the dirty hay, and puts the new hay in, and feeds the horses, and cleans up their piss. It's not a good job. It's miserable, but someone has to shovel the shit so the family can enjoy what they have. That is how he framed it for me. 'You shovel the shit so your family, so the United States, can have what we have and live the way we do.'"

That night when their squadron boarded a nondescript passenger jet heading to Afghanistan, Heath asked Adam, "You got your waders?" To which Adam replied, "Oh yeah. Let's go shovel some."

At the DEVGRU compound in eastern Afghanistan, the day after they arrived on March 1, Adam's squadron began work on operations.

The tempo of missions in Afghanistan was never as high speed as in Iraq, with its more populated areas and flatter landscapes. And it was unlikely that anything in these SEALs' careers would match their rotation in 2008, when they'd obliterated the network of insurgents and IED builders in Iraq with back-to-back nightly raids and sometimes back-to-back raids in a single night.

In Afghanistan the terrain, the intelligence process, and the enemy were extremely complex, requiring more deliberate planning. Since 2008,

DEVGRU's intelligence networks had been tracking a Kunar Taliban leader, code-named Objective Lake James, who "had more blood on his hands than any other Taliban leader in his district," says an Army officer familiar with operations in the Pech River Valley.

The latest attack James had claimed was on February 20, when his fighters killed twenty-nine-year-old U.S. Army Staff Sergeant Michael Cardenaz with a rocket-propelled grenade as Cardenaz was assisting a mortar team setting up security for the Chapa Dara District Center. Recently constructed in the remote province of Chapa Dara, the building was a town hall of sorts housing the local police force, government offices, a medical and veterinary clinic, and other infrastructure services of the national government.

James was doing his best to upset the local attempts at stability, and killing Americans in the process. "He earned himself a high spot on our list of targets," says one of Adam's teammates, "and that didn't mean we thought we'd find intel that led to bin Laden or anything. They weren't all romantic missions for us—few of them were. They were ugly, dirty, hard-fought battles to protect our Army and Marine brothers who were trying to stabilize Afghanistan. We all assumed that bin Laden was living safely in Pakistan and that it would take an act of God to find him and a second act of God to be given the go-ahead to get in there and kill him.

"There are many snakes in Pakistan and Afghanistan, and cutting the heads off of each one is crucial to demolishing enemy forces and their resolve. That was what Objective Lake James was—a snake, and we had to find where his hole was."

Exactly two weeks after he'd kissed his family good-bye, Adam sat on his bed in a small room within the compound studying for the GMAT, his books spread out on the blanket. Taped to every wall were pictures that Nathan and Savannah had drawn.

On the dresser to his right was his laptop, the screensaver a rotating montage of family photos he never tired of watching. The song he was listening to through his headphones made him think of Kelley, and he sent her a quick e-mail to let her know:

> I am so proud, happy and fortunate to have you as my wife. I listen to all these songs, and I realize I have the girl I always dreamed of. I wonder how many people can really say that and mean it. Not many, I reckon. My kids are awesome too. Both of them could not have been drawn out any better in a Disney movie.
>
> Y'all have a good day.
> I love you,
> Adam

Three days later, on March 15, Kelley was about to sit the kids down for a late dinner when her laptop chimed at 6:45 p.m., 3:15 a.m. Afghan time.

"It's Daddy!" she told Nathan and Savannah, who ran to the computer.

Via a Skype live chat, Adam wrote that he had "just got off work" (his third mission) and was going to study for a couple of hours before bed, but wanted to talk to his babies first. Nathan and Savannah took turns typing him messages about school, the books they were reading, the bowling trip they'd taken, a new martial arts class they were in, what they were having for dinner. "I wish I was having taco salad for dinner," replied Adam. "I sure miss you. Y'all being good babies for Mommy?"

"Very good," wrote Savannah, inserting an angel icon. "I miss you sooooooooo much," she added.

"Are you helping Mom out around the house?" Adam asked Nathan. "Doing the little things goes a long way."

After more than twenty minutes, Adam signed off: "I miss you. You are my favorite little girl and boy in the whole wide world."

And then to Kelley he wrote, "It's good to stay involved. I love y'all, and will talk to you soon."

"I love you too," she typed back. "Bye, bye, baby."

March 17. Just after sunrise, the crunch of footsteps on gravel broke the silence within the squadron's compound. A man started laughing.

"Keep dreaming!" Kevin Houston chided Adam as they faced each other alongside the plywood building. "You straight up *suck* at basketball."

Content with talking smack, the two friends had yet to have that one-on-one tournament they'd been threatening for more than a year. For now, they held lacrosse sticks, Kevin tossing a ball in one hand. This time of day they should have been snoring away, but Adam wanted to learn lacrosse from "the master" (according to Kevin), so they had notched a half-hour "playdate" into their schedule for Adam's second lesson.

"Let's go!" Adam said, holding up his stick. Kevin lobbed one over, and Adam caught the ball and hucked it the twenty yards back.

"Hey, ease back," said Kevin, who describes a lacrosse ball as "a cross between a baseball and a hockey puck." Given the right speed it'll do serious damage, and there was Adam, holding the net near his right cheek.

"Wing it at me!"

Now he's a pro, thought Kevin, envisioning the ball accidentally punching out Adam's good eye. "Naw, man," he said, "keep it mellow till you get the hang of it."

"I got it!" said Adam. "Come on, just throw it! Don't be a pansy."

For the next half hour Kevin wouldn't throw the ball as hard as Adam wanted him to, and Adam wouldn't stop calling Kevin a pansy, among other things—right up until their master chief busted them for being awake during a sleep cycle and barked at them to "get some f—ing rest."

Turning in, they slept through most of the day. At three o'clock, teammate John Faas poked his head into Adam's room and found him on his bed, reading.

As his high school's valedictorian and the quarterback of its football team, John "could have done anything he wanted with his life," says Kelley. "But he chose to serve his country, and Adam really respected him for it." The two SEALs were always swapping books and having long talks about history, religion, politics, and war. The rest of their squadron ribbed them endlessly for watching hours of Book TV on deployments and training trips.

"What ya got going there?" John said from the doorway, lifting his chin toward the book.

"*Tender Warrior*," Adam replied and showed John the cover. "You can read it; I'm almost done. Check this out," he said, thumbing backward through the pages. "It was written by Stu Weber, a Vietnam veteran, Special Forces. He became a chaplain." Stopping at a passage, he handed the book to John, who read,

> The Warrior function is…unmistakable in Scripture.… Within the epistles, the mature believing man is often described in militant terms—a warrior equipped to battle mighty enemies and shatter satanic strongholds.
>
> The heart of the Warrior is a protective heart. The Warrior shields, defends, stands between, and guards.… He invests himself in "the energy of self-disciplined, aggressive action."

By Warrior I do not mean one who loves war or draws sadistic
pleasure from fighting or bloodshed. There is a difference
between a warrior and a brute. A warrior is a protector.…
Men stand tallest when they are protecting and defending.

The brotherhood of DEVGRU SEALs.is built upon a foundation of
mutual respect, and just as Adam aspired to what he considered John's
"genius"—academically and as a warrior—John aspired to Adam's ability
to juggle and, in his opinion, master the apparently paradoxical roles of
fierce warrior and loving husband and father. After reading a few more
passages from Weber's book, he realized that the term "tender warrior"
perfectly described Adam.

John handed the book back, then Adam jumped off the bed, stood
tall, and grunted while flexing his arms and chest. Laughing, John shook
his head as Adam swaggered into the hall, flexing again for Brian Bill,
who shielded his eyes from the vision of his fellow SEAL, naked except
for his Batman briefs.

"Man," said Brian, "put some clothes on and make us some coffee."

Inside the small living room central to their hooch—one of numerous small portable buildings that housed the squadron—was a flat-screen
television, couches, and the coveted high-end espresso machine, the one
luxury item Adam brought with him on deployments because he couldn't
stand what he called "drip garbage" coffee. Adam made his usual brew of
rocket fuel and poured cups for John, Brian, and Kevin, then the four
men headed, coffee in hand, to the squadron meeting at 1300 Zulu time,
5:30 p.m. local time.

Before they even made it across the compound, gestures from fellow
SEALs—a nod, a thumbs-up—told them a mission was on the table.
"How far we walking?" Kevin asked when they entered the briefing room.

"It's going to be a long one tonight," replied Tom Ratzlaff, the senior sniper and reconnaissance team leader. "Five hours minimum. Shit terrain."

"Up or down?"

"A lot of both."

The number of SEALs on an assault force executing a direct-action raid varies from mission to mission and remains classified, as do the Special Operations Command (SOCOM) military units sometimes attached to these operations. That said, more than a dozen but fewer than fifty highly trained warriors had gathered to review the available intelligence and study the images and infiltration routes that gave them a semi-clear picture of what they would face that night. In one word: *brutal,* and that didn't even include the enemy target, Objective Lake James.

"It was a classic DEVGRU mission," says one of Adam's teammates. "High-value target in a high-danger environment. American forces had never been to the valley where Objective Lake James was holed up. The whole area was bad guys; we expected zero compliance from anybody. We needed to get in, hit everything real hard and fast, and get out before we encountered too much resistance. If the sun were to come up, we'd be running out of bullets because it would have been us against the entire valley.

"But the risk was well worth it, because this person that we were going after was going to keep on killing our brothers in the Army and whoever else was based at that FOB, using those roads. Our intel told us he was going to attack soon; it was a race against time. Because he had proven to be so effective in his tactics, there was no doubt he would be successful. More Americans would die if we didn't get him."

James's résumé had been scrutinized—he and his fighters were not the type to surrender. "When you get there," a briefing officer informed the assault force, "be ready for a fight."

———

About forty-five minutes into the squadron's meeting, Kelley sent Adam a message on Skype, hoping he was there. "Hi, sweetie," she wrote. When she didn't receive a response within a few minutes, she sighed and set about helping the kids get ready for school. It was Wednesday, Saint Patrick's Day, and both Nathan and Savannah were wearing green. While Savannah chattered on in her usual manner about what the day had in store, Nathan was subdued.

"He was quiet that morning," says Kelley, "which is how Nathan gets when he's sad. I didn't have to ask why; I knew it was because he missed his daddy." What Nathan didn't tell his mother and sister was that he had awakened that morning worrying about his father, a feeling he couldn't shake.

After dropping the kids at school, Kelley spent some time with Michelle, taking an aerobics class, having a smoothie, then shopping for household supplies at Target. "It was Saint Patrick's Day," says Michelle, "and Kelley has never liked the color green, but everything in the store was green that day, and out of the blue she said, 'I think I'm starting to like the color green. I'm going to start embracing the color green from now on.'

"Okay," said Michelle. "You do that."

Soon after night fell, the assault force was driven to the tarmac, where double-rotor MH-47 helicopters awaited. Their crews performed the final flight checks as the men loaded their gear and piled in for the "commute" to work.

In the lead helicopter, Tom Ratzlaff and his sniper team settled into their seats. On liftoff he silently recited his usual prayer when heading into someplace hot: *Our Father in heaven, hallowed be Your name. Your*

Brown family archives

While his teammates wore double-eyepiece night-vision goggles, Adam was easily identifiable as the lone operator with a mono lens. He is shown here post-raid during a mission in an undisclosed location.

kingdom come. Your will be done on earth as it is in heaven... He followed the Lord's Prayer with, *Lord, take care of my wife and kids, protect them and watch over them. Protect my buddies and forgive them of all their sins and me of all my sins. Amen.*

Then it was game on. As with the rest of the team, Tom focused completely on the operation, mentally reviewing the enemy-occupied terrain they were infiltrating. He and his fellow snipers had helped choose the landing zone and mapped out the route over which they would lead their teammates through the mountains to Objective Lake James. Once on target, the snipers' job would be to position themselves so they had eyes on the SEALs that would be assaulting the target, to cover their brothers and put a bullet through the head or chest of any enemy presenting a threat.

Tom never prayed for protection for himself; he considered that God's decision. Instead, he devoted his body and soul to protecting the team. In his role as overwatch, Tom had never lost a man.

In the Hindu Kush mountains, the helicopters hugged the terrain, flying low and fast along a steep ridgeline. Kevin, who was in the second MH-47, felt the helicopter slowing down. The engines' pitch changed while the helicopter banked and descended into the mouth of a small side canyon.

Out the window to Kevin's right, only a granite ridgeline was visible; it was nearly vertical at the top and spilled downward into a steep and rocky slope. Taking in the greenish night-vision hues of the landscape, he leaned toward the window for a better look but could see only treetops— a dark swath of evergreen forest concentrated in the deepest recesses of this narrowing chasm. To the sides and above the helicopter, the jagged slopes appeared to squeeze in on the spinning rotors that labored to keep the machine airborne and steady. The pilots held their altitude, hovering as they searched for a suitable opening to land these dual-rotor beasts.

Gnarly, thought Kevin. Hands down, this was the most hellacious landing zone he'd encountered in his entire career. *Nobody in his right mind would fly a helicopter into this ravine,* he thought—exactly *why* it had been chosen as their LZ. The elite pilots of the 160th Special Operations Aviation Regiment could fly and "park" these "buses" like sports cars just about anywhere.

Generally, these types of infiltration happen in seconds, but on this night the pilots circled back up and out of the gorge and came in a second time. Finally, the message came over radio headsets: "We're roping in."

As the SEALs led the assault force by sliding down ninety-foot "fast ropes" into the enemy's backyard, Chris Campbell slammed into a boulder the size of a van. From the boulder he bounced against a slope that he estimated at sixty degrees. Sliding on his rear in the loose granite, he hustled to get out of the way before the next guy landed on top of him. Dust from the rotor wash gave the scene a misty, sinister appearance through his night-vision goggles.

Minutes later the MH-47s disappeared, and the assault force made its way down into the forest, which was nourished by a creek that tumbled through the gorge. Though the area had been thoroughly scouted from above, Chris could see that being in the bottom of the ravine, with high ground above them, was a no-win situation if an enemy machine gun emplacement had been overlooked. They would be cut to ribbons.

The sniper team led the way through the rocky, wooded chaos, followed by the assault force that included a small contingent of Afghan Special Forces soldiers with an interpreter, and two groups of American light infantrymen who would take up blocking positions as the SEALs carried out their raid. Two of the infantrymen had hit the ground so hard roping in that they'd broken their night-vision goggles. Hobbled but determined, they had no choice but to buddy walk, virtually blind, over the brutal terrain.

After a couple of hours spent negotiating cliffs, traversing avalanche paths, and fording rivers and streams, the Afghans—renowned for being both hearty and nimble in their mountainous element—could not keep up the pace. The interpreter, the strongest Afghan, later described the SEALs and their American military counterparts as "machines." "They would not stop," he said.

The inclusion of these Afghan troops, their physical endurance aside, was a political partnership that none of the SEALs were particularly happy about. While the SEALs carried around fifty or sixty pounds, they'd made sure the Afghan loads topped out at thirty. At one point Adam shouldered an Afghan's rucksack on top of his own load, giving the man a half-hour breather while the line moved forward. At three hours, the same man lay down on the ground and moaned that he couldn't go on. Adam picked him up and pushed him down the goat path. At four hours, the man slipped, falling thirty yards down a steep granite face, and Adam hurried down to him with the interpreter.

"Look," Adam said forcefully. "You gotta man up; there's no other way out of here. When the sun comes up, we're either going to get swarmed by enemy or we'll be gone. The only way out is down this valley and through the target. So get up or we're going to leave you right here."

About three-quarters of the way to the objective, after the assault force's route merged into a man-made trail, a dog began to bark ferociously from a small enclave of rock-and-timber huts that air reconnaissance had missed. When an unarmed man wearing a *shalwar kameez* appeared in a doorway, a contingent of SEALs stopped to speak to him and search the premises. They found tools, cooking utensils, clothing, and bedding—no radios or weapons—but they informed the Afghan that he and his family of seven were being watched, and instructed him to keep everyone inside their homes until after sunrise. If they did not follow these instructions explicitly, they would be killed.

The doors to the rest of the huts were closed up tight, not a sound heard from within, and the SEALs continued toward Objective Lake James.

At the rally point, a few hundred yards outside the mountain hamlet where the target resided, the sniper team radioed back its status. There was no time to rest. It had taken over two hours longer than expected to reach the area, and morning was fast approaching. As soon as the rest of the assault force began to arrive, the snipers moved forward to recon the village.

Along with women, children, and the elderly, every single building Tom and his fellow snipers passed likely held the enemy as well. Tom knew they were completely surrounded and outnumbered, but "after eight years of war," he says, "we'd been doing it so much, I felt, 'I've got every advantage in the world on these guys.' I was superconfident."

Adding to that confidence, there was no smell from cooking fires and the "eyes in the sky"—intelligence, surveillance, and reconnaissance (ISR)—reported thermal images of people sleeping throughout the valley and almost no movement. From thousands of feet overhead, every SEAL on the ground was immediately informed when an Afghan male stepped outside a hut to urinate, then quickly went back inside. Without night-vision goggles, the world was black, and in the blackness the SEALs found comfort.

It had taken over six hours for the final remnants of the assault force—the Afghans, prodded by Adam the entire way—to reach the objective rally point. This was late, but not late enough to warrant aborting the mission. No man had completed the journey without numerous falls; one SEAL estimated he'd gone down at least fifteen times, and they were all bloodied, bruised, and fatigued. There was no time to acknowledge any of that, though. The sun would be up in a few hours, and every one of the Americans remembered clearly the intelligence officer's final remark that capped their briefing:

"When you get there, be ready for a fight."

18

I Got It!

"It's hard to describe to somebody who hasn't been in these mountains, and visited these villages, just how badass the Objective Lake James op was," says an Army NCO (noncommissioned officer) who was on a mortar team at one of the forward operating bases that James had been attacking.

"Think of it like they infiltrated a hornet's nest, which is way gnarlier than just kicking it. That whole area was swarming with hard-core Taliban, so they snuck into that valley like it was the entrance to the nest, and they crept past all these hornets who were asleep and went straight for the queen that was James. And then they went ahead and kicked him right in the head, knowing the entire swarm was there on top of them and they still had to get out of the nest. Crazy thing is, these guys were okay with that."

Deep inside the hornet's nest, the assault force moved in staggered formation down the sides of the village's main thoroughfare: a narrow, rutted dirt road. Stone and earthen-walled dwellings built into the face of a rugged mountain flanked their left side. On their right were a few sporadic buildings whose roofs they could literally step onto, as the slope continued dropping off steeply into farming terraces, all the way to the valley floor a quarter mile below.

The road veered left, following the contour of the mountain, and buildings appeared on the opposite side of the valley in more stair-stepping terraces, a sleeping honeycomb of enemy intermixed with the local population. Amid the confluence of crowded structures on the left and descending terraces on the right was James's compound. A bit wider and perhaps twice the length of a basketball court, it was built on its own terrace and surrounded by eight-foot walls. Its western wall—one of the short sides of the rectangular compound—was against the mountain, while the remaining walls jutted out and overlooked the valley.

Spreading out, a primary assault team of SEALs enveloped the compound, including Adam, who moved to the eastern wall. Meanwhile, Heath Robinson topped the southern wall, where the main gate was. From the images he'd reviewed in planning, Heath already knew there were two structures, a residence spanning the western wall and a smaller barn with animal pens at the northeast corner. Now he took a mental snapshot of the inside of the compound: the number of doors and windows, a tree in the center of the large courtyard, and a porch—inset into the residence—on which two men were asleep.

As the SEAL assault team moved closer, one of the men on the porch abruptly sat up and scanned the darkness. Then "he picked up his AK," says Heath. "He heard something, and then he pointed his gun at me. And I was only thirty feet away. Besides the AK, there were some other identifying factors that told me, without a doubt, this was a Taliban fighter. And by the way he handled his weapon, he knew what he was doing."

Because the stars on this clear, cold night offered, at best, shadowy definition for the naked eye, the SEALs were concealed by darkness as they peered into the courtyard. From atop the wall Heath read the fighter's body language, and when the man—whom Heath was all but certain was James—moved his finger onto the trigger, "that's when I pulled the trigger, because I wasn't going to take the chance." Heath's suppressed shot was a *click* no louder than a staple gun, and the fighter dropped instantly.

The other man immediately rose up, spraying bullets with his AK-47 out into the night. Positioned on high ground beyond the northwest corner of the compound, Tom monitored the situation through his rifle's scope. *Okay,* he thought, *that woke up the neighbors.*

The second fighter dropped as quickly as he had risen. More gunfire followed as another man ran into the courtyard, firing toward the gate and compound walls. At least three SEALs, including Tom, simultaneously took him out: three of the enemy were now dead, within ten seconds. A moment of complete silence followed; the smell of gunpowder hung in the air.

Two doors on opposite sides of the porch flew open and people ran out of the residence, screaming. Holding their fire, the SEALs, communicating via radio headsets, reported five women and five young children. Three of the children huddled on the porch, bathed in the dim glow of a kerosene lantern or candle inside one of the rooms. The other two followed the women as they moved in a group to a dead fighter, crying out frantically, throwing up their arms, and wailing—"which we've learned can be part of an act," says Heath, who remained vigilant, his finger poised by the trigger of his rifle.

One woman pulled a military chest rack bulging with ammunition from a body, and the wailing group returned to the porch, where she hid it under some bushes. Says Heath, "You know you're dealing with bad guys when the women are trained to create a diversion to retrieve and then conceal weapons and ammo. It's rehearsed. They're hiding the evidence, and then they tell everybody that these guys were unarmed."

In the same fashion the crying women removed the chest racks from the other two bodies. "It was chaotic," says Tom. "The women were jumping around and the interpreter was doing all he could, shouting out in the local dialect that they were surrounded by coalition forces and to freeze and put their hands up." At that moment a SEAL blew the lock on the gate and swung it open, providing an exit for the women and children as well as any remaining fighters who might surrender.

The women appeared to be lining up per the interpreter's instructions when Heath reported on the radio, "The one in the dark-colored robe just picked up an AK. She's hiding it under her robe." Tom confirmed seeing the same action from his angle, and the assault team leader, Rick Martinez, relayed this to the interpreter, who yelled something along the lines of, "We saw that, lady! Drop the weapon!"

Instead, she pulled the AK-47 out and began to wave it about wildly, endangering numerous concealed SEALs. At least three trained their gun sights on her. "The bad guys have spread the word that we're heartless, mindless killers," says Tom. "We are not. We play by the rules. We had the right to drop her where she stood, but everybody showed restraint."

From eight feet up on the wall, Heath diligently watched the woman's trigger finger as she continued to brandish the weapon. "Drop it!" the interpreter shouted again. "Drop the weapon now or you will be shot."

The children, on the porch and pressed up against the four other women, cried and screamed as the armed woman advanced on the gate, appearing both angry and determined. Machine-gun fire sounded, outside the compound's walls but nearby; from their flanking position, the light infantrymen were firing warning shots ahead of approaching locals, some of whom were armed but had not raised their weapons.

"As all that's going down," says Heath, "a guy with a pistol in his hand comes out of a door on the near side of the porch and crouches behind the kids while he bolts across the porch. I'm tracking him but I can't get a shot—I don't want to shoot the kids. He runs into the door on the far side and slams it shut."

Outside the open gate, four SEALs were against the wall, ready to move in. The armed woman was now only a couple of strides away from the gate, and Heath was going to have to make the decision to shoot her. It was the last thing he wanted to do, but any minute she might charge through the gate and open fire. She was directly below him when he bellowed out in Pashto, praying she would listen, "Drop it! Now!"

Startled, the woman looked up, set the gun on the ground, put her hands over her head, and walked through the gate. She was searched and seated along the wall, then quickly joined by the other women and the children. As Afghan soldiers guarded them, a SEAL asked who lived in the compound, who remained inside, and whether that included any more women and children. He briefly held a red-lens flashlight on each of their faces so they could account for those present.

"They were adamant," says Brian Bill. " 'There is nobody inside the building,' they said. We told them, 'Okay, we are going to blow the building up, but we don't want anyone to get hurt. Do you want to reconsider your answer?'

" 'Nope,' they said. 'Nobody is inside. We are just simple farmers.' "

From inside the residence an unseen shooter, presumably the man who had darted across the porch, began to fire randomly through the windows into the courtyard. At the same time, the assault team began to take what is known as ineffective fire—mostly AK-47, but some light machine gun as well—from buildings both close by and across the valley. "When you hear a bullet whack the wall by your head," says Brian, "you know how *effective* that *ineffective* fire could have been."

It had been confirmed via multiple intelligence sources and surveillance techniques that the men in this compound were James and his Taliban militants. With three fighters dead, it had already been a semi-successful mission, but there was no way for the SEALs to verify that James was among them without exposing themselves to the shooter in the residence. And when asked about James (using the Taliban leader's real name), the women "of course had never heard of him," says Brian.

Now, less than five minutes after the first shots were fired, support aircraft overhead reported movement all over the area. Says Heath, "People knew we were there. Explosions had already gone off; the enemy was starting to wake up and mobilize. We got multiple reports such as 'Okay, you got five to ten personnel maneuvering to the southwest across the valley.'"

But without being able to positively identify whether they were women, children, or armed males, "our air assets could not engage them," says Matt Mason.

The precariousness of the situation escalated by the minute, with some of the assault force pinned down by increasingly steady fire coming from virtually all directions, yet the primary SEAL assault team remained calm and focused on the shooter inside the residence. They were "working the problem," methodically rooting the snake out of its hole.

"We were being flanked, maybe even surrounded. It was a bad situation," says Heath. "And our scale for what is a bad situation is significantly different from normal people's. A bad situation for us is catastrophic for most people. So yeah, it was not a good place to be in."

At three o'clock local time, Adam caught a glimpse of the shooter through a window of the residence and confirmed his location: "I got a shooter moving in building one, window one," he reported.

"Can anybody get a grenade in there?" Rick asked.

"There's no way," said Heath, "too much exposure." No SEAL was positioned close enough to throw a hand grenade through the window without becoming fully exposed to the shooters. "A forty-mike might work," Heath added, referring to a 40mm grenade fired from a grenade launcher.

"I got it," was Adam's immediate response.

Of course you do, thought Kevin, hearing Adam's words through his headset as he repositioned himself beyond the compound's northern wall. "Adam was Mr. 'I Got It,'" he says. "It didn't matter what it was. Nobody knows what was going on in his mind, but I was thinking, this target is going to shit, guys are pinned down, and we still have a long walk to a helicopter, so let's get this Taliban, let's get his ass out of the gene pool and go home before we see what this place looks like in the daylight."

Still positioned along the south side of the compound, Heath watched Adam top the east wall, swing a leg over, and scan the now-quiet courtyard. From Adam's perspective, the interior to his left was bare ground all the way down the long wall to the gate, then the residence with the shooter in it beyond that. To his right were the animal pens, shaded by a thatched roof and backed by the small barn. In the center of the courtyard and in front of Adam, the branches of a barren tree blocked his view of the window where the shooter was.

A rock wall about four feet tall extended from the compound's outer east wall inward toward the tree, whose branches Adam would aim through. Lowering himself onto this foot-wide catwalk, he began to inch forward, the stubby 40mm grenade launcher in his hand, his carbine slung across his chest.

It had been about ten minutes since the assault began.

Halfway to the tree, Adam paused and aimed the grenade launcher through the branches, but was apparently unable to get a clear shot and continued forward. Not more than fifteen feet away, Kraig Vickers, an

EOD, was on the roof of the barn. A burst of gunfire echoed from within the courtyard. "Where's that coming from?" Kraig said urgently into his headset.

A longer burst of AK-47 fire erupted, and sparks flew from bullets raking the wall Heath was behind. He instinctively ducked down as small rocks and debris showered his helmet and shoulders. Noticing the sparks, Kraig called out to Adam, "Get down! They're shooting at you!"

An instant later, Adam cried out in pain.

Looking over the wall, Heath saw Adam—who had fallen when he was shot through both of his lower legs—lying on his back on top of the shorter rock wall, tangled in the branches of the tree. "Roll off the wall, Adam!" Heath spoke urgently into his radio. "Roll off the wall!"

Struggling to free himself from the tree, Adam waved his arm toward the barn. "They're over there," he grunted angrily. "In there." At that moment, this newly identified shooter sprayed the tree and wall with a long volley of bullets, many of them hitting Adam's exposed left side between his armor plates. Only then did Adam speak the code word that signaled an American was down.

The other shooter in the residence started up again, turning the courtyard into a deadly crossfire of bullets.

The SEALs were trained for the worst-case scenario, and it didn't get much worse than this. They were deep within the hornet's nest, facing at least two barricaded fighters shooting from opposite ends of a compound, with a severely wounded teammate fully exposed between them.

"Let's go get him! We gotta go, we gotta go, we gotta go!" Brian said urgently, peering around the open gate. As Rick formulated a split-second plan, Heath stood atop the southern wall and poured cover fire over Adam and into the barn's door and windows. Kraig ran across the barn's flat roof and leaned over the edge, first firing his weapon down at the well-barricaded shooter, then taking out a grenade.

Both of his hands were on the grenade ready to pull out its pin when there was another burst of AK-47 gunfire, this time directed not at Adam but through the roof at Kraig. A bullet struck Kraig's wrist, forcing him to his knees and knocking the grenade out of his hands—just as five of Adam's teammates stormed through the compound gate.

Seeing Kraig go down, Kevin jumped up on the roof and helped him into the alley north of the compound, then squeezed his wrist to stop the bleeding. "Just give me my aid kit and go!" Kraig said, and Kevin tore around the corner toward the main gate. Immediately, Kraig slapped a pressure bandage on his wrist, bound it tight, climbed back on the barn roof, and pulled out another grenade.

In the courtyard John Faas and Matt Mason went right and Rick went left, all three laying down cover fire into the residence and the barn. Brian Bill and Nick Null ran straight to Adam, who was motionless when they reached under his shoulders and pulled him through the branches and off the wall. They repositioned their grip on his belt and the shoulder straps of his chest rack, lifted some 250 pounds—Adam's weight with the equipment and weapons still slung across his chest—and in a crouch half shuffled, half ran for the gate, Adam's feet dragging on the ground behind.

Kraig moved forward and threw the second grenade through a window of the barn. He waited for the explosion, then swung his weapon over the edge and started shooting downward into the building. In the courtyard Matt gripped Adam's collar while shuffling backward, helping to pull Adam toward the gate as he continued to fire between Nick and Brian at the barn. John, Heath, and Rick pounded both the residence and the barn with gunfire before throwing numerous fragmentation and thermobaric grenades into every window.

At last the enemy gunfire ceased, but searching the buildings and identifying the dead was no longer the priority. Adam was.

Less than one minute after Adam was shot, Brian, Nick, and Matt set him down outside the wall, and Zeke, one of the assault force's medics, frantically went to work pulling off Adam's armor and cutting away his cammies to assess his wounds. Matt unrolled a casualty litter, while Kevin moved the women and children being guarded by the Afghan soldiers farther away from the compound. Nick helped Zeke pack the wounds, and Brian held Adam's hand. "Talk to him," Zeke said to the two SEALs. He slapped Adam's cheek. "Stay with me, Adam!"

There were bullet holes through Adam's legs, along his left side, under his left arm, and in his abdomen. The side angle from which the fighter had shot the AK-47 could not have been more deadly.

The bleeding was severe.

Zeke rolled Adam onto his side, found an exit wound, patched it with a dressing, then felt along every inch he couldn't see to be sure he wasn't missing a bullet hole. Through it all Adam remained conscious but groggy, looking up with tired eyes but never saying a word. As Zeke cut through the rest of Adam's pants, he paused for a moment, as did Nick, Matt, and Brian.

"The world stopped for a few seconds," says Brian, "and we just stared. He was wearing the Batman underwear his kids gave him."

At the Brown residence in Virginia Beach, it was eight in the evening and Kelley was cleaning up the kitchen, Nathan was reading, and Savannah was playing with her stuffed animals when the doorbell rang. "It was dark out," says Kelley, "and my heart kind of stopped. Nobody rings the doorbell at night, and with Adam deployed… So I peeked out and it was my neighbor, bringing over something I'd bought from their kids' fund-raiser."

As Kelley closed the door, the smile of greeting dropped from her face and she put her hand to her chest, thinking, *That hurt. That was scary.*

A half hour later, the kids were in bed and Kelley checked to see if Adam had replied to the e-mail she'd sent earlier that day. He had not. That's when "I got this sick feeling," she says. "Out of the blue I pictured having a funeral for Adam, and I'd never had that happen before. I'd have worries, but never, ever a funeral. It was so sad, and horrible, and I literally shook my head trying to get the thought out of there."

She took a hot shower and cried, then put on one of Adam's T-shirts, checked e-mail again, and got into bed, thinking that maybe her feeling of dread was because "he was unhappy and missing us. That was always the hardest thing for him. I prayed for him right then. I prayed that he was safe and that he wasn't sad—that he would have peace being away from us."

Hurrying out the compound gate, Heath dropped to his knees beside Adam and asked Zeke what he could do to help. Grenades continued to explode in the background as Zeke placed Heath's hand atop a bandage on Adam's side and instructed him, "Push! Hard!"

"I was putting pressure," says Heath, "and looking at Adam, talking to him. I've seen it enough; you can see when somebody's not all there, like it's bad. I saw Brian was holding his hand, and I yelled, 'Adam! Hang in there, buddy!' That's when he looked right at me. He looked at all of us who were there. We've got this red light on so he can see our faces a little, and he says, 'I'm okay. I'm okay.' That's standard Adam—he's good, he's good with it."

—

"I'm okay. I'm okay."

Adam closed his eyes after those words, but no doubt in his heart remained the essence of the letter he'd written to Nathan and Savannah years earlier during his initial combat deployment in Iraq, the first time he'd seen death on the battlefield: "I'm not afraid of anything that might happen to me on this Earth because I know no matter what, nothing can take my spirit from me.... No matter what, my spirit is given to the Lord and I will finally be victorious."

Zeke finished strapping Adam onto the litter and told Matt, who was relaying status on the radio, "Get that 47 spun up! We need to get Adam on a helicopter now!"

The original plan had been to push through the compound and village to the helicopter landing zone farther down the road and just outside the hamlet. But the steadily increasing gunfire meant that reaching the first HLZ was no longer an option, and neither was an immediate onsite pickup; the helicopter was at too great a risk of being shot down.

Instead, the assault force began to follow Tom and his sniper team's directives, away from the compound down to an emergency HLZ below the terraces and almost at the base of the valley. Adam's litter was carried at first by four men, one each at his head, feet, and sides, with Zeke and another medic alternating between helping carry and monitoring Adam. Soon that number increased to eight, four on each side, their body armor a shield surrounding Adam and the extra hands mandatory as muscles began to burn and shake. An AC-130 gunship thousands of feet overhead engaged the enemy that could be positively identified by their weapon fire.

The men moved as quickly as they could down the steep, muddy terraces, shuffling forward maybe twenty yards before setting Adam down so that Zeke could do chest compressions. Then they would pick him up and repeat the process, "a nightmare," according to every man there.

Halfway down the terraces, a light infantryman was shot through the bicep, which led the assault force to believe that the enemy had night-vision capabilities. Those who carried Adam traversed the slope, attempting to distance themselves from the line of fire, only to enter a different line of fire.

At one point during a set of chest compressions, Zeke switched on his red-lens penlight, which was barely discernible to the naked eye but lit up like a circus tent to someone wearing night-vision goggles. Instantly, bullets started whizzing by and sparking off the rocks along the terrace walls a few feet away. "I know you're doing what you need to do," Matt said to Zeke, "but is there any way you can do it without that light on?"

"There were a few times where it was sheer madness," says Brian. "We were getting shot at from so many different directions, you couldn't even tell where it was coming from. And we were smoked."

Every man was on the brink of exhaustion following the six-and-a-half-hour foot patrol and the ongoing battle, but the terraces went on and on, some of them so narrow there was barely room for the men bearing Adam's litter. Kevin found his heels hanging over the edge as they side-stepped, then lost his foothold and released his grip on the litter, falling fifteen feet into an irrigation ditch filled with water. His rifle dug into his thigh, which he had to punch repeatedly to relieve a paralyzing muscle spasm before he could climb back up and limp onward.

Each terrace was a riddle, requiring a new technique to move Adam to the next level. Sometimes that was sliding the litter down an opportune slope adjacent to the terrace; sometimes that was lying prone, then lowering Adam horizontally or vertically to the waiting hands reaching up from ten feet below. The medics performed CPR every minute of the maddening descent.

Only a few hundred yards below, the sniper team had marked the new HLZ, but it took over an hour to carry Adam there. Nearly every

SEAL had done his part to carry, talk to, breathe for, or encourage Adam to hold on, that they were "almost there," that he'd "be home very soon."

"I don't think anybody gave up hope," says Matt. "He'd been through so many injuries. If anybody could pull through, it was Adam."

At the HLZ, a helicopter came out of nowhere, hovering only long enough for the medics and immediate litter team to scramble on board with Adam. They screamed down the valley and over a mountain pass. In less than ten minutes they were at a forward operating base, offloading Adam into the waiting hands of a surgical team.

The remainder of the assault force crowded into a second MH-47 and landed at the FOB soon after the first. Both helicopters' rotors remained spinning at low power while every man on board waited for news. On their helicopter, Heath and John moved away from the others, down to the end of the open ramp, and stood looking out at the light blue hues of morning spanning the eastern horizon.

"We need to be prepared," Heath said quietly. "We need to keep it together and be prepared for what's going to come out of this."

"What do you mean?" John asked.

"Adam's gone, man."

"What? No. I'm not ready for that… You sure?"

"I'm not positive, but it didn't look good to me. I don't see him making it."

Silently, the two SEALs continued to stare at the brightening sky until the grave voice of their master chief came over their radios a few minutes later.

"Adam didn't make it."

A handful of SEALs—some of Adam's closest friends—filed slowly off the helicopter, across the tarmac, and into the trauma center for a private moment with Adam. Afterward, they gathered outside and one by one thanked Zeke, who was sitting on the ground, head in hands. "He was a hero," says Tom. "He fought so hard to keep Adam alive and pretty much collapsed once he got him into surgery. The doc told him, 'If he'd been shot up like this and landed right here on this operating table, we could not have saved him.'"

"So, what happens now?" Rick asked the surgeon, who stood solemnly nearby.

"We'll get him prepared to move, then someone will fly in and take him down to Bagram, where they'll fly him to Germany and then to the States...usually one of the rotation flights that we get in here."

"Well, screw that," said Brian. "Can we just take him right now?"

"That's not protocol," said the surgeon, "but I'm not going to stop you."

"We'll take him," said Rick. "We'll bring him home."

Two hours later Adam was back on the MH-47, flying to the DEVGRU home base, surrounded by his brothers in arms, who planned to give him a proper warrior's send-off.

Staring at the body bag on the floor of the helicopter, Kevin thought only of Kelley, Nathan, and Savannah. *God*, he prayed, *if you're up there, I'm not too happy with you right now, but we'll work that out later. If you're listening, be with Kelley and the kids. They're going to need you.*

19

Unconquerable Soul

KELLEY HAD BEEN BOTH PRAYING and crying at ten thirty (seven the next morning in Afghanistan), the last time she'd looked at the clock before falling asleep.

An hour and a half later, two black Suburbans entered the quiet cul-de-sac, their lights dimming as they pulled to a stop. In the backseat of the vehicle in front, Christian Taylor stared blankly out the window, remembering all the times Adam had invited him over to visit; yet he'd been busy, he'd kept putting it off, and this was the first time he would see their new house. At midnight, Christian, Dave Cain, and a SEAL in dress blues exited the vehicles, and Dave knocked on the front door.

Kelley heard the knocking as if in a dream, but when the doorbell rang she knew. It hit her like a shot of adrenaline. "The sad thoughts, the crying, the vision of a funeral. Adam had been telling me good-bye."

How much it pains me to think about never kissing Kelley's lips, Adam had written in that letter years before, *and not watching my boy excel in life, or giving my little baby girl away in marriage. But don't worry, Kelley, I'll kiss you again someday.*

"He was dying," she says, "and he was telling me, 'I'm leaving, and I'm sad.'"

Outside the door waited a SEAL in uniform, standing between

Christian and Dave, both of whom Kelley knew were on Adam's casualty assistance calls officer (CACO) form. The uniformed SEAL began, "Mrs. Brown, I'm sorry to inform you…" Kelley didn't need to hear any more; the words drove her straight to the floor.

Gently, Christian and Dave helped her up.

"Are you sure?" Kelley sobbed. "Are you sure?"

"Yes," Dave said. "We're sure. I'm very sorry."

When the SEAL finished his mandatory words, Michelle Michaels, who had been called by the notification team and was waiting down the street, ran to Kelley and held her as she cried. "What happened?" Kelley managed to ask through her tears.

"We don't know yet," Dave said.

"But you're sure?" Kelley asked him again.

"I'm so sorry, but yes. We're sure."

"You're sure?" she said again and looked to Christian, who nodded. "I'm so sorry, Kelley," he said.

"Why Adam? Why my Adam?" she asked him.

Says Christian, "My own guilt translated 'Why Adam?' into 'Why not you?' Kelley would never say or imply that, but I was mad it wasn't me. It *should* have been me. I messed up my family, was unfaithful to my wife, and Adam didn't and never would. He would have kept being the great father and husband that he was, not like me. I asked myself why would God take somebody like Adam, who is an example—a moral compass for so many of us—instead of me?"

"I just don't know," he replied.

In an instant of composure, Kelley said, "There's got to be a reason." Then she began to sob again.

———

"Mama?" Nathan said from the top of the stairs. "Are you okay?"

"Hey, buddy, we're just talking with your mom," said Dave. "Why don't you crawl back in bed?"

Quickly Michelle climbed the steps, led Nathan to his room, and sat on the side of the bed as the ten-year-old closed his eyes. But he didn't sleep.

"The minute I saw Daddy's friends there," he says, "they didn't have to tell me what happened. I think God had been telling me all day. I already knew."

On the living room couch, Kelley sobbed for a while longer before asking Dave to bring the children down. Barely awake in Michelle's arms, Savannah started crying as soon as she saw her mother's face, while Nathan walked stoically beside Dave, tears running down his cheeks.

Putting her arms tightly around Nathan and Savannah, Kelley told them softly, "Daddy's not coming home. Daddy's gone to be with Jesus. He's in heaven."

While a small jet carried another notification team from Virginia to Hot Springs to inform Janice and Larry that their son had been killed in action, the MH-47 helicopter with Adam and his teammates on board landed at 9:00 a.m. at the airfield servicing DEVGRU's compound in eastern Afghanistan.

The squadron's entire air and ground support staff were on the tarmac, dozens of uniformed men and women standing at attention and forming an aisle between the ramp of the helicopter and a pickup truck. Members of Adam's assault team, including Rick, Brian, John, and Heath, carried his body to the vehicle and then crowded in around him for the drive to their compound.

Bringing a body bag through the thick layers of security surrounding

their base in Afghanistan was uncharted territory. "We basically comman-
deered Adam's body," says Tom. "It couldn't have been legal—we never
checked. We were going to bring Adam in so we could say good-bye."

But there were no questions, only salutes for Adam as the group passed
through multiple security checks. Inside the squadron's compound, Adam's teammates laid his body on one of the benches that encircled their fire
pit, near an American flag lowered to half-mast. They sat with Adam and
passed around bottles of whiskey, and every once in a while one would
kneel beside his body for a moment alone, saying a good-bye, saying a
prayer. "We know that you are still with us," said Adam's teammate Rob
Reeves. "You will be with us on our next op, and on our next deployment,
and forever."

When it was his turn, Kevin ripped their squadron patch off his
shoulder, set it on the body bag, and pressed it against Adam's chest. "Go
easy, brother," he said.

Larry had started that Thursday morning the way he always did: with
coffee and his Bible. As active as ever with their church, he now also volunteered with the Garland County jail ministry. Almost every Sunday
evening for the past decade, he had walked through steel doors and into
the cell blocks, where inmates called him Preacher Larry—a man whose
son had been behind these same bars and by God's grace had turned his
life around and become a U.S. Navy SEAL.

Someone knocked at the door and Larry closed his Bible, one of
several he and Janice had literally worn out over twelve years of study.
They loved and trusted Jesus with all their hearts, but when Larry opened
the door and saw four SEALs in dress blues, his faith was stretched to the
breaking point.

Oh God, he thought. *You got this wrong. You didn't do right here.*

—

If Adam's teammates were the best-trained warriors, they were also some of the best at providing aid and comfort to the families of the fallen. So, too, were their wives, who immediately began showing up at Kelley's house to help in any way they could.

During that long, terrible first night, Kelley never stopped asking, "Why my Adam?!" Sometimes she screamed as if she were having a nightmare. At one point she searched for a hat, a jacket, anything of Adam's that hadn't been laundered. Finding a ball cap, Kelley held it closely to her face, closed her eyes, and breathed in, almost hyperventilating in the attempt to memorize Adam's scent as Michelle rubbed her back. Then she composed herself and insisted on cleaning the house.

"It made her feel normal," explains Michelle. "We encouraged the kids to do things like watch movies and play video games, and they all just tried to escape reality. It was such a horrible fog, and we were there to help guide them through it." While Kelley washed dishes, Michelle stood beside her and dried them, aware of the sheet of paper on the refrigerator in Adam's handwriting. "Pray for the little girl with cancer." Adam had put it there as a reminder in February after seeing a frail child wearing a surgical mask at their church.

Around sunrise Nathan began to throw pillows around the living room, then toys and books and magazines. He yelled at God and he yelled at the world until Kelley held him and the anger subsided into tears. When he was calm again, he took aside Jeff Buschmann, who had arrived shortly after Michelle, and said, "I need to know something. Did they get the guy who killed my dad?"

Jeff had just gotten word from Christian, who had received the information from Intelligence. "Yes," he was able to tell Nathan definitively. "Your daddy's teammates got him. And then some."

Nathan nodded his head for a few seconds before saying one word: "Good."

Vindicated by confirmation of the death of Objective Lake James, Adam's team loaded back into the helicopters that night and escorted his body from eastern Afghanistan to the military airbase at Bagram, where uniformed servicemen and women, hundreds this time, waited on the tarmac. They stood at attention, flanking the team as they carried the flag-draped coffin into the cavernous hull of the transport plane that would take Adam to Germany, then the United States.

Brian, John, and Kevin remained in the plane to accompany Adam home, while the rest of the men returned to their compound. There they built a roaring fire in the fire pit, and in turn, each committed a piece of Adam's blood-soaked kit to the flames.

"No matter how late Adam came home from a deployment," says Michelle, "Kelley always loaded up the car and met him at the gate. She was determined to meet him this time as well."

Grief stricken, Shawn, Manda, and their families flew to Virginia Beach with Janice and Larry on Friday morning. That evening Janice and Larry joined Kelley, who was escorted by Adam's commander, on a private military jet to Dover Air Force Base in Delaware. For two days Kelley had not slept and had hardly eaten. "She could barely stand," says the commander, "but she found the strength somehow to welcome him home like she always had. These SEAL wives are a dignified bunch, and Kelley Brown showed me that night that she was a warrior in her own right."

Adam returned to Hot Springs on March 23, met by the pallbearers

Brown family archives

At the Hot Springs airport, Adam was carried home
by his friends and teammates.

he'd named in his CACO form: friends from his youth, Jeff Buschmann, Heath Vance, and Sean Merriott; his brother and brother-in-law, Shawn Brown and Jeremy Atkinson; and his SEAL brethren, Dave Cain, Austin Michaels, and Christian Taylor.

Although Christian did not realize it at the time, he had taken the front-right position on the casket, the same position he'd had on their boat team at BUD/S a decade before, opposite Adam's front left. Led by Chaplain Tim Springer, whom Adam had met during his planning for Nate Hardy's funeral in 2008, the men carried Adam from the plane to the waiting hearse, between rows of American flag–bearing Patriot Guard Riders standing at attention behind Kelley, Nathan, Savannah, Larry, Janice, and Manda.

Before the casket was put into the hearse, Chaplain Springer addressed the crowd of hundreds who had known and loved and respected Adam. As Adam had instructed in the event of his death, the chaplain preached the story of the Resurrection, the "one thing," he said, "that gave Adam comfort and hope."

After the chaplain's brief message, the hearse drove through the streets of Hot Springs, whose residents had turned out by the thousands. American flags waved, citizens saluted, and autos respectfully paused at intersections. The billboard at Lake Hamilton High School read in bold letters ADAM BROWN AMERICAN HERO.

Later that afternoon and on into evening, Brian Bill, John Faas, Kevin Houston, Dave, Austin, and Christian escorted the members of the Brown family, guarded Adam's casket, and greeted the public during a viewing that spanned hours. Adam had requested that if killed in combat, he would be buried in his dress blues. His SEAL Trident was prominent on his chest, accompanied by ribbons, medals, and awards his family had no idea he'd received. Missing was the Silver Star still under consideration for his actions the night of his death.

While Nathan and Savannah did not attend the viewing, Kelley carried for them special items to give to their daddy, whom she looked upon sadly but with the absolute clarity that his spirit was gone from his body. She, too, tucked something special into the casket, as well as the one thing Adam had requested—his favorite photograph of his family of four. Shawn included the Arkansas flag he had given Adam the previous year, the one Adam had worn between his body armor and uniform on all his ops.

Once the viewing was over, John shut the door to the room, and the six SEALs stood at attention while Austin took a shiny new Silver Star out of his pocket, pinned it on Adam's uniform, and closed the casket. "It was way out of protocol," says Christian, "but we felt in our hearts that he deserved it."

On March 24, 2010, more than a thousand people crowded into the dimly lit Hot Springs Baptist Church for a celebration of Adam Brown's life. As the last were seated and the family was led to the front row, a song by Tim McGraw broke the silence of the hushed crowd. "If You're Reading This" relays the words from heaven of a soldier who has been killed in combat and contains the refrain,

> And know my soul
> Is where my momma always prayed that it would go.

Two poster-size photographs—Adam kneeling in front of a group of Afghan children, and Adam with Nathan and Savannah—were displayed on either side of his flag-draped casket. Leaning against the podium behind the casket was the wooden paddle SEAL Team TWO had presented Adam four years earlier, "The Ballad of Adam Brown" inscribed on its blade.

Chaplain Springer welcomed those attending, and the service began with a prayer and a reading from a psalm written by King David, a great warrior himself:

> Be merciful to me, O God, for men hotly pursue me;
>> all day long they press their attack.
> My slanderers pursue me all day long;
>> many are attacking me in their pride.
>
> When I am afraid,
>> I will trust in you.
> In God, whose word I praise,
>> in God I trust; I will not be afraid.
>> What can mortal man do to me? (Psalm 56:1–4, NIV)

Then, for nearly two hours, Adam's friends, teammates, and spiritual mentors took their places at the podium to share verses from the ballad that was Adam Brown's life.

Pastor Mike Smith spoke of Adam's dark time and how he had accepted the Lord into his heart while on his knees in the Garland County jail—a shocking revelation to those in the audience who had never heard about those years of struggle. On his CACO form Adam had encouraged people to talk about his drug addiction and what he had put his family through, "probably the most selfless and fearless thing he ever did," says Christian.

Says Austin, "He must have known he'd be a hero if he were killed in action, but he gave the go-ahead to humble himself, to let the world see those skeletons in his closet, to share his testimony."

Pastor Smith was followed by Chaplain Springer, who said that Adam "surrendered only once, and that was to Jesus Christ."

Jeff elicited laughs when he told about some of Adam's stunts and described him as "the wild guy, the crazy guy. But," he added, "I remember his compassion, and how he didn't think about himself, ever." He talked about how Adam had faced the young man with the loaded shotgun the night Jeff was stabbed. "Adam saved my life. He was a hero long before he was a SEAL."

In the eulogy Heath Vance said, "Whether it was a game called wall ball we played as kids or training as a Navy SEAL or being a husband to his wife, a father to his kids, he defined commitment. Adam was not reckless; he was in command of his fears. He never cheated death; he earned life. He was driven in a way few of us can comprehend. To fail at something was acceptable. To fail to *try* was not."

And in his remembrance, John Faas said, "Adam is the hardest man I have ever met. Over the course of his career he sustained more significant injuries than most of us combined, but he just kept on operating.

Adam would not quit, he would not accept defeat. Not ever.

"Adam's devout Christian faith matched his toughness and fearlessness. It was the cornerstone upon which he built his life and the compass that he turned to for guidance. To truly live one's faith, in word and deed, is a mighty, and a daily, struggle; and Adam embraced that struggle and devoted himself to it.

"A couple of days before Adam died, he showed me a passage from one of the books he had brought with him on this deployment, titled *Tender Warrior,* written by a Vietnam veteran who served in the Special Forces: 'A warrior is one who possesses high moral standards and holds to high principles. He is willing to live by them, stand for them, spend himself in them, and, if necessary, die for them.'

"Adam was the rarest and truest of warriors in that he combined fierce and unwavering resolve on the battlefield with deep and genuine compassion off of it." John paused, looking over the vast, hushed crowd, many of them wiping away tears. Christian was sobbing, the first time he'd broken down since Adam died.

"Adam was a protector and a defender, and his individual actions reflect the same purpose that is at the core of the actions of this country; a country that Adam loved dearly. No country has shed more of its own blood for the freedom of other people than America. One need only take a glance at recent history to see the proof of this. America turned the tide in World War II and defeated the murderous regimes of Nazi Germany and Imperialist Japan. America stood watch up on the walls of the Western World for the long years of the Cold War, and ultimately defeated communism, whose menace was responsible for the deaths of untold millions. And who is doing the heavy lifting now, in civilization's current struggle with fundamentalist Islamic jihad? America.

"This fight is every bit as significant as the struggles against the fascism of the Third Reich and the murderous communism of the Soviet

Union. All of these ideologies share a common thread: an utter lack of respect for the dignity of individual human life. And it is precisely that respect for individual human dignity that characterizes our Constitution and our willingness to help those who cannot defend themselves.

"Ultimately this is more than just a fight between America and the Taliban or al Qaeda, just as World War II was more than just the Allies versus the Axis. This is a struggle between the forces that would protect and nourish human dignity and freedom, and those that would destroy it. Adam Brown was a part of that struggle. It is a struggle that is of eternal significance, and Adam's contribution to it is of eternal significance.

"A week ago, on Saint Patrick's Day, Adam's team was given a challenging mission. They were tasked to go into a remote area of Afghanistan that was without American presence. A place that was a sanctuary for the insurgents, a place where they felt safe and beyond the reach of the American military. No one else but members of Adam's team had the skill, fortitude, or audacity to infiltrate this area undetected and engage the enemy in their own backyard. This was exactly the kind of challenge that Adam Brown relished.

"In the fight that followed, Adam acted aggressively and selflessly. He fell protecting his teammates. Adam died a warrior's death. Adam Brown is a hero."

John stopped again. Willing his composure, he took a deep breath and continued. "Adam, we miss you, brother. We miss your goofy grin, your crazy eye, your hilarious stories, and your warm-hearted presence. In the days to come we will miss your untiring work ethic, and your fearlessness under fire. We will aspire to the example that you set for us, and we will tell the young warriors who join us about you and the standard that you set.

"Mr. and Mrs. Brown, on behalf of the men of Adam's team, I want to tell you that your son Adam was a man of the highest caliber, the truest character. Adam lived by his faith and by his principles and he did not compromise, period.

"Kelley, Adam was our brother, and you are our sister. We will support you always, and whatever your need, great or small, we will be there for you.

"Nathan and Savannah, we are your uncles and love you very much. Now, and as you grow older, it will be our honor to share with you the man that your father was, as we knew him: warm-hearted, goofy country boy, rabid Razorbacks fan, patriot, hero, warrior-brother, friend.

"And to Adam's brothers in arms: Today we mourn the passing of our brother and we celebrate his life and the example he set for us. Tomorrow, we avenge him. Today we honor the passing of Adam's unconquerable soul into the eternal glory of Christ Jesus and into the halls of Valhalla; tomorrow, we dispatch the souls of Adam's enemies to the hell that surely awaits them. Tomorrow, we bring that hell to their doorstep.

"Long live the brotherhood."

Adam was buried in a small cemetery bordered by woods and farmland, the funeral a coming together of his past and present, the crowd a checkerboard of starched Navy uniforms and citizens dressed in their Sunday best. In front of the casket, Kevin and Brian had lined up chairs, exactly twenty-four, the number on Adam's high school jersey that had been his favorite ever since. With the family's approval, Kevin and Brian had arranged his military burial, with full honors, for the twenty-fourth day of March.

The three-round volley from the honor guard's rifles got the cows mooing, making Austin smile. *So, Adam,* he thought. *This is Arkansas. It's perfect.*

A wall of men in blue faced the casket throughout the service, until the flag was lifted and ceremoniously folded and Captain Pete Van

The front page of the Browns' hometown newspaper,
the day after Adam's funeral.

Hooser—Adam's commander from SEAL Team FOUR—broke ranks
to present it to Kelley.

Janice and Larry, too, received a flag, then the chaplain closed in
prayer. Upon his final words, Van Hooser removed the golden Trident
from his chest and walked to the casket. He had pinned Adam with his
Trident when Adam was born a SEAL a decade before, and today he
would complete the cycle and pin his casket.

Setting the Trident at the head of the casket, Van Hooser raised his
arm, clenched his fist, and brought it down with a *thud*—driving the pin
into wood. One by one, every SEAL present removed his Trident and
rendered the same honor to his fallen teammate. The only sound was the
Thud! Thud! Thud! as more than fifty Tridents were pounded in.

After the burial, strangers walked up to the SEALs and thanked
them for their service. A woman shook Kevin's hand and asked if he had

been friends with Adam. "One of my best," he replied, then asked the woman how she had known Adam. She told him that Adam had noticed her standing awkwardly by herself at a school function in the ninth grade…and had asked her to dance.

Others reunited—like Richard Williams and Ryan Whited, who hadn't seen each other in more than a decade. Janice and Larry embraced Captain Roger Buschmann, then Larry thanked him for what he'd done for Adam. "We were so worried about you when you vouched for him," he said. "We were worried that we were going to really do you some harm if he messed up."

Now retired, Captain Buschmann said, "You know, Adam thanked me too every time he'd get a promotion. He'd call and say, 'I owe my life to you, sir.' And I told him what I'll tell you both now: bringing Adam in was the best thing I ever did the whole time I was in the Navy."

In fact, Captain Buschmann had second-guessed this very decision when he'd learned of Adam's death. "I don't think *anything's* ever hit me that hard," he says. "But I'm proud I had a part in his life. Adam Brown epitomizes exactly what I would want to be myself and what I would wish for any child. He epitomizes what a real man is. He's honorable, he cares deeply about his family. He's not just a tough guy; he's a gentle giant, no question. He's one of the most unique men I've ever known. If you have a son and your son turns out to be half the person Adam Brown was, warts and all, it's the luckiest day of your life."

If ever a story could come full circle, it was the headstone donated to the Browns by Dick Holden, whose business was making memorial markers and whose thirty-five-year-old son, Richard, was the boy with Down syndrome whom Adam had stood up for in middle school. When Dick told Richard that Adam had gone to be with Jesus, tears ran down his son's face. "I miss him," Richard replied. "I miss Adam Brown."

Once Adam was laid to rest, the entire Brown family headed straight to Virginia Beach for a second, private memorial service on March 26 at the Little Creek Naval Base. There, more of his teammates provided remembrances, including Austin, who recounted the blade incident, and Christian, who explained how Adam had gone from being his competitive nemesis at BUD/S to a best friend.

Standing before a crowd of hundreds, seven-year-old Savannah demonstrated that the fearless gene ran strong in her when she gave her father one final gift. Adam had always loved it when she sang to him, so she did just that, performing an impromptu solo of "Proud to Be an American."

"That was so brave, Little Baby," Kelley told her when she hurried back to her seat.

"I know," said Savannah. "I did it for Daddy."

A little over a week after Adam's death, Kelley asked Larry to drive out to that special property in Hot Springs where she and Adam had stood in the tall grass and envisioned the home they wanted Nathan and Savannah to grow up in. The lot had been sold, but Larry later located the owner; after hearing the circumstances, the man immediately sold it to Kelley for the same price he'd paid.

Kelley, Nathan, and Savannah stayed in Virginia Beach while Larry championed the planning and building of Kelley and Adam's dream home. Though this provided a distraction for everyone, Adam's absence was no less painful.

While Nathan's and Savannah's grief came in waves of despair that would last a couple of days or sometimes a few weeks, they were able to live normally in between, reassuring Kelley that her children would one day be okay. Kelley's grief, however, was constant—and agonizing.

In her darkest moments of despair, she asked God again and again why Adam had been taken instead of her: the survivor's guilt of a military spouse. *He was the fun one,* she thought. *The kids will remember the fun stuff. They are going to remember all that, but I'm not the fun one. We were a partnership and God took the wrong one.* Then she would bury her face in a pillow and sob.

Unable to sleep one night, Kelley was looking through a box of old papers when she found a letter she'd never seen, written in Adam's familiar script at least nine years before:

> I'm lying here about to sleep, and all I can think about is how awesome my life is with you and Nathan, and I was thinking what if something happened to me this week and you never really knew how much I love you, and how I love being married to you, how much I love my life and how awesome it is to be NaNa's father. You are the greatest, purest, sweetest, and most beautiful woman I have ever met, much less I get to be your husband....
>
> Nathan holds a part of my heart that is unexplainable, and that I did not know existed until he came into our lives.... May he always know that the greatest man on Earth is Jesus Christ, may we always show him that. I am so blessed, it makes my blood burn with a completeness and happiness I have never had. You are so precious. Although I miss you so deeply, the Word says, "This is the day the LORD has made; let us rejoice and be glad."...
>
> With Love Through Eternity,
> Adam

As Adam always did in his letters, he added a bit of Scripture.

> 1 Peter 5:10: May the God of all grace, who called us to His eternal glory by Christ Jesus, after you have suffered a while, perfect, establish, strengthen, and settle you.

A calm came over Kelley as she read this postscript, a flood of resolve and renewed faith. She knew at that moment that Adam had intended for her to find the letter when she needed it the most. He had always said that the answer to anything you ever question could be found in the Bible.

Holding the letter against her chest, she thought, *It's Adam, reminding me to hang in there. Reminding me about what's important.*

Four months after Adam was killed, two busloads of SEALs who had been at war and missed the funeral arrived at his grave in Hot Springs. Larry was moved by how many had come to see where Adam was buried, near his grandfather's grave in Adam's beloved home state. "I just knew Adam was smiling down on us," he says.

Larry stood with the SEALs and told them the story of the Resurrection. "I miss my son dearly," he said, "and I know many of you do too. But Adam would have wanted me to tell y'all that there *is* hope, and if you'd like to see him again someday, you just need to invite Jesus into your heart."

Later that summer, seventeen of Adam's friends from DEVGRU headed to Arkansas; some of them, like Brian, Kevin, Austin, and John, had met the Browns at the funeral, and nearly all of them, including Heath, Matt, Kraig, and Tom, had been with Adam the night he died.

They spent a few days in Hot Springs visiting with different members of the Brown family and those from Adam's past. Chris Dunkel invited them to Stubby's for southern barbecue, pointing out the fire pit where Adam had worked. Jeff took them to the high school and Wolf Stadium, and then to Janice and Larry's home, where the SEALs swam in Lake Hamilton, within view of the 70 West bridge.

It was still hot and humid when ten of Adam's teammates, their battle-scarred and tattooed bodies clad in swim trunks, peered down at the deep blue water from the bridge where Adam had made his legendary nighttime leap.

"You sure this is safe?" one of them asked Jeff, who stood with them.

"It's pretty safe," he replied. "Adam would do gainers off it. Look, you don't want to embarrass Adam in his hometown, do you? Don't be a bunch of wussies. You're going to disgrace the whole SEAL community." He grinned.

And so the warriors climbed up on the narrow concrete wall, spread out along it, and with all the Browns watching from the shore, they jumped—for Adam.

Every SEAL from Adam's DEVGRU troop jumped from the 70 West bridge to honor his memory.

Brown family archives

Epilogue

ACROSS THE NATION AND INTO THE FAR REACHES of the World Wide Web, Adam Brown was hailed as a hero, his photograph in newspapers, on websites, on television, and—perhaps most meaningful to his teammates—on the memorial wall of a forward operating base in the Pech River Valley, Kunar Province, Afghanistan.

A week after Adam's death, leadership from the Army battalion based at the FOB, the unit that had been repeatedly attacked by Objective Lake James, requested a picture of Adam to post alongside those of the battalion's own men killed on their yearlong deployment in the Kunar. "We didn't have any more problems from the James gang after March 17," says an officer from that battalion. "Officially, we lost nine men in Kunar, but we always say we lost ten. Adam was our tenth man."

On Friday morning, August 20, 2010—five months after Adam died—the Navy Band, playing the hymn "Eternal Father, Strong to Save," could be heard across the Lake Hamilton school campus. A congressman, a county judge, and representatives from the school district stood before Kelley, Nathan, Savannah, and the rest of the Brown family, who had gathered with a number of other Hot Springs citizens for a dedication ceremony: Old Airport Road, which ran alongside the campus, was being renamed Adam Brown Road.

Adam's old coach, Steve Anderson—now the district's super-intendent—began the dedication by recounting the speech he'd made to students just days after the attacks on September 11, 2001, and followed up with, "When I read those words in 2001, little did I know the price that America would have to pay in the War on Terrorism…that one of Garland County's own sons would pay the ultimate price, that one of my boys, Adam Lee Brown, would sacrifice his own life in a faraway province in Afghanistan."

A couple of months later, Kelley sold their house in Virginia Beach, and Nathan and Savannah became students at Lake Hamilton Elementary School, walking the same halls and playing sports on the same fields as their daddy had two decades earlier.

After dropping them off in the mornings, Kelley would drive to the new home that Larry, Shawn, Jeremy, and other family members and friends had completed for her and the children in just eight months. There was no doorbell on this house—the sound haunted Kelley. Every time she heard one, it jolted her back to that horrible midnight that still seemed like yesterday.

Once inside, she would step into the office and glance down at the wood floor the way she always did. The planks weren't perfect—upon closer examination, the dings and dents were apparent—but every time Kelley saw the mahogany planks, she could almost hear Adam sighing loudly, followed by, "Gall darnit! I cut the dang thing wrong again!" She could almost hear the hammer as he pounded the boards into submission.

These floorboards were so special to Kelley that she'd had them torn up from their house in Virginia Beach to be installed in this room

Brown family archives

Kelley with Adam's teammate Heath Robinson during the ceremony
when she was presented his Silver Star more than a year after his death.

overlooking the wide-open space that was now Nathan and Savannah's backyard. The view out the office window faced the spot where Adam had parked on the property nearly three years earlier. "Right there," Kelley says, pointing. "Adam drove into the middle. The grass was up to my neck, and he made me get out and we walked the lot. He loved it. Now we love watching the deer and the birds. It's everything Adam thought it would be—I can feel his presence here more than anywhere."

On shelves in Daddy's room were mementos: his helmet from BUD/S Class 227 beside a Lake Hamilton Wolves football helmet. His beloved espresso machine and the inscribed paddle from Team TWO. On the desk, his Bible. The walls, covered by photos, certificates, insignias, and awards, including his bachelor's degree, the Bronze Star with valor, and the posthumously presented Silver Star for Chief Brown's actions

> as part of an assault force that executed a daring raid deep
> into mountainous enemy-occupied terrain in northeastern
> Afghanistan...while numerous enemy fighters simultaneously
> engaged the force from the surrounding mountains.... Reacting
> immediately, and without regard for his own safety, Chief
> Brown...

Says Kelley, "Adam would hate having all these awards on the wall. He never, ever thought of himself as a hero, but he would have, in an instant, called every man on his team a hero for what they did after he was wounded. Kraig went in a second later with a grenade to stop the guy from shooting at Adam, and *he* got shot, then Brian, and Nick, Matt, John, Heath, all those guys rushed in with bullets flying everywhere to pull him out. Kevin, Tom, Chris, Jonas, Lou, and a bunch of others— they went through hell getting him out of there. The pilots, the medics that worked on him...

"He always said, 'I work with heroes,' but he never called himself one. Not ever. But he's my hero and he's Nathan's and Savannah's, and that's who this room is for. It's for them."

Kelley has continued to honor Adam by "doing the best I can as a mom," she says. "I have good days and bad days, but I've changed: I don't cook like I used to, and the house gets messy sometimes. I always return to that verse Adam left me, that I will suffer for a while and then God will direct my path. I'm being patient, waiting for God to lead me. Janice and Larry's steadfast faith has been an inspiration—they have channeled their grief into something positive."

Despite their initial disappointment with God, Janice and Larry ultimately remain firm in their belief that Adam's death, like his life, is part of God's plan. "We were faced with some tough decisions," says Larry. "Are we going to abandon our faith or *apply* our faith? Allow our grief to make us bitter, or allow God to use that grief to make us *better*? How are we going to live so that our Lord and Adam are honored by our lives while we wait to join them in heaven?"

Just a few months after Adam died, Janice and Larry befriended Jill and Brad Sullivan, who had lost their young daughter, Hannah, to cancer. Together they confronted their grief and began to heal, finding comfort in their shared circumstances and beliefs. The Sullivans and the Browns would go on to organize "While We're Waiting" faith-based retreats for bereaved parents.

On the evening of May 1, 2011—a little over a year since Adam's death—Kelley sat down to relax on the couch after an emotionally draining trip to Pittsburgh with Janice and Larry for the debut of a documentary called *The Adam Brown Story* on the NRA Life of Duty online television network. She cuddled up with Nathan and Savannah, switched on the television, and saw that President Obama was about to speak.

Osama bin Laden was dead, the president announced to the world.

Janice and Larry by the just-unveiled sign
at the Adam Brown Road dedication ceremony.

"A small team of Americans carried out the operation with extraordinary courage and capability. No Americans were harmed. They took care to avoid civilian casualties. After a firefight, they killed Osama bin Laden…"

"Nathan burst into tears," says Kelley. "They were happy and sad tears. He's only eleven, but he's smart, and the kids are not sheltered anymore. Their daddy was killed; they know what war is.

"Nathan was nodding while I said, 'I bet it was Daddy's friends!' When we listened to Obama, I flashed back to what John Faas had said at the funeral: 'We *will* be hunting you down, and we *are* going to deliver you to the doorsteps of hell.' This was coming from Team SIX. He was talking to the men, but he was looking at the kids, and I heard it as, 'We are going to avenge your father's death.'

"I just knew it was his team. It was such a release. It validated everything Adam did. We got him, and I was really happy about it.

"And little Savannah, she's so insightful. She asked, 'Are we supposed to cheer because somebody died?' I explained, 'Your daddy was gone all these years to protect us from this man and others like him. They are not good; they're evil. They killed thousands of innocent people, not just SEALs. It's okay to feel good that this man is gone, that he will never again do the things he did. The world knows that we won't ever put up with anybody else who does either.'"

Janice and Larry experienced the same closure, embracing Kelley when she dropped Savannah and Nathan off at their home a few days later on her way to the airport. They, too, had remembered John's words and had rejoiced in the death of a man they considered evil.

Kelley flew to Virginia Beach the same day the media announced it had indeed been SEAL Team SIX that took out bin Laden, and attended a get-together with her family of SEALs and their wives. They lifted their glasses to Adam and to another fallen teammate, whose widow stood beside Kelley. They toasted all the men from their command who had been killed in nearly ten years of war, then they toasted those who had lost their lives on September 11, 2001.

As the night wore on, one of Adam's friends took Kelley aside and told her that bin Laden's death was further proof that Adam had not died in vain. "It was a team effort, and Adam was a team player. He loved his country, God, and he loved you, Nathan, and Savannah more than anything in the world. When those guys were flying in, I bet they could feel Adam there with them, Kelley. I bet they could feel *all* the guys we've lost."

Although the DEVGRU SEALs I met with would occasionally bring up the bin Laden capture/kill mission during the many hours of interviews I conducted with them over the next few weeks, the topic was always in conjunction with Adam—specifically how he would have loved to have been there. "Adam would have been badgering his team leaders for the primary roles," said one SEAL with a laugh. "I can just hear that Arkansas accent: 'Don't worry, y'all—ah got it!'"

The laughter would often bring with it tears; Adam's death was a deep wound, far from healed.

Kevin Houston had just finished recounting Adam's death when he broke down and cried. Apologizing, he walked outside on the balcony of the hotel room in Virginia Beach and stared out at the Atlantic Ocean, the same stretch of water where he and his SEAL brothers had trained over the years.

Then he went on to tell me that he had spent a year pondering the question "How does this happen to a man like Adam?" He had ultimately concluded that the trials and tribulations of Adam's life were "grooming for a future job. I think that the Lord himself had one of his right-hand men—like an angel or however it works in heaven—set to retire and Adam got called up to fill his place."

Two weeks later Kevin went to church with his family and Austin and his family, and sat in the same pew they'd always shared with the Browns. At the end of the service, Kevin accepted Jesus into his heart and asked him to be his Savior.

"Adam really got him thinking," says Kevin's wife, Meiling, who called Kelley right afterward to tell her, "He finally did it, and I just want you to know, Adam's life was the seed that inspired him."

On August 6, 2011, six weeks after that interview with Kevin, I was in the Sierra Mountains enjoying a camping trip with my wife, our children, and some friends when Adam's teammates, now deployed in Afghanistan, were called upon to assist a combat element under attack and in need of immediate reinforcement.

Seven of the ten men I had met with from SEAL Team SIX—Brian Bill, Chris Campbell, John Faas, Kevin Houston, Matt Mason, Tom Ratzlaff, and Heath Robinson—were locked and loaded on a CH-47 helicopter that was approaching a landing zone in Wardak Province when an insurgent-fired rocket-propelled grenade struck the aft rotor blade, causing the CH-47 to crash into a dry creek bed and explode. Everyone on board was killed: thirty U.S. forces and seven Afghan soldiers.

As my family and I left the mountains, our car filled with the laughter of grimy, happy kids, my cell phone coverage came back, delivering a voice-mail box full of terrible news. Never could I have imagined that nearly every SEAL I'd visited with and spoken to about Adam Brown would perish in the single worst loss-of-life incident in Naval Special Warfare history.

—

When Kelley sat Nathan and Savannah down, she couldn't contain her tears.

"Who got killed?" Nathan immediately asked. "That's what happened, right?"

"I'm so sorry, babies," said Kelley. "Some of Daddy's friends."

Their faces dropped, says Kelley, as "they rattled off the nicknames— Big Bird? Fozzy? Uncle Juicy?—and I nodded after each one, seventeen men. They knew all of them. Most were like uncles."

"Why?" said Nathan in tears. "Why is God doing this?"

Says Kelley, "I tried to be strong; I thought, *What would Adam want me to say?* So I was honest."

"I don't know," she told the children, "but let's pray for them and their families."

Over the next three weeks Kelley traveled from state to state, attending thirteen funerals to honor the men from Adam's team, putting aside her own grief and painful memories in order to comfort the widows and families, as she herself had been comforted the year before.

Those few of Adam's close military friends either not on the squadron that was hit or not deployed at the time, including Austin, Christian, Dave, and Jeff, joined her.

The people who knew and loved these men, and the people who knew and loved Adam Brown, continue to ask why. Though the answers to this question vary, they share a common result: solace.

When Austin spoke at Kevin's funeral, he explained how he envisioned Adam taking Kevin's hand—and the hands of the others who had perished—and welcoming them to heaven as God's warriors.

Brian Bill   Chris Campbell   John Faas

Kevin Houston   Matt Mason   Nick Null

Tom Ratzlaff   Heath Robinson   Kraig Vickers

Faces of some of the fallen Naval Special Warfare
warriors who appear in this book.

Heath Vance leans heavily on the story of a German colleague whose father's family had lost almost everything toward the end of World War II. An American GI brought food to the then ten-year-old boy to share with the rest of his family, "an act of kindness by a lone American soldier," says Heath, "that impressed the boy so much he eventually named his first son after the GI.

"War heroes get celebrated," he says, "but it makes me incredibly proud to think about Adam and what those gifts of shoes may have done to win the war. How many Afghan kids will remember his name, and how might that heal our world just a little bit? Adam didn't have an ulterior motive; he wasn't pushing hard to win the hearts and minds. He did it because he saw children with cold feet and he wanted them to be warm."

One SEAL returns often to a letter he keeps tucked in his Bible, written by Adam's commander in Afghanistan two days after he was killed and sent out to every DEVGRU operator. A copy of the same letter is in Larry's desk drawer, in Kelley's box of special papers, and in a file meant for Nathan and Savannah when they're older.

"Adam gave his life for his teammates during a mission which can only be defined as classic SEAL Team SIX work in Afghanistan," the letter begins. It ends with, "Adam was a friend, teammate, and brother in arms. Adam was a husband and a son and a father. Adam will always be a hero. His actions on his final mission were indicative of the way he lived his life. Fearless."

Adam's final resting place in Hot Springs, Arkansas.

AFTERWORD

One of Adam Brown's final wishes, written by hand on his CACO form, was that his spiritual testimony—his *complete* story—be told, including "my life before I met Jesus Christ and Kelley." You can appreciate now just how fearless Adam had been when he requested others to share that dark period from his past. Even in death, he selflessly and publicly risked tainting his own legacy so that others might be inspired to seek faith and overcome their own struggles.

This was a special request that Kelley, Janice, and Larry Brown were determined to uphold.

A few months before his final deployment, Adam and some of his fellow SEALs had met Rick Stewart, executive producer of the NRA Life of Duty online television network, whose mission is to honor those who serve our country. At the time, Rick was producing a documentary about a Special Forces A-team of Green Berets, ODA 574, based on my book *The Only Thing Worth Dying For,* which chronicles 574's mission into southern Afghanistan in the weeks after 9/11.

In March 2010, Tom Ratzlaff contacted Rick about Adam's death. This resulted in *The Adam Brown Story* (www.nralifeofduty.tv/patriot -profiles/video/a-tribute-to-adam-brown, www.fearlessnavyseal.com), a documentary that was set to debut in April 2011 at the NRA Convention and annual meeting in Pittsburgh, the same venue where I was going to speak about ODA 574.

Rick picked me up at the airport, got me checked in to my hotel room, then opened his laptop and allowed me to preview *The Adam Brown Story*. From the opening scene with eight-year-old Savannah bravely describing her daddy, I was just as riveted, emotionally invested, and inspired as Rick had been when he was moved to produce the documentary.

"So, would you be interested in writing a book about Adam Brown?" Rick asked.

"I'd be honored," I replied without a second thought. "I'd call it *Fearless*."

"That's great," he said, "because Kelley, Larry, and Janice Brown are flying into Pittsburgh tonight and want to meet you."

Unbeknownst to me, Rick had told the Browns about my previous books, casting his vote for me to write Adam's story. At dinner that night, I had the pleasure of meeting the Browns, and with their very first hugs and handshakes they made me feel like family. It had been barely a year since Adam had died, and as I told each of them how sorry I was for their loss, the sadness in their eyes conveyed how fresh and deep the pain still was.

While we were being seated, the hostess took my coat and handed me a coat-check card with the number 24 on it. The significance escaped me, but for the Browns—who noticed the number as I tucked the card into my shirt pocket—it was a sign from God or Adam or both. They had been praying for guidance about telling Adam's story, and at that moment they were all but certain I would be the author.

After dinner we drove to the Browns' hotel, where Kelley checked in, then walked over to us and held up her key envelope: room 24 on the 24th floor of the hotel had randomly been assigned to her. That's when she and Janice explained that 24 had been Adam's favorite number, and further, it was his and Kelley's secret code; if he came home late, he would call out "Twenty-four!" to let her know who it was.

"First your coat check, now this," Kelley said to me. "I know this is

Adam talking to me, and I would love it if you would tell his story." I looked at the Browns and thought, *Are you sure? We've just met.*

"You should read my other books," I said, and Larry responded, "We'll read them, but it feels right. You're the one."

The next day the Browns and I walked the convention center floor with Rick, who introduced us to Ted Nugent, an avid supporter of the military who had just seen the debut of *The Adam Brown Story*. Kelley informed him that I would be authoring the book about Adam and he handed me a business card, asking me to send him a copy when it was published.

Glancing at the card, I immediately got chills at the address. *Okay, what are the chances?* I thought. Within a day, the coat check, the hotel floor, the room number, and now the meeting of a rock'n'roll icon who lives at 2424 Something Street?

I mulled over this string of 24s and Larry's statement to me— "There is no such thing as coincidence"—all the way through my arrival in San Diego the following night. Disembarking from the plane, I made my way to the baggage terminal, noticing the groups of people gathered around television screens that were tuned to CNN. I paused at one. Osama bin Laden was dead.

At home, I gave my sleeping kids a kiss, then headed to my computer, where I discovered an e-mail from Kelley with the subject line "Osama bin Laden." "Eric, I'm almost certain it was Adam's team that got him!" she wrote. "I can just feel it in my heart."

A few days later, the media announced that in fact it was.

Despite the impact and magnitude of the bin Laden mission, Adam's story stands on its own. Throughout his life he inspired scores of people, and his story has continued to change the lives of many—including mine. He's reminded me to appreciate every moment with my family, to be goofy rather than grumpy, to get back up no matter how hard I might get slapped down, to sometimes buy my children a cupcake when I pick up coffee in the morning but to call it a muffin "because," as Adam would tell Savannah, "as long as you call them muffins, they're okay to eat for breakfast." And though I hadn't opened a Bible in more than twenty-five years, his faith encouraged me to question my own questioning about religion.

Even with the knowledge that Adam truly was ready—body and soul—to give up his life in the line of duty, the final chapters of this book were heartrending to write. I knew what was coming, but I hoped for a different outcome...somehow.

Equally devastating and shockingly sudden was the loss of life on August 6, 2011, including Adam's friends and teammates, several of whom had sat with me for hours to ensure that his story would be rich in detail, to illustrate—so I might convey to the world—just how special he had been. While describing Adam, they had unknowingly defined themselves: fearless in their own right, selfless, and not only willing but also proud to sacrifice their lives for the freedoms we enjoy every day.

ACKNOWLEDGMENTS

Thank you, Adam Brown.

Thank you, Brian Bill, Chris Campbell, John Faas, Kevin Houston, Matt Mason, Tom Ratzlaff, and Heath Robinson.

Thank you, Kelley, Nathan, Savannah, Janice, Larry, Shawn and Tina Brown, and Manda and Jeremy Atkinson for your steadfast resolve to share Adam's story and for trusting me to tell it.

Thank you, Rick Stewart, for your confidence and enthusiasm.

Thank you to the entire Naval Special Warfare community, and to those SEALs—both active duty and retired—and their wives who helped me navigate through Adam's Naval career. Thank you to those in the Army battalion who spoke to me about Objective Lake James, as well as the individuals from the FBI, Special Forces, Marines, and OGA who provided insight into operations in Iraq and Afghanistan.

Thank you, Steve Anderson, Thaddeus Bruce, Jeff Buschmann, Roger Buschmann, Chris Dunkel, Mike Glisson, Wayne Gray, Dick Holden, Kenneth Moore, Pastor Mike Smith, Heath Vance, Helen Webb, Ryan Whited, Curtis Williams, and Richard Williams for your candid interviews.

Thank you to everyone else who devoted time to making sure Adam's story was told right.

Thank you, Bruce Nygren at Random House, WaterBrook Multnomah Publishing Group: I cannot imagine a better editor for Adam's story. Thank you to the rest of the dedicated team there, including Lori Addicott, Laura Barker, Ashley Boyer, Heather Brown, Steve Cobb,

Carie Freimuth, Allison O'Hara, Renee Nyen, Kristopher Orr, Michael Palgon, Ken Petersen, Beverly Rykerd, Karen Sherry, and Laura Wright.

Thank you, Christy Fletcher, my longtime agent and friend, Melissa Chinchillo, Alyssa Wolff, and all of Fletcher & Co.

Thank you to Rita Samols, my tireless and meticulous copyeditor, and my researchers, Rebecca Edelston, Mike Hennessy, and Maxine Keene.

Thank you, Chris Adams, Matt Baglio, Nicole Buschmann, Rick Bychowski, James Campbell, Amber Coutts, Craig and Kathy Cupp, Erika Daniels, Ed Darack, Brandy DeGlopper, Suzi Drennen, Lacey Duffy, Danny Fallis, Chaplain Bob Freiberg, Justin Geiger, Dan Green, Kurt Johnstad, Alyssa Lair, Christy Lewis, Scooter Leonard, Alison Margo, Kevin McMillan, Rob Olive, Richard Oesterheld, Wilson Phillips, Carlos Royal, Joy Sheppard, Anthony Sitz, Madison Tybroski, Mike Weaver, Ryan Welch, Janet Wendle, and Colter Wilhoite.

Thank you to my ever-supportive and patient family and friends.

Thank you to my wife, editor, and best friend, Lorien, for always making me look good. And thank you to our incredible children for reminding me what's important in life.

IN MEMORIAM

U.S. Naval Special Warfare, East Coast

Lieutenant Commander (SEAL) Jonas B. Kelsall, 32, Shreveport, Louisiana

Special Warfare Operator Master Chief Petty Officer (SEAL) Louis J. Langlais, 44, Santa Barbara, California

Special Warfare Operator Senior Chief Petty Officer (SEAL) Thomas A. Ratzlaff, 34, Green Forest, Arkansas

Explosive Ordnance Disposal Technician Senior Chief Petty Officer Kraig M. Vickers, 36, Kokomo, Hawaii

Special Warfare Operator Chief Petty Officer (SEAL) Brian R. Bill, 31, Stamford, Connecticut

Special Warfare Operator Chief Petty Officer (SEAL) John W. Faas, 31, Minneapolis, Minnesota

Special Warfare Operator Chief Petty Officer (SEAL) Kevin A. Houston, 35, West Hyannisport, Massachusetts

Special Warfare Operator Chief Petty Officer (SEAL) Matthew D. Mason, 37, Kansas City, Missouri

Special Warfare Operator Chief Petty Officer (SEAL) Stephen M. Mills, 35, Fort Worth, Texas

Explosive Ordnance Disposal Technician Chief Petty Officer Nicholas H. Null, 30, Washington, West Virginia

Special Warfare Operator Chief Petty Officer (SEAL) Robert J. Reeves, 32, Shreveport, Louisiana

Special Warfare Operator Chief Petty Officer (SEAL) Heath M. Robinson, 34, Detroit, Michigan

Special Warfare Operator Petty Officer 1st Class (SEAL) Darrik C. Benson, 28, Angwin, California

Special Warfare Operator Petty Officer 1st Class (SEAL) Christopher G. Campbell, 36, Jacksonville, North Carolina

Information Systems Technician Petty Officer 1st Class Jared W. Day, 28, Taylorsville, Utah

Master-at-Arms Petty Officer 1st Class John Douangdara, 26, South Sioux City, Nebraska

Cryptologist Technician Petty Officer 1st Class Michael J. Strange, 25, Philadelphia, Pennsylvania

Special Warfare Operator Petty Officer 1st Class (SEAL) Jon T. Tumilson, 35, Rockford, Iowa

Special Warfare Operator Petty Officer 1st Class (SEAL) Aaron C. Vaughn, 30, Stuart, Florida

Special Warfare Operator Petty Officer 1st Class (SEAL) Jason R. Workman, 32, Blanding, Utah

U.S. Naval Special Warfare, West Coast

Special Warfare Operator Petty Officer 1st Class (SEAL) Jesse D. Pittman, 27, Ukiah, California

Special Warfare Operator Petty Officer 2nd Class (SEAL) Nicholas P. Spehar, 24, Saint Paul, Minnesota

U.S. Air Force Special Operations Command

Technical Sergeant John W. Brown, 33, Tallahassee, Florida

Staff Sergeant Andrew W. Harvell, 26, Long Beach, California

Technical Sergeant Daniel L. Zerbe, 28, York, Pennsylvania

U.S. Army General Support Aviation Battalion

Chief Warrant Officer David R. Carter, 47, Centennial, Colorado

In Memoriam

Chief Warrant Officer Bryan J. Nichols, 31, Hays, Kansas
Staff Sergeant Patrick D. Hamburger, 30, Lincoln, Nebraska
Sergeant Alexander J. Bennett, 24, Tacoma, Washington
Specialist Spencer C. Duncan, 21, Olathe, Kansas

This information was provided by the U.S. Department of Defense.

Adam's Legacy

Since *Fearless* released a year ago, a day has not passed that I haven't received at least one e-mail, and sometimes dozens, addressed to me or the Brown family, sharing how Adam's story has inspired them. One reader, a singer/songwriter named Mark Dowdy, was so moved by Adam's life story and what he overcame during his rise to the top tier of the United States military that he produced a song to honor Adam and the Brown family. (You can listen to *Fearless* the single by going to www.fearless navyseal.com or downloading it on iTunes or at www.cdbaby.com.) Mark, who was born blind, told me he hoped the song would inspire others to, as the lyrics suggest, be brave, stand tall, and live fearless—like Adam. The following letters, just a few excerpts out of thousands, are a testament to the depth and reach of Adam's legacy. After reading them, if you'd like to share how Adam's story impacted you, please post it on my Facebook page at www.facebook.com/ericblehm or e-mail me at ericblehm@fearlessnavyseal.com. Thank you for taking the time to contact the Brown family via these means.

Eric Blehm
San Diego, California
Spring 2013

A Strength and Pillar

My father is a veteran from the Korean conflict. He is now passed, but he instilled in me and my siblings a fierce loyalty and devotion to our grand country and its blessed military members. I honor their sacrifice and service every day. Since I was small, I have been taught to love and revere our great warriors, both men and women, who serve selflessly for our benefit.

As a mom of four, married twenty-seven years to the same wonderful man, and having lived enough of life to respect what it takes to actually get *through* it…I only feel more keenly the beauty, love, and commitment of our present-day warriors. *Warrior*—love that word. What a beautiful description of a worthy individual. Thank you for sharing this magnificent story of this magnificent warrior. What a strength and pillar he can and will be to all Americans. What a strength and pillar his family can and will be to all Americans. Mostly, I know that God speaks to those who listen. Adam Brown listened and selflessly gave what only he could give.

Renewed Pride

I have spent ten years in the U.S. Army, and mainly through my career I have been on cruise control. I lost my pride for my flag and my uniform. I guess deep down I forgot there are great men like Adam who wore the uniform and fought for the same reason we do in the Army.

Reading his story has renewed my pride in the flag I wear and my uniform. Regardless of my being in a different branch, it truly was amazing to read a story of such a great man. It helped me see my job in a different view. No longer will I sit on cruise control. I lost sight of my goals to become an elite soldier in the Army. Somewhere deep down I lost my fight. But again, Adam's story renewed the fight inside me to stand up no matter what and fight for what is right in this world.

From here on, I will hold my head high, I will show pride in the flag I carry on my uniform, and I will always fight for what is right no matter the obstacles.

PURSUIT OF DIEHARD EXCELLENCE

My son gave me this book yesterday. Finished it this morning. I just wanted you to know that it spoke to me very deeply and touched places in me that I hadn't thought about in many years.

I went into the service out of high school to be a U.S. Army Ranger in 1981. Long story short, I quit the Rangers and quit the Army. Came back home and hit bottom with drugs, etc. Adam's story, his struggles, his values, his relationships…as I said, spoke to me very deeply.

I can't redo my past, but I can be relentless in my pursuit of diehard excellence as a father and a husband. Thank you for sharing the realness of Adam's life. It touched the realness of mine!

REAL HEROES

Ever since I was a young boy, I had wanted to be a member of the elite U.S. Navy SEALs. To this day, at the age of thirty-seven, I still have hero worship when I am around those guys.

I enlisted in the Navy in 1994 and suffered an asthma attack (which I lied about to enlist) during a swim qualification. I was crushed to know that my dream would never come true, so I pursued the closest civilian route that I could take: law enforcement. I was a member of a SWAT unit for over five years and eventually became a deputy United States marshal. During my career as a law enforcement officer, I have had the pleasure, and what I consider an honor, to train with some of Adam's comrades.

I grew up with recruitment posters of SEALs on my wall rather than sports figures, and I now teach my children that these elite men are real heroes and not some guy who can score thirty points in a basketball game.

A Lasting Impression

I selected this book rather randomly while at the bookstore and could not believe what a lasting impression it has left. I was born and raised in Stamford, Connecticut. My oldest brother, Michael, was a Navy pilot who was killed during flight operations in the North Arabian Sea in July 1984.

I pursued my dream of becoming a firefighter by joining the FDNY in 1998. On September 11, 2001, I found myself at the base of the North Tower just prior to its collapse. So the connections between the U.S. Navy and the War on Terror are quite clear to me and something I have very strong feelings about.

What was even more ironic was the fact that you interviewed Brian Bill for the book. Although I did not know Brian personally, I and several FDNY members came to Stamford to pay our respects at his funeral. I had the honor of attending the after affair at Sterling Farms and was simply amazed to be in the company of the SEALs he served with. Although our time together was short, I cannot begin to explain the lasting impression these men left on me—I was truly proud to be an American. The story of Adam Brown only reaffirms my feelings and high regards for these brave men.

"I Got This!"

I am a nurse in a small rural hospital. Last week my team acted to resuscitate a child whose heart and breathing had stopped due to an accident.

I was 180 pages into *Fearless* on that day. I am not a religious person. I am a spiritual person, like Adam was. I believe that our hands were guided and, as the lead nurse, I was guided in the decisions I made that helped us save this baby. I believe that had I not been reading about Adam's life, his struggles and triumphs, I would not have felt the peace I felt while leading this resuscitation. I was able to remain completely calm and, by doing so, was able to help others stay calm.

When the baby first got to us, having never used the phrase before, I told the team *"I got this!"* and dove straight in and started compression on this tiny chest. Afterward, I recalled that this was Adam's catch phrase and smiled to myself, all the while knowing that had I not "got it," the baby's chances of making it [would have] dramatically dwindled. I silently thanked Adam for lending me his phrase and went about my business.

After resuscitations like this, there is mental and physical exhaustion and always a few quiet tears (usually kept to myself). I have to be the strong one. We normally have a debriefing after such events that I lead. It is sometimes hard to keep my composure. I "had it" this time. I came home and stayed up to finish the book, sacrificing sleep for the friend I had found in the story of Adam Brown. I finally let myself cry it out while I was reading the rest of Adam's life. It made sense to me that I was able to use his story as my own personal debriefing.

This book has renewed my faith. I am stronger and better for it. So, without knowing me, and even after his passing, Adam has witnessed to me in a way I never expected. Grateful doesn't even begin to describe the appreciation I have for Adam opening up his life, insisting on having his story told and, in turn, you all opening up your lives to share Adam with the world.

A common theme throughout the book, to me, was how humble Adam was all his life. Adam is my new heavenly mentor. I'm sure he'd be okay with that. I know that even though my life will never have the impact on this world that Adam's did, I will strive to make the greatest impact possible, keeping him in mind. Adam was a hero. You are all heroes. My heroes.

A Lasting Depth

I teach at a day-treatment facility. The focus of our program is social/emotional training and skills for at-risk youth. Often, I tell Adam's story to my students when they feel like they are at the point of no return. I have a student that has made tremendous progress this past school year, so we are discharging him from our program. I gave him *Fearless* as a gift on what was supposed to be his last day of school. There was one more day left, but he didn't have any tests the last day, so there wasn't a reason for him to return. However, he showed up with his copy of *Fearless* in tow. He stopped me in the hallway and was eager to tell me that he had already finished reading four chapters. He then continued walking and stopped again and said, "You didn't tell me they [the Browns] were poor." Adam's story touches different people in different ways but with a depth that is lasting. Thank you, Adam, for inspiring us.

Many Good Lessons

I am a father, a veteran, and a federal agent. I have a young son who seems to have many of the traits of Adam. I'm a drug agent, and I worry about him and the temptations of the future. I read *Fearless* in one day. I'm going to make my son read it when he is twelve. There are so many good lessons about faith, family, service, and the temptations that can derail all of those things. I'm going to reread it as well, to remind myself how tough a job parenting a teen and young man can be.

I've been through some dark times, nothing compared to what [the Brown family] and Adam have gone through, and this book gave me wonderful perspective to see how blessed my life is, and it also renewed my interest in developing a relationship with God and his family. Thank you for having the courage to come forward with Adam's story. God bless you on this Memorial Day and every other day.

PEOPLE NEED TO KNOW

Thanks for sharing the life of this warrior with the world. People need to know these are the type of men that are allowing us the freedom we enjoy. The media loves to share stories when a few bad soldiers do stupid things but fail to mention the many men such as Adam.

CLOSURE

Thank you for allowing your son's life to be shared with us. His story has caused two feelings that I never expected when I began reading. The first is simply inspiration—to be a better father, husband, and person. The second, oddly enough, is guilt. I lost my best friend / brother on September 11. Reading Adam's story makes me wish I had done more and tried harder to serve my country and remember my friend. But with the guilt, also strangely, there is closure. Adam's story made me face and deal with emotions I had long held back.

GOD NEEDED A RIGHT-HAND MAN

This story has moved, touched, inspired me in more ways than I can count. You see, I, too, have been on the wrong side of life, been in for DWIs, not owning up for my mistakes, not living as I should. I found

God again back in October of last year and found a good church home.

I was reading some books on Kindle, and *Fearless* showed up as one I might like, so I ordered it. When I started reading it, I found I could not put it down. The more I read, I found myself asking, *What have I done?* I haven't done anything that even remotely comes close to what Adam did. But after I finished it, I am telling myself that if God can help someone like Adam, then there is hope for me. His story has renewed my own faith.

I am sorry for the loss of Adam and his teammates. Someone said in the book that if God needed a right-hand man, he could not have chosen someone better. Once again, thank you for your son's unwavering, unselfish, inspiring service for my freedoms. Thank you for allowing me a glimpse into yours and Adam's life.

Incredibly Humbled and Inspired

Before reading this book, I had no sense of direction in my life. I am a twenty-seven-year-old mother of four, and two years ago I fled from my children's abusive father and was homeless for a while. I currently work full time, and I'm going to school to earn my bachelor's degree.

There are days when I find it hard to go on and feel like giving up. I was feeling this way before I read *Fearless,* and thanks to Adam's incredible life-changing story, I have finally realized what was missing in my life—God. I am incredibly humbled and inspired to keep going and to keep fighting through this life, and I know that all things are possible with faith and love.

I am deeply saddened for your family's loss of such a courageous soul, but please know that Adam did not die in vain and my life has been forever changed.

A Debt of Gratitude

First of all, "thank you" is definitely not enough. I have never served in the Armed Forces; however, I have family members who have served. One grandfather served in the Navy Seabees, one grandfather served with General Patton's Third Army at Bastogne, an uncle served as a B-52 crew chief in the Air Force, and countless friends have served. I am a proud and patriotic American who greatly appreciates the freedoms and liberties defended by our dedicated servicemen and women and their devoted families who sacrifice while their loved ones are away. It is a debt of gratitude I can never repay.

Drawn to a Photograph

I would like to start by saying my son is with the [SEAL] teams. In May of last year my son was shot, and I went to his aid as soon as he was brought home. His rehabilitation was long and arduous. At this point he is fine and back with his team, but during his rehab I would go to the team gym and work out. I was always drawn to a photograph on the wall with a Trident below it. The caption below the photograph read, "We will never forget you, Chief Brown."

I would always pay my respects, knowing the great sacrifice that this man and his family had given. I would swell with pride knowing that he must of been an outstanding person. I didn't feel compelled to ask anyone about Adam; I just knew some day the story might be told and I would know about him. By the way, it was the only picture hanging on the wall. I never met Adam, but I can tell you he and I had a few moments together in the gym that will always be special to me.

TRULY FEARLESS

I'm an Assemblies of God church pastor, so I have no doubt that Adam is with his Father in heaven this very moment. Yet I am also a family man and a patriot who just doesn't feel worthy of Adam's sacrifice. My prayers are with you all. Words cannot express my incredible sense of gratitude to you for releasing Adam to do what he was created to do, in spite of the price you were willing to pay. You are all truly fearless.

A LUCKY MAN

As a Canadian Airborne Regiment soldier, I am proud to have served with Americans who help protect us all from terrorists. He was a lucky man to have found Kelley to support him. God bless.

PERSONALLY SATISFYING

I served in the Army in 1993–96, nothing special, just a simple military police corrections officer. Later I worked for the Colorado State Penitentiary and then moved back to Ohio, where I worked for a county juvenile center until I landed a career as a police officer.

For the last fourteen years as a street cop, I have dedicated my career to drug-related offenses, trying to clean up my zone and building relationships with the citizens. It feels like an extended family. I have seen drugs ruin professional people, such as doctors and business owners. I have seen average persons whose families and friends have been destroyed. Rarely do I ever see anyone come around and stop using. It was personally satisfying to see that Adam finally overcame drugs with the help of his family, friends, the service, and God.

A Warrior in the Truest Sense

I am from a small town in South Wales, United Kingdom, and read a lot of books about military special forces operatives. I am not in the least way religious, but reading *Fearless* was one of the most inspirational books I ever read and makes me wonder how the USA and UK produce guys of this caliber. But Adam seems to be a warrior in the truest sense of the word, as described in the Bible. It makes me want to be a better person every day of my life going forward.

I know I will never meet you, but I know Adam is still with you in spirit every day and that Savannah and Nathan will grow up to be the most amazing people. I will be visiting Arlington National Cemetery next month on my first visit to New York and Washington DC and will be remembering people like Adam and other warriors I have read about recently, keeping us safe at night.

I Can Make it

I'm eighteen, and I'm a diabetic and have been struggling with taking care of myself. Seeing that Adam made it through his addiction really touched me that I can make it through being a diabetic. I laughed, I cried, but most of all I realized how God, family, and friends can help me take care of myself better and live my life better.

A Magnificent Life Force

My son works at DEVGRU and was in BUD/S Class 228. Reading about Adam makes me realize again that some lives are larger than others. What a magnificent life force Adam was, but a life force that would not have been so magnificent without his family.

I've had the pleasure to get to know some of my son's teammates and to hear the kinds of stories you have also heard. Both my wife and I had a similar reaction to reading the book: Adam sounds a lot like our son—wild, funny, willing to do anything, kind, sweet (he would object vigorously to these terms), devoted to his wife, fiercely patriotic, and loyal to his mates. It is truly a brotherhood like no other.

Reading about Adam has helped me get a little deeper inside my son's mind and heart and to understand a little better this incredible band of brothers and the bonds between them. Thank you for sharing your lives and Adam's life with the rest of us. It means much more than I would have imagined when I began reading.

A GAME CHANGER

I just finished your book, *Fearless,* and all I can say is that Adam's story is a game changer for me. The inspiration that Adam has given me is undeniable. His work on earth continues with his story and your words. His story reminds me to always value the time with my kids and wife and to never take it for granted. His drive inspires me to always strive to be the best, and his unshakeable faith causes me to reflect on my own beliefs. His life story reminds me to be the good guy and just enjoy life and live a good life.

Thank you for this book, and thanks to the Brown family for allowing this story to be told. I am a firefighter in Canada, and although my role is nowhere near that of Adam and his fellow SEALs, their story inspires me to be the best I can be, love what I do, and help when called on. God bless all those serving in our Armed Forces and their families that fight the good fight at home.

Thank You for Your Sacrifice

I am a Marine, and I want to say thank you. Thank you for allowing not only Adam's story to be written but your family's story. Thank you for your sacrifice. Adam gave his life for us, for me, for our country. But truly you are the ones who are sacrificing for us. For that I cannot thank you enough. Have solace in the fact that his story will touch millions, and if one person makes it out of their dark days because of it, know that it is your victory as well.

I have been truly inspired to go for the things that I want and to overcome my hurdles. Although I am not religious, my spiritual side feels renewed by Adam's devotion and that of his teammates to you and our country. I thank you for allowing us into your life and giving us one of the greatest stories I have ever read. Adam will forever be in my thoughts, especially during hard times. Knowing full well there was a man who struggled more and overcame to become greater than most but remained humble will help me through my life's goals. I thank you!

Renewed Hope

Reading the book *Fearless* has given me renewed hope for the future. For most of my life I have had a desire to serve in the military. About six years ago I decided to train and prepare for the Navy SEALs. Two years ago I joined the Navy with a SEAL contract, but just one week after that, I began to have problems with my left eye. The doctor told me my retina was being detached, and I was permanently disqualified from all armed services. The news was absolutely devastating, but I have faith that God is in control and has a reason for this.

To be honest, I don't believe my dream of becoming a Navy SEAL is over with; I still feel God's call to it. The book really showed me the power of prayer, and I know it is only through God that I have a chance of ever joining the military again.

I just wanted you to know that the life of Adam Brown has had a big impact on my life in many different ways and has given me that renewed hope for the future. Thank you very much for all the sacrifices you have made.

A Great Legacy

To the entire family of NSW Operator Adam Brown, I would like to first and foremost express my family's gratitude and our deepest and sincere condolences in your loss of such a fine young man as Adam. I would like to also thank the family for not only sharing Adam's story but the story of a loving and caring family who were able to come through some pretty difficult times in his (and your) life.

Larry, Janice, Manda, and Shawn, thank you for sticking together through those rough times. I have been in law enforcement for twenty-four years and have seen the effects that drugs can have on families.

Kelley, thank you for believing in Adam and for supporting him through the rough times as well, and for supporting him throughout the training and deployments. Too many people take for granted the sacrifices that our military members and their families make. Thank you for sharing some of the family (at home) sacrifices.

Nathan and Savannah, your father left a great legacy. He is a hero to our family and this country, and his spirit lives on forever with you.

Words cannot express the emotions that I experienced while reading *Fearless*. I would just like the family to know that he is not and will not be forgotten by a grateful nation.

The Footsteps
of Many Great Men

I am a senior at the United States Naval Academy and have recently decided that I want to attempt to try for the Naval Special Warfare Group. I realize why I wanted to be a part of this community: it is people like SOC Adam Brown who really invigorate me to constantly strive to be better. I want to follow in the footsteps of many great men, such as him, into the SEAL community. I really respect him for his sacrifice to country, and I really respect the parents who raised him to be the man he became and the wife who gave everything for him. God bless, and may God watch over all of you.

Love from
a Tough Father

My father gave this book to me, as he does a lot of books, all of which (except this one) I never read. I had to go on a business trip, so I grabbed it on the way out the door. I started reading at the airport and could not put this book down. I started out rooting for Adam, then became angry at him, only to come back to rooting for and admiring him.

Let me please say thank you from the bottom of my heart for your sacrifice. But most of all, thank you for never giving up on Adam. I know some of his troubles, as I have been there as well. I overcame mine with love from a tough father. There is a part in the book where Adam wrote something to his father: ["If I become half of the man you are, I'll be happy of who I am."] I wrote the same thing to my father about eight years ago.

I don't know what to say. I have thought about Adam every day since

I read the book. I think about his family and how I hope they have found peace. I hope your lives are filled with joy. I also think to myself *I got this* with any troubles I have, though they seem so small compared to what he did.

ANYTHING IS POSSIBLE

I have just finished reading *Fearless,* and let me tell you, I hope one day I can become half the man Adam Brown was. He is now my hero for being such a great person / family man and for being one of the greatest warriors to ever walk this earth. I'm currently in the process of joining the Navy to try and become a SEAL. Reading about Adam made me realize that anything is possible and to tackle life with a never-quit attitude. I am sorry for your loss, and thanks for telling us the story about such an amazing man.

ADAM'S GOT YOU COVERED

Where I work, part of my job is to receive the Department of Defense casualty notifications. I reprinted Adam's death notification and I stared at the name. As I read this book, Adam became more than "just a name" to me. That name became your son, your brother, Kelley's husband, Nathan and Savannah's father. It has been an honor and privilege to have met you all through reading this book.

There was spiritual reasoning (24) behind Mr. Blehm being the writer. Never have I read any book that evoked so much pride, spirit, or heartbreaking sobbing tears. I will pray for you all every day. I will pray for Adam every day. May God bless and hold you close in his heart. Adam's got you covered.

THE LORD'S WARRIOR NOW

Thank you. It's two simple words and doesn't seem adequate enough for the sacrifice that your family has made for our great nation. I've never read a story that has touched me so much and inspired me to be a better man. There are so many great lessons Adam has left us.

God bless you all, and Nathan and Savannah, there is no greater hero in the history of this country than your father. To the rest of the Brown family, thank you for sharing Adam's story with all of us. He is the Lord's warrior now, doing as much for mankind in the heavens as he did for mankind on earth.

Thank you for your gift of freedom, Adam.

The Adam Brown

1 Peter 5:10

Legacy Foundation

Adam Brown left his legacy...
What will *your* Legacy be?

ALSO BY ERIC BLEHM

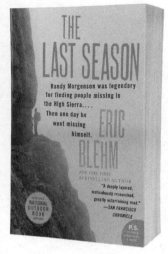

THE LAST SEASON

"A legendary tale of wilderness devotion
—Aron Ralston, author of *Between a Rock*
a Hard Place

Destined to become a classic of adventure
literature, *The Last Season* examines the
extraordinary life of legendary backcountry
ranger Randy Morgenson and his mysterious
disappearance in California's unforgiving Sierra
Nevada—mountains as perilous as they are
beautiful. Eric Blehm's masterful work is a gripping
detective story interwoven with the riveting
biography of a complicated, original, and wholly
fascinating man.

THE ONLY THING WORTH DYING FOR
HOW ELEVEN GREEN BERETS FOUGHT FOR A NEW AFGHANISTAN

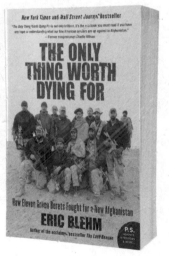

**"*The Only Thing Worth Dying For* is not only
brilliant, it's the one book you must read if you
have any hope of understanding what our fine
American soldiers are up against in Afghanistan."**
—Former Congressman Charlie Wilson

Eric Blehm, author of the award-winning *The Last
Season*, is back with another true adventure story.
Set in the immediate aftermath of 9/11, *The Only
Thing Worth Dying For* chronicles the untold story
of the team of Green Berets led by Captain Jason
Amerine that conquered the Taliban and helped
bring Hamid Karzai to power in Afghanistan.

🏠HarperCollins*Publishers* | HARPER ⬤ PERENNIAL
DISCOVER GREAT AUTHORS, EXCLUSIVE OFFERS, AND MORE AT HC.COM.

Available from *New York Times* bestselling author

ERIC BLEHM

Available wherever books are sold